W9-DEK-135

Cops, Soldiers, and Diplomats

Explaining Agency Behavior in the War on Drugs

Tony Payan

LEXINGTON BOOKS

A division of
ROWMAN & LITTLEFIELD PUBLISHERS, INC.
Lanham • Boulder • New York • Toronto • Oxford

Cops, Soldiers, and Diplomats

LEXINGTON BOOKS

A division of Rowman & Littlefield Publishers, Inc.
A wholly owned subsidiary of The Rowman & Littlefield Publishing Group, Inc.
4501 Forbes Boulevard, Suite 200
Lanham, MD 20706

PO Box 317
Oxford
OX2 9RU, UK

British Library Cataloguing in Publication Information Available

Library of Congress Cataloging-in-Publication Data

Payan, Tony, 1967-
Cops, soldiers, and diplomats : explaining agency behavior in the war on drugs / Tony Payan.
p. cm.
Includes bibliographical references and index.
ISBN-13: 978-0-7391-1221-2 (cloth : alk. paper)
ISBN-10: 0-7391-1221-X (cloth : alk. paper)
1. Drug control--United States. 2. Administrative agencies--United States. 3. Bureaucracy--United States. I. Title.
HV5825.P332 2006
363.450973--dc22 2005036005

Printed in the United States of America

∞™ The paper used in this publication meets the minimum requirements of American National Standard for Information Sciences—Permanence of Paper for Printed Library Materials, ANSI/NISO Z39.48–1992.

Contents

Abbreviations

AFB	*Air Force Base*
ASA-IL&E	*Assistant Secretary of the Army for installations, Logistic & Environment*
CDEP&S	*Coordinator for Drug Enforcement Policy*
C^3I	*Communications, Command & Control Centers*
CINC	*Commander-In-Chief*
DCM	*Deputy Chief of Mission*
DEA	*Drug Enforcement Administration*
DIRECO	*Dirección de Reconversión de la Coca*
DOD	*Department of Defense*
DOM	*Directorate of Military Support*
FBI	*Federal Bureau of Investigation*
FDIN	*Federal Drug Identification Number*
FLIR	*Forward-Looking Infrared Radars*
FM	*Field Manual*
FORSCOM	*Forces Command*
FSO	*Foreign Service Officers*
GAO	*General Accounting Office*
GPS	*Global Positioning System*
HC	*Host Country*
INM	*Bureau of International Narcotic Matters*
IRS	*Internal Revenue Service*
ISC	*International Standing Committee*
JTF	*Joint Task Force*
LANTCOM	*Atlantic Command*
LEA	*Law Enforcement Organizations*
MOU	*Memorandum of Understanding*
NAS	*Narcotics Affair Section*

NAU	*Narcotics Affairs Unit*
NG	*National Guard*
NORAD	*North American Aerospace Command*
NSC	*National Security Council*
OI	*Office of Investigation*
ONDCP	*Office of Natural Drug Control Policy*
OOTW	*Operations Other Than War*
OPTEMPO	*Operating Tempo*
OTH-B	*Over-The-Horizon Backscatter Radar Program*
PACOM	*Pacific Command*
SOF	*Special Operations Forces*
SOP	*Standard Operating Procedures*
SOUTHCOM	*Southern Command*
TACLET	*Tactical Enforcement Team*
U.S.	*United States*
USCG	*United States Coast Guard*
VBSS	*Visit, Board, Search & Seizure*

Preface

The United States government has waged a war on drugs for nearly thirty-five years, since 1972 when President Richard Nixon opened the first front on the "scourge" of psychotropic substances by declaring a "war on drugs." Since then, the war on drugs has cost billions and billions of dollars and many lives; fed a correctional-industrial complex that is becoming a burden to society; wreaked havoc with the Judicial System; soured relations with other countries and irked many a world leader, particularly in Latin America; and created and expanded an enormous bureaucracy. Yet, in spite of all its mostly unpleasant consequences, US anti-narcotics policy has had practically no results in stemming the flow of drugs into the United States or in curbing Americans' thirst for mind-bending substances. Simply put, as we enter the 21st Century still waging the longest war in US history, the results are abysmal. Illegal drugs of all kinds, from marijuana to cocaine to heroin to confection drugs, are just as available as ever not only in the large and medium size cities but increasingly in the rural areas of the South and Midwest. And they are certainly cheaper than they were at any time since President Nixon declared a war on drugs. Almost any high school or college student can readily attest to both their ready availability and their low cost. Abroad, the production of illegal drugs continues apace, from Colombia to Afghanistan. And although drug trafficking cartels come and go, every new one is just as strong as the ones that have preceded them.

Yet, the war on drugs grinds on, on a quasi-mechanical, monotonous, dehumanizing routine. There is no sign that the United States government, its enormous bureaucracy, or the American public are ready to acknowledge that the war on drugs has been largely a failure, in spite of the multiple tactical successes against drug cartels and drug dealers. If anything, the war on drugs enjoys enormous support. Politicians are fond of calling themselves "tough on crime," a stand that translates into unwavering support for current drug policy. Those who disagree with the policy approach to illegal drugs silence themselves. The political cost of honesty is too high. Similarly, government bureaucrats engaged in the drug war, from agency heads to street-level bureaucrats, are addicted to the dollars, the jobs and the careers that are made in the business of fighting the drug war. There are every year more people, more buildings, more equipment, more technology and more budgets that increase the perks and the prestige of the bureaucrats making a living off fighting illegal drugs. Hardly a bureaucrat will acknowledge publicly the enormous failure of the government's efforts to end illegal drugs—though many do so in private. The official stand in interview after interview with drug war bureaucrats was generally that more of the same was needed. Among the American public the drug war enjoys enormous support as well, largely because most Americans are oblivious to the real costs of the drug war and unwilling to accept the futility of its battles. Often a moralistic overtone underlies public support for the drug war. And, unlike with the Iraqi War, the costs and casualties of the drug war are barely perceived by the day-to-day news reader or listener, if at all.

The overall consequence of this is that almost no one in America today can successfully advocate a different approach to the drug war. The few groups that do are generally on the fringes of liberalism and increasingly shoved aside in a more and more conservative society. Thus, the nation is torn apart by illegal drug producers, traders and consumers who push in the direction of their concupiscence and business interests and by the government and the general public bent on pushing the way of prohibition. In between is a failed policy that promises no more in the future than it has already delivered in the past.

To demonstrate the futility of the drug war overall, it would be necessary to assess the entire drug war, all its actors, all its facets, and all thirty-plus years of it. There is plenty of evidence over three decades to arrive at the conclusion that it is a long-drawn and largely fruitless policy. Yet, to argue that the war on drugs is a failed policy is not the major goal of this book. A general assessment of the drugs war or an argument for or against it lies beyond the scope of this book. Instead, I want to look at the drug war to learn something about why governments do what they do. I want to explore what motivates government agencies and agents to draw out policy lessons for all who must deal with government and for bureaucrats themselves. Thus, here I take up a single aspect of the war on drugs—agency behavior—that becomes at once sufficient to lay bare the kinds of problems that plague the efforts of the United States government from within to fight the drug war. This approach, coupled with a single significant period in the drug war (1989-1992), is perhaps the most revealing of the types of problems that afflict efforts to end the production, trade and use of illegal drugs from within the government itself. Specifically, this work looks at the three main bureaucratic groups that have been forced over time to deal with the drug war: law enforcement, the military, and the diplomatic corps. In doing so, we analyze how each of these groups responded to their own mandate in the drug war. I hope that by examining the various US bureaucracies engaged in the drug war, this work demonstrates that the war on drugs is a poorly put together patchwork of efforts that has not been well thought out, well coordinated, or well implemented inside the government. (And it certainly has not produced the results expected.) On the contrary, the bureaucratic quilt that is the war on drugs has produced unhealthy inter-agency competition and organizational rivalries; jurisdictional ambiguities; duplication of efforts and inefficiencies; policy fragmentation; and even attempts to sabotage some drug war efforts, all the while trying to hide the grand failure of America's longest war. And explaining why this happens is the chief goal of this book.

The value of this work thus lies in the fact that it is crucial to study and understand this great public policy effort by the US government because it contains many lessons that can be drawn for future reference. Observing the way the drug war was conceived, created, implemented and funded can help us discern certain problems in policy design and implementation and the perils of a broad, vague policy. In this sense, this book is as valuable to academics as it is to policy makers.

One of the greatest lessons of this study is that the modern, rationalized bureaucracies of the US government are hardly equipped to deal with what is paradoxically an ancient yet postmodern problem such as psychotropic substances. The modern, rational government agency is saddled with all the systemic trappings of a highly inflexible organization with rigid standard operating procedures, a vertically-organized structure, and an unbendable hierarchy of accountability. In addition, agencies develop material interests that they pursue, often regardless of their effect on the overall policy goals of an administration. Moreover, agencies develop hard-and-fast organizational cultures that make them even more inflexible in their hierarchy of preferences and unable to respond lithely to a new mandate or a new situation. The result of this essential reality is that government agencies can easily turn into dinosaurs, hardly able to move and adapt. And this is precisely the type of bureau that is pitted against a postmodern, highly flexible, versatile, horizontally-organized, adaptable, ever-changing enemy: the illegal drugs producer and trafficker, the so-called "drug cartels." In other words, the very way the US bureaucracy is organized collides with the rather opposite nature of criminal organizations. And evidence shows that US bureaucracies are at a disadvantage. The tool kit of modern bureaucracy is simply insufficient to deal with the problem of today's criminal organizations. The structure of government, coupled with the awkward nature of the policy itself, has created a perverse structure of incentives and disincentives that lead bureaucracies and bureaucrats to seek interests that often contradict and undermine the policy itself. Yet, there is little bureaucrats can do to escape the dilemmas of their own existence. This reality undermines the very efforts of the government's policy against illegal drugs and makes the war on drugs unwinnable.

Moreover, given the events of September 11 and the ensuing bureaucratic reorganization that resulted in the creation of the Homeland Security Department, there is an even more pressing lesson that can and should be drawn from this study. Bureaucracies are not merely instruments of government. They are organizations unto themselves; with their own lives. They develop their own interests and goals, independent of the interests and goals of politicians and the public. Then bureaucracies seek and defend these goals, which may not always be agreeable with the public policy that has been entrusted to them. Often this conflict is resolved in detriment of the public policy goal. It is pressing to understand why and how such bureaucratic pathologies occur in order to stem the negative effects of this reality. If the US bureaucracy is to succeed in its current efforts to fight world terrorism—the war on terror—the lessons of the drug war are quintessential. As combating terrorism becomes a public policy goal, heavily entrenched in the daily life of the nation, much like the drug war became, it is important to organize bureaucracy and create policies that will not undermine the ultimate national goal, whether the war on drugs or the war on terror.

I hope then, that this book will serve politicians and policy makers to understand the workings of bureaucracy; to academics as a contribution to the study of public policy and administration; and to the general public interested in understanding how government works and why sometimes it does not work. Ultimately, it is the public that should be most interested, given that it is the public that pays for the bureaucratic infrastructure of our national government.

In preparing this volume I want to acknowledge the many people that helped me along the way with their academic, moral and financial support and tolerated the many hours that it took to complete this book: Andy Bennett, Bill Gormley, John Bailey, Kenn Kern, Nivien Saleh, Ralph Scott, Edmundo Rodríguez, Gail Tillman, Michael Forge and Alfonso Sánchez.

I dedicate this volume to my mother, Piedad Alvarado.

Chapter 1
Bureaucracies, Politics, and Culture

This book focuses on the behavior of governmental organizations. Identifying and evaluating the motivations behind bureaucratic behavior clarifies not only why governments do what they do but also why policies look the way they do. Thus, our concern here is to expose the motives behind the action of bureaucracies. We seek to contribute to a better understanding of the way government divides and organizes its parts, the quantity and quality of the jurisdictional authority and the resources each part possesses, and the manner in which these parts relate to each other. Each is key to exercising effective democratic control over government and to forming and achieving functional policies. Since September 11, 2001, understanding these behaviors is even more pressing, given that the federal government has undertaken the largest reorganization of the bureaucratic apparatus since 1947.

What this Book is about

This book begins with an assumption: the primary units of government are organizations called bureaucracies. They constitute the essential organs of governmental administration. When we ask questions about the government, we must necessarily turn to an analysis of its structural parts. Thinking of the state as a bundle of organizational units each with its own "personality" and interests is a much more accurate way of understanding how government functions and is a much more effective way of explaining its behavior. It thus follows to ask what exactly shapes and colors bureaucratic behavior. This book endeavors to give an answer to this question. We aim here to analyze the agencies involved in the federal government's war on drugs from two distinct perspectives: *bureaucratic politics* and *organizational culture*. By bringing together the war on drugs and organizational theory, this book sheds some light on the behavior of U.S. governmental organizations. To accomplish this, two *testable* versions of bureaucratic politics and organizational culture are developed (the rest of this chapter). Then the models are tested by applying them to the agencies operating in the war on drugs (Chapters 2, 3, and 4). The result is twofold. First, the study offers plausible explanations for the behavior of the bureaucracies in the anti-narcotics policy space. Second, the study draws general conclusions about the utility of organizational theory in explaining agency behavior (Chapter 5).

Why the War on Drugs?

A considerable number of empirical realms are conducive to examining bureaucratic behavior. Trade, war, health policy, environmental policy, and many other areas could serve as the ground for the study of bureaucratic behavior. But among these policy areas, the United States anti-narcotics policy in the period between 1989 and 1993 is ideal. Through the late 1980s and early 1990s, the U.S. government substantially escalated its efforts against the production of mind-altering substances and their trafficking to the United States. This generated hundreds of programs and activities that involved an increasing number of bureaucracies. During the George H. W. Bush administration, the anti-narcotics "policy space"[1] grew considerably in monetary funding, overall "tools for the trade," and the number of bureaus dealing with the issue.[2] Consequently, anti-narcotics policy became increasingly fraught with all the dangers of overlapping jurisdictions, potentially conflicting arrangements for sharing information and resources, complicated inter-organizational efforts, multi-layered joint programs, and diverse interpretations of the issue and how to deal with it. Thousands of bureaucrats from many agencies constantly defined and redefined the issue and its possible remedies; planned and implemented programs jointly; and dealt together with multiple strategic, operational, and tactical issues of the so-called war on drugs. The rich inter-agency environment of U.S. drug policy helps highlight important aspects of bureaucratic behavior that can only be observed studying agencies working together in a single policy space.[3] Because of the attributes of the drug war between 1989 and 1993, this book examines this time as an ideal laboratory for the study of bureaucratic behavior from the perspective of organizational theory.

Why Organizational Theory?

There are several reasons to focus on organizational theory. First, it is unrealistic to attempt to understand governmental action as the purposive act of a unified national government. Governments are composed of organizational units and these units often conflict with one another on national goals, organizational ends, and political objectives (Allison and Zelikow, 1999, pp. 4-5). Often, when scholars open the black box of governmental processes for analysis, theorizing relies on systemic, psychological, or rational perspectives to understand bureaucratic behavior. Organizational theory, however,

a) offers an alternative and perhaps more accurate perspective;[4]
b) offers an alternative view that goes directly to the heart of how governments are organized to make policy;
c) moves away from the excessive *sui generis* nature of psychological approaches and the idealistic scenarios of systemic or rational theories
d) allows us to understand the unintended irrationalities that creep into the behavior of governments and which result from the individual *and* the collective actions of bureaucracies;
e) offers the opportunity to build middle-range theories, whose scope and conditions of applicability neither brush over important differences nor are too particularistic;
f) is useful because it cuts across methodological paradigms.
g) draws theoretical instruments from rational choice, economic theories, psychological perspectives and cultural analyses.

This integration of methodological perspectives offers the flexibility to conduct studies that can yield plausible explanations of agency behavior. Jerel Rosati (1981), for example, introduces a situational variable (crisis) and an individual-level variable (presidential interest) to offer a model of the conditions under which bureaucratic politics processes will most likely occur. Paul t'Hart (1994) argues that psychological effects of inter-group and intra-group relations underlie groupthink and bureaucratic politics predictions. Brian Ripley (1995) offers ideas from his organizational culture research and social cognition to enrich bureaucratic politics as an explanatory model. In the field of public policy, Ellison (1995) argues that government managers in autonomous agencies show competitive behavior when the core tasks of the organization are threatened. Ellison's work is an example of an approach to the study of bureaucratic behavior because it combines political features with organizational culture considerations. Page and Wouters (1994) show the interplay between the prevalence of bureaucratic politics and the level of agency control by political leadership. Kunioka and Rothenberg (1993) examine competition among agencies demonstrating that agencies put far more stress on agency autonomy than on competition—including competition for greater resources. At most, they argue, bureaucratic competition gives politicians a greater set of choices. Finally, Headrick (1992) shows how the studies produced by four U.S. governmental agencies to explain the causes of the 1987 stock market crash actually served each agency's political and bureaucratic ends. The theories, the methodological variations, and the very definition of the problem actually fed the political orientations of the agencies' analyses.

Bureaucratic Politics

After World War II, political scientists began to study governmental organizations, paying attention to their workings and component parts. They asked some of the crucial questions: Who are the people behind the state? How do they reach decisions of state, for what motives, and by what processes? Roger Hilsman, Samuel Huntington, Richard Neudstadt and Warner Schilling gave important insights into the politics that affect governmental policy. They spoke to the assumption that governmental behavior is centrally coordinated, rational and purposive. The key components of the policy process, wrote Schilling (1962), are "an elite structure characterized by a large number of autonomous and competing groups; and a mass structure characterized by a small, informed stratum, attentive to elite discussion and conflict, and a much larger base normally ignorant of and indifferent to policy and the policy-making [process]." Hilsman (1959) pointed out that there was a tendency to regard the state as a monolithic entity, identical to every other state in aims, motivation, and behavior. Complex abstract theories about governmental workings were elaborated without reference to the people in the states, the different goals they sought, and the different procedures they followed.[5] This generation of scholars argued that power is never centrally concentrated. They studied governmental hierarchies, political bosses, and extra-governmental and environmental pressures on the policy process. Huntington (1961) spoke of the role that domestic politics, interest groups, political parties, and social classes with conflicting interests and goals played in foreign policy. He also argued that there is a struggle between the administration and bureaucracy because each is trying to appeal to different forums or capitalize on different resources. Hilsman (1959) pointed out that the policy process is one of building consensus and persuading or dissuading. Skills and the power of persuasion were held to be crucial in the process. With no figure having all power, *politics* was crucial to convince others of what they should do for their own interest. Negotiation, bargaining, and compromise have a prominent place. There is behind government, Hilsman (1959) wrote, a complex set of informal relationships between the different participants in policy making, a pattern of pressure and counter-pressure, debate, persuasion, and coercion that marks their interaction. He further stated that,

> the patterns of relationships among these groups would cut across institutional lines . . . and the participants would perform a variety of roles, though not necessarily the same role on two different issues or even through time on the same issue. The roles would consist of originating ideas; debating and testing ideas; persuading or selling a policy proposal within a departmental structure; persuading or selling more widely in government to other agencies or to the Congress; bargaining within a department or other agencies . . . developing policy proposals . . . aggregating alternatives; modifying, vetoing, appraising past results; and enlisting public support where necessary" (Hilsman, 1959, p. 366).

Schilling (1962) wrote that a satisfactory settlement may be a direct compromise on the issue concerned or a bargain reached by bringing into the negotiation another issue in dispute, thereby permitting each to give up something of less value than that which it receives. The process required the reconciliation of a range of values and goals and of alternative means and policies. Hilsman (1959) argued that the process was one of accommodation for arranging mutual concessions so as to maximize values gained and minimize sacrifice.

These scholars believed that policy is a *political* resultant that reflects the intervening interests. Even if it were true, as Neustadt (1960) put it, that in foreign policy politics stops at the water's edge, there is certainly a lot of it before it reaches the shore. Policy processes are not, as rational choice theory would have it, a "systematic and comprehensive exploration of the whole range of values and means but one of trial and error in which policy changes by zigs and zags, reverses itself, and then moves forward in a series of incremental steps" (Hilsman, 1959, p. 363). This generation of pioneers in the study of the influence of politics in policy processes left only works that never cohered into a defined research program. They demonstrated that *politics* mattered in governmental policy, but they did not demonstrate that *bureaucracies* mattered. Their fascination with politics did not translate into *bureaucratic politics*.

It was later that bureaucratic politics qua bureaucratic politics was born. Graham T. Allison systematized the relationship between *bureaucracies* and *politics* in the late 1960s and early 1970s. In *Essence of Decision*, Allison (1971) proposed that in thinking about foreign affairs, scholars should view the behavior of government as the resultant of games among organizational and individual players who have different perceptions, motivations, positions, powers, and exercise various maneuvers in the direction of their policy preferences. Allison complained that foreign policy is often compared to

> moves and sequences of moves in the game of chess . . . in which the observer could see only a screen upon which moves in the game were projected, with no information about how the pieces came to be moved. Initially, most observers would assume . . . that an individual chess player was moving the pieces with reference to plans and tactics toward the goal of winning the game.

But, Allison objects,

> a pattern of moves can be imagined that would lead some observers, after watching several games, to consider . . . [another] assumption: the chess player might not be a single individual but rather a loose alliance of semi-independent organizations, each of which moves the pieces according to a set of procedures . . . [or] a number of distinct players, with distinct objectives but shared power over the pieces.

Allison's bureaucratic politics model made four assumptions. First, the government is composed of individuals and organizations with varied objectives. Second, governments are loosely-held-together alliances where no one individual or organization is preponderant over the others. If the President is involved, he too becomes another participant, although his influence may be considerable. Third, the policy making process is fundamentally a *political* process. The various individuals and organizations involved pull and haul in the direction of their policy preferences; they negotiate, bargain, accommodate, compromise, and give and take. Fourth, the final decision or policy outcome is a *political* result. The policy adopted may not be what any one participant desired but an amalgamation of various compromises.

Allison argues that when a decision is completed, one must ask: who did what to whom that yielded the action in question? Policy is the product of "pulling and hauling" by bureaucrats pursuing their interests. The game is played inside bureaucracies; the information available to central players is asymmetrical; the options available to the players are varied and can change from one moment to another; and the final outcome is not known to any one player until the end. The basic unit of analysis is the behaviors of bureaucrats which occur along certain channels of action among the players. The channels of action (regularized ways of interaction among players, formal and informal) constitute an important variable because they determine who has access to whom and how quickly. Action channels can determine some advantages or disadvantages in the process for any one player because the ability to influence other players and draw them in the direction of one's preferences depends on one's 1) bargaining advantages; 2) skill and will in using one's advantages and neutralizing one's disadvantages; and 3) other player's perceptions of the first two ingredients. While the result can be policy—a decision—it can also be the avoidance of a decision. Not making a decision can, for example, represent an impasse of power among the various players as well as their inability to persuade or dissuade one another in regards to a particular course of action. The bargaining advantages of a player come from formal authority and responsibility and control over resources for carrying out an action. Control over information is crucial (Allison deals obliquely with this issue) as is the ability to determine whether a decision is going to be implemented. Persuading those in charge of implementing a decision is crucial. Without their collaboration the decision making process can easily turn to naught. What is underneath the behavior of agencies can be summed up as the pursuit of individual and organizational interests. The game is politics.

Critique of the Bureaucratic Politics Paradigm

Bureaucratic politics has received mostly critical attention.[6] Robert J. Art (1973) argued that Allison's work contains internal inconsistencies and logical flaws because it fails to consider the effects of different issue areas and types of problems. Art's critique is correct. Allison's model throws multiple and complex variables together, with the potential for contradictory explanations and predictions of the same case. Also, the model does not typologize issue areas to determine where bureaucratic politics matter more. Do bureaucratic politics matter more on budget and procurement matters than, say, deployment of U.S. armed personnel in a foreign conflict or the process by which environmental policy is made?[7]

Stephen D. Krasner's (1972) critique focuses on the role of the executive in the policy process formation. His major focus is Allison's disinterest in the "president as king." The President, Krasner argues, can compel bureaucracies to obey him and he alone chooses the policy he regards optimal from among those presented to him by the bureaucracy. Krasner is uncomfortable with the normative implications of bureaucratic politics because Allison's model implies that the president is paralyzed by sinister and powerful bureaucrats.

David A. Welch's (1992) critique focused on the nature, purpose and methodology of Allison's models. He argued the model fails not because bureaucratic politics do not matter but because the model is poorly conceptualized and not carefully specified. The theoretical propositions of the model are not clear, suffer from implausibility and are difficult to test. In addition, history has shown that bureaucracies do not matter equally in everything, everywhere, all the time. To discern where they do, they must be studied diachronically for variations to discern under what conditions they matter, when, where and how.

Jonathan Bendor and Thomas H. Hammond (1992) argued that while Allison's model shows that the study of bureaucratic influence on policy is both feasible and desirable and that *Essence of Decision* placed the study of bureaucracy's influence on a more scientific foundation, the logic behind the models is beginning to show its age. Their general critique centers on three arguments. First, it is difficult to discern the assumptions underlying the model. While some are evident, others are obscured by complexity. The model is more thematically, than deductively, constructed. It is more discursive and not explicitly theoretical. It also misconstrues the nature of the executive branch because it ignores that policy making takes place within a hierarchy. Second, Allison's hypotheses seem loosely related to the original assumptions of the model. It is possible to show, on logical grounds, that several key propositions are incorrect. Third, parsimony is sacrificed. The model is too complex. It is analytically too intractable to yield a good number of testable hypotheses. Bendor and Hammond propose that Allison's model be revisited; that it be more rigorously formulated and tested; and that propositions be derived rigorously from the original assumptions in order to subject these assumptions more easily to empirical corroboration. Finally, Allison ignores crucial actors in the environment of a bureau. An agency's clients, regulated interests, and opposing interests are critical. Participation of individuals and pressure groups in a policy space is crucial for determining the political behavior of bureaucracy. An interest group can pressure Congress to impel a bureau in a certain direction; give it protection or support to extract resources, etc. Allison's model can be criticized for ignoring all of these factors.

Organizational Culture

In the study of culture as an organizational variable, there are four different strands of theorizing: 1) organizational culture, 2) political culture, 3) strategic culture, and 4) global culture. All the literature on culture shares several assumptions. First, culture is an adequate way of explaining behavior, regardless of whether the unit of analysis is organizational, national or global. Second, culturalists favor medium-range theories and are rather skeptical of grand theory. They are suspicious of aspirations to universality in explaining behavior. Third, culturalists are dissatisfied with positivism, which excludes culture because, positivists argue, that it is not "scientific enough."[8] They reject the notion that economic and structural theories suffice to explain behavior. For them, culture is just as, if not more, important in explaining behavior. Cultural theories (Johnston, 1995), rather than rejecting rationality *per se* as a factor in strategic choice, challenge the ahistorical, non-cultural framework for analyzing choices.

Organizational culture itself has a long history. In sociology, culture has long been used as a powerful explanatory element of organizational behavior. From as early as the 1930s to the 1950s, Robert K. Merton touted organizational culture as a way of understanding why governmental agencies do what they do. Merton argued that as a result of their day to day activities, bureaucrats develop special preferences, antipathies, discriminations and emphases. He contended that bureaucrats often appropriate the aims of their organization at a personal level, involving their own attitudes and sentiments. The instrumental values of the organization become the terminal values of the organization's members. Although Merton claims that such "pronounced character of the mind" leads to rigidities, the inability to adjust readily, and to formulism, ritualism, and the punctilious adherence to formalized procedures, the important point is that these behaviors are the byproducts or the manifestation of what is fundamentally the sentimental internalization and personalization of an organization's instrumental values by its members. The process is gradual and imperceptible.[9] Coercion is not necessary. By 1944, Herbert A. Simon began to look into the mechanisms by which the organization exerts its influence on its members. Organizational influences, he argued, put limits on the exercise of discretion by an organization's members, on the degree of loyalty they exhibit to the organization, and on the way an organization's members carry out the organization's goals and aims when the people at the highest levels are not looking. Simon was concerned with the decision-making process and the mechanisms of administrative control; he clearly began to uncover the ways by which culture exerts its influence over the members of an organization.[10] Then Allison and Morton Halperin used the concept of organizational culture in their 1972 article "Bureaucratic Politics: A Paradigm and Some Policy Implications."[11] Allison and Halperin (1972) called it "organizational essence," arguing that the members of an organization go about their organizational activities keeping in mind what they view as the essence of the organization's activity. Halperin (1974) defined "organizational essence" as the "view held by the dominant group in the organization of what the missions and capabilities should be." He argued that,

> (1) An organization favors policies and strategies which its members believe will make the organization as they define it more important; (2) an organization struggles hardest for the capabilities which it views as necessary to the essence of the organization. It seeks autonomy and funds to pursue the necessary capabilities and missions; (3) an organization resists efforts to take away from those functions viewed as part of its essence. It will seek to protect these functions by taking on additional functions if it believes that foregoing these added functions may ultimately jeopardize its sole control over the essence of its activities . . . (4) an organization is often indifferent to functions not seen as part of its essence or necessary to protect its essence. It tends not to initiate new activities or seek new capabilities even when technology makes them feasible. (5) Sometimes an organization attempts to push a growing function out of its domain entirely. It is chary of new personnel with new skills and interests which may seek to dilute or change the organization's essence.

Thus, an organization translates its essence (culture) into strategic, operational, and tactical preferences. What an organization does is related to its "essence." Allison and Halperin later dropped their references to "organizational essence" and brought some of its hypotheses into a broader bureaucratic politics paradigm.

In the late 1980s, organizational culture received some attention in the work of James Q. Wilson. But for Wilson, organizational culture as an explanation for bureaucratic behavior is only part of his more comprehensive theory of bureaucratic behavior. In fact, by the end of his work, Wilson (1989) states pessimistically that he doubts that anything worth calling "organizational theory" exists. He declared that "[t]heories will exist, but they will generally be so abstract or so general as to explain rather little. Interesting explanations will exist, some even supported with facts, but these will be partial, place- and time-bound insights" (pp. ix-xii). Nevertheless, Wilson develops a concept of culture which he claims is "to an organization what personality is to an individual." He defines culture as "those patterned and enduring differences among systems of coordinated action that lead those systems to respond in different ways to the same stimuli."[12] Culture speaks to "the central tasks of and human relationships within [the] organization." An organization has a sense of mission when its culture is broadly shared and endorsed by operators and managers. The sense of mission an organization possesses is developed during the first stages of its life. This sense of mission has both benefits and costs. While organizational culture enables an organization to cohere internally, to minimize uncertainty and to respond more or less effectively to external stimuli, a mission-oriented organization has to pay a price,

> (1) those tasks that are not part of the culture will not be attended to with the same resources as are devoted to tasks that are part of it; (2) organizations in which two or more cultures struggle for supremacy will experience serious conflicts as defenders of one seek to dominate representatives of the others; (3) organizations will resist taking on new tasks that seem incompatible with their dominant culture (Wilson, 1989, p. 101).

Thus, while the benefit of possessing an organizational culture is that it enables an organization to minimize its costs and maximize its mission, an organization's culture is often the source of struggles, conflict, and, in extreme cases, stagnation (resistance to innovation or refusal to adapt) and, potentially, death. Wilson offers valuable insight into the issue of innovation and change. He argues that organizations resist innovation and are supposed to resist it.[13] Organizations do not like sudden changes. They prefer to change only glacially and predictably. The embodiment of an organization's culture is its standard operating procedures (SOPs). Through its SOPs, an organization minimizes uncertainty and supplants randomness, preserving the organization's identity. Tasks that are not seen compatible with the organization's culture will not be accepted; those that are seen as peripheral to the organization will receive only minimal attention and resources; and new tasks that are seen as compatible or central will be embraced and accepted. What organizations abhor is—"redefining"—changes that threaten the core of an organization's essence are opposed. Most changes in an organization occur not because they are internally generated but because they are either externally imposed or because the executives of the organization consider them vital to the continued health of it. Still, Wilson's work gives organizational culture a limited role in explaining why bureaucracies do what they do. His work, *Bureaucracy*, is an amalgam of diverse approaches. It includes principal-agent theory elements, organizational cultural elements, bureaucratic politics elements, and democratic accountability theory elements. Wilson helps himself to every useful variable he can find. The result, fortunately, is an insightful book about all that makes organizations tick. Unfortunately, *Bureaucracy* is also a multi-layered, complex theory of bureaucracy that is hardly testable.

Some organizational culture studies have focused on the military. In *The Culture of National Security*, Jeffrey Legro et al. (1996) focused on the factors that shape the culture of specific military forces in various countries, paying particular attention to how armed forces come to develop idiosyncratic cultures that make them respond differently to the same external stimuli. Their attention addresses the way in which external forces shape military cultures. Their interest, however, is not with the organizational culture of the armed forces but with the external determinants of an armed force's organizational culture, which is shaped by ideas, interests, national culture and domestic politics. They do not consider whether the determinants of the culture of an organization originate it, with the social function it was created to perform, the characteristics it possesses, and the factors inherent to the organization rather than external to it. In reality, an organization's culture develops within the organization, from its intrinsic characteristics.

Other scholars have argued that organizations are self-consciously cultural. Organizations gain legitimacy by manipulating "cultural" symbols. These symbols enable organizations to cohere internally, gain legitimacy among their masters and the public, protect their sense of self and cope in consistent, systematic ways with their environment.[14] There is little agreement on what culture is or how it affects organizational behavior, but there is general agreement that all organizations have a "way we do things around here."

Organizational culture does not lend itself to easy definition or uncomplicated operationalization. Lean and mean organizational culture theories are practically non-existent. Thus organizational culture remains untested. The same pessimism about the study of organizational culture expressed by Wilson is perhaps what led Allison and Halperin to abandon the paradigm altogether. The foregoing observations notwithstanding, we propose here a testable model of organizational culture. We define culture; operationalize it; and proceed to make explicit the mechanisms by which culture influences behavior. Finally, we test the model.

Critique of the Organizational Culture Paradigm

Several challenges face those who study organizational culture. The first is the problem of definition. This problem has haunted culturalists for a long time and has made some suggest that culture has slipped into a "degenerate research program."[15] Others have argued that culture has no conceptual clarity.[16] Rogowski (1974) argued that the available definitions of culture make it very hard to formulate testable theories. There is, he said, a fundamental failing in the theory that makes definitions uncertain; uncertain definitions make for uncertainty about strategies and measures; and so long as measures remain uncertain, convincing tests of the theory are impossible. He also points to the problem of operationalizing culture. Defining culture as the collectively held ideas, beliefs, and values, for example, leaves the concept too broad, imprecise and difficult to measure.

A second difficulty with organizational culture is that it is hard to establish plausible causal mechanisms. How does culture work as explanation? By what causal mechanisms does culture influence behavior? How to establish causal relations between a perception, a feeling, an idea, a value, a belief, a worldview, or an assumption and actual, concrete, observable behavior? Organizational cultural cannot rely on the *content* of culture for causal mechanisms because the content varies from organization to organization. Content is what makes organizations act differently, not similarly. Relying on cultural content is a way to explain one case but not to generalize across cases. The culture of a private school is far from the culture of the U.S. Marine Corps or Microsoft or the Department of Energy. Relying on content is unwise because each organization is *sui generis*. Using the content of culture as an explanation for behavior can at best make for configurative-ideographic studies. How a *particular* culture exerts *its particular effect* on the behavior of the members of *a particular organization* is only of secondary interest. Of greater interest are the general mechanisms by which culture affects behavior, regardless of content. So, what are the systemic elements of culture on which to build theory? This is the question that must be answered to go beyond the impasse on the *sui generis* challenge. Despite differences in cultural content, generalizations about the effects of culture should be possible. Some scholars believe that culture is amenable to science.[17] Others, like Clifford Geertz, are skeptical,[18] but, we argue, it is possible to have a "science of culture" by stepping outside content and then, once generalizations about cause-effect have been made, stepping back into cultural content to test the theory.

Building Testable Models of Politics and Culture

Bureaucratic Politics

Among scholars of bureaucratic politics, there is no agreement on many of the features of the theory. There is, for example, no common definition of "politics." There is a great deal of confusion about the idea of political motivation (e.g., whether it is ideological or material). Some scholars focus on the policy process; others focus on the policy outcome. Some scholars rely on personality variables; others rely on organizational variables. Some focus on relations with Congress or the Presidency; others focus on intra-agency dynamics; others focus on inter-agency dynamics. At times, the only thing that these studies have in common is their theoretical claim to bureaucratic politics.[19] These disagreements over bureaucratic politics theory have generated very different models of bureaucratic politics.

The existing models can be put on a "spectrum" ranging from the most simple to the most complex. At the simplest level, some authors offer exceedingly parsimonious models of bureaucratic politics. William Niskanen's work (1971), for example, offers one of the simplest. The central theoretical claim of Niskanen's model is an economic claim: all governmental organizations seek to increase their material resources. All agencies are conjectured to be "budget-maximizing" because the higher the budget, the better off the bureaucrats, the higher their utility. The utility function of bureaucrats is equal to the salary, perquisites, reputation, patronage, power, output, ease of making changes, and ease of managing the bureau. This claim has been tested with mixed results.[20]

Other proponents of bureaucratic politics offer overly complicated models. They mix all kinds of systemic, organizational and individual variables. By combining several types of variables, some bureaucratic politics scholars try to explain what they correctly view as a complex phenomenon: organizational behavior. In building exceedingly complex models, however, these scholars fail to clarify the import of each variable (or type of variable) in the model and even whether the object of explanation is the policy process or the outcome. The methodological problems with these models are formidable. Complex models of bureaucratic politics have consequently drawn criticism for their lack of parsimony and the difficulties of putting their complexity to the test. Sifting through existing works, this study builds a testable model of bureaucratic politics. The goal is to build a model that neither exhibits the nearly fruitless simplicity of Niskanen's model nor the unwieldy complexity of Allison's model. It is a bureaucratic politics model designed to test the fundamental claims of bureaucratic politics.

What Governmental Agencies Desire the Most

Governmental organizations develop a distinctive set of interests to preserve and enhance their existence and prosperity. As Clark and Wilson (1961) argued, few organizations disband willingly, as neither their executives nor their members are eager to end an activity that rewards them. An organization is always interested in creating conditions that ensure its survival and prosperity. Bureaucratic organizations strive to do so, regardless of the personal attributes of the individuals in them. There is really no way in which a governmental organization can survive and prosper if it does not become an advocate for itself. No agency would live long or prosper if it did not look after its interests with as much vehemence and dedication as it looks after fulfilling its social function—some look to their survival and prosperity with even greater eagerness than to fulfilling their social mission.

The most obvious way for an agency to survive and prosper is to achieve increasingly favorable positions in terms of 1) resources and 2) organizational autonomy within the policy space it inhabits. Greater resources are desirable because they result in an overall betterment of the members of the organization, including salary, perquisites, reputation, power, patronage, output, ease of making changes, and ease of managing bureaucrats. As Niskanen put it, "all of these variables...are a positive monotonic function of the total *budget* of the bureau during the bureaucrat's tenure in office."[21] Resources put an agency in a more favorable position from which to compete for more resources (Clark and Wilson, 1961, p. 158). Organizational autonomy is desirable because competition and confused jurisdictions vex the health of the organization before the public, the media, and its political bosses—partly because it is not in a position to take all the credit for the good and it can more easily be blamed by its competitors for what goes wrong. Although agencies recognize that mechanisms of bureaucratic control and accountability are necessary, they prefer as little oversight as possible and as much autonomy from the principal agents that might curtail their ability to make decisions not only in terms of their policy mandate but also in terms of the fundamental interests of the organization. A bureaucratic organization dislikes overlapping jurisdictions because sharing its policy space with other agencies truncates the organization's discretion on how to view the policy problem and how to solve it.[22] Discretion is a highly desirable good.

Thus, our bureaucratic politics model premises that an agency's fundamental interests lie in maximizing both its material resources *and* its organizational autonomy. An agency prefers to have increasing amounts of both *ad infinitum*. If this were possible, bureaucratic politics would not exist. But because both material resources and organizational autonomy are scarce commodities, agencies must engage in "politics" in order to maximize one, the other, or both—or even to "defend" one, the other, or both, when these come under encroachment by other organizations sharing the agency's policy space. Inevitably, it often happens that governmental organizations must make trade-offs among themselves.[23]

Defining Resources and Autonomy

Having defined what governmental organizations desire most, we must now supply precise definitions of what is meant by resources and autonomy. Our model views resources from a strictly materialistic view. "Resources" means budget, staff, and assets. A budget is the annual appropriation of money that Congress makes for a bureaucracy. By staff it is meant the members of the organization—anyone who draws its livelihood from the organization's payroll. By assets we mean the material goods that an organization has at its disposition—buildings, vehicles, machinery, equipment, etc. Organizational autonomy is defined as "a legally and politically recognized area of distinctive competence" (Rachal, 1982, p. 41).

A governmental agency enjoys autonomy when 1) it has sole jurisdiction over the set of tasks relevant to its mission and 2) can act independently of some or all of the groups that have authority to constrain it. The first can be difficult to achieve in a system where there is a high level of fragmentation of power and authority and multiple actors are found to share jurisdiction over a single policy space. The second is difficult to achieve in a political system where bureaus are subject to the supervision of many political bosses with disparate goals, the watchful eye of social and interest groups, and the competition of public and private organizations that can provide the same good or service as the governmental agency of concern. The mechanisms of oversight by Congress also matter. These mechanisms of oversight are many and varied. In any one event, an agency can come under the scrutiny of a committee, a freelancing legislator, a member of the congressional staff, its departmental boss, the courts, the media, the public, etc. Oversight can take a variety of forms that include judicial challenges, challenges to appropriations, hearings, protests, media criticism, and other instruments of control, formal and informal. An agency would like to be free of any of these constraints.

The Environment of Government Agencies

All government agencies operate in policy spaces populated by at least several other actors and every agency is obliged to deal with its "fellow dwellers" in that space. According to Downs (1967), the relevant actors for any one agency in the policy space it inhabits can be classified into the following categories: 1) political masters (elected and appointed officials and even members of the judiciary, friendly or not); 2) suppliers; 3) rivals and allies (other agencies); 4) beneficiaries and sufferers; and 5) regulatees. I would add two more categories: 6) the media and 7) public opinion. Neglecting any of these can cost an agency support and maybe even bring about a degree of hostility in its environment. Lack of support or outright hostility makes the operations of an agency difficult—or worse, they can jeopardize the agency's budget and autonomy. Artfully cultivating and nourishing these relationships can make a bureau's work easier and more successful.

A bureaucratic politics model computing the weight of each relationship on the political behavior of an agency is bound to be a complex model. To avoid excessive complexity, this work considers only those actors that can *directly* impinge on a government agency's policy space, both in regards to its budget and its organizational autonomy. These two types of actors are an agency's 1) political masters and 2) other agencies that claim competence on the issue area. More narrowly, an agency's political masters are Congress and the Executive; and its fellow dwellers in a policy space can be either its rival or its allied agencies. All other actors, while relevant to the behavioral choices of an agency, are held "constant" in order to focus on the two relationships of greatest interest here: 1) the relationship between a bureau and its political masters and 2) the relationships among the agencies that share a given policy space. These two categories of actors are the most influential actors shaping an agency's "political" behavior.

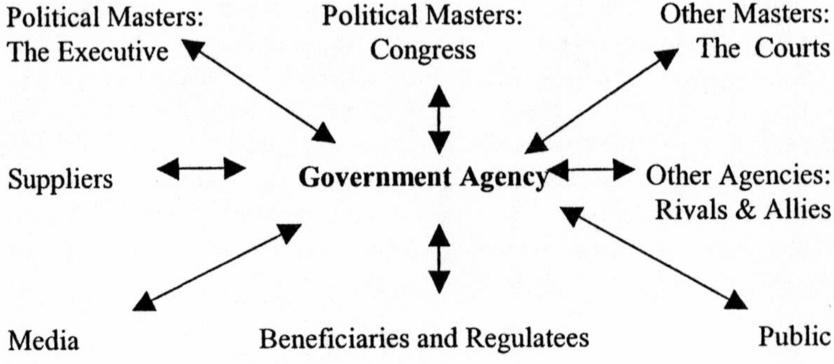

Figure 1.1 The environment of an agency (from Downs, *Inside Bureaucracy*, 45).

The Political Masters of Government Agencies

The executive is a crucial actor in the environment of an agency. It can substantially affect the policy space within which an agency operates. Although the executive cannot in the very short term change the distribution of "bureaucratic power," it has many ways of affecting the environment of a bureau. The executive can offer considerable support for the work of an agency, making its work a lot easier. It can provide political cover when an agency comes under congressional scrutiny. Similarly, falling from the graces of the White House can result in the loss of clout and in having to defer to agencies whose presidential standing has risen (Halperin, 1974, p. 221). More dramatically, an executive can initiate a reorganization that can profoundly affect an organization in positive and negative ways. Such reorganization can bring considerable uncertainty to an agency's life and even result in the detriment of its resources or autonomy, if not its very existence. For these reasons, agencies cannot afford to alienate the executive. It is not surprising that agencies seek to cultivate good relationships with the executive. Bureaucracies ignore the executive at their own peril. Besides the White House and its administrative organs, governmental agencies must also pay close attention to the actions of their departmental executives. In departmental heads, an agency has a superb ally or a formidable enemy. For most bureaus, maintaining good relations with the department in which they are located is a highly valuable asset.[24]

The other key actor in the environment of an agency is Congress. To understand the politics of bureaucracy, it is necessary to understand how the structure and dynamics of Congress shape, delimit, and provide opportunities for organizations to bring about their preferences—resources and autonomy. Agencies constantly take stock of the wishes and whims of the legislative branch, including its committees and subcommittees, staff, and oversight organs, in addition to paying particular attention to any freelancing legislator who may launch a special initiative on an issue of the agency's competence.[25] A freelancing legislator has indeed become very important in this scenario. Specific members of Congress matter because they choose to be "entrepreneurial" on particular issues of their personal interest. These freelancing legislators constitute political sponsors or enemies to whom bureaucrats must respond.[26] If an agency finds favor with a legislator, that legislator can make things very easy for that agency. As Rourke (1984) argued, there is no better lobbyist for an agency than a legislator. Failing to tend to its relationships with congressional actors can prove dangerous for an agency. Congress has not only the legislative power to alter the policy space an agency inhabits but also wields the considerable powers of the purse and oversight. These powers over bureaucracy dictate that agencies respond more or less effectively to the demands of congressional actors. A congressional enemy can make an agency's life wretched, just as a congressional ally can make an agency's work easier (Rourke, 1984, pp. 66-72). The power and dynamics of Congress are such that they "cause" bureaucracies to behave politically. Congress provides agencies with what they most want: 1) resources and 2) statutory authority in the area of their competence. But just as Congress provides these, it can also take them away. Agencies know Congress has the power to affect their policy space in regards to these goods. Besides looking to Congress for the provision of resources and autonomy, agencies also seek congressional allies for their protection when they come "under attack" by a master or a rival agency. Bureaus also keep a close eye on Congress for another reason. Congressional budgetary or legislative action on an issue area can sometimes set in motion a revision of the distribution of "bureaucratic power" in a policy space—a redistribution of resources or autonomy. Agencies "affected" by such change are left to cope with uncertainty and a change that they did not necessarily desire. The ability of Congress to change circumstances is considered a crucial variable shaping the "political" behavior of bureaucracies. It is hard to know when reorganization will be initiated, such as the 2002 Homeland Security Act that reshaped the configuration of many agencies.

Politics is a "between" phenomenon. Bureaucratic power and prerogatives vis-à-vis Congress must also be measured. Bureaucracies are not entirely powerless before Congress. They are important for members of Congress because the projects that Congress funds are implemented by bureaucracies. A good relationship between an agency and the congressional actors relevant to its policy space allows members of Congress to claim credit for a project or a new or improved service to a constituency. Taking credit for something in turn enhances the Congress member's chances for reelection. As Rourke (1984) put it, at times it seems that Congress itself has a vested interest in the growth of bureaucracy. Bureaucracies have a high level of control over information; have developed a level of expertise often lacking among Congress members or their staff; and even help create ideologies concerning the manner in which a subject should be treated. Given these factors, a Congress member's needs for information, expert advice and ideological guidance can often give bureaucracies considerable leverage on Capitol Hill. Relative to the bureaucracy, legislative organs are understaffed and underspecialized. Even when Congress has the staff and specialized knowledge, it rarely has the time to collect information from sources outside the bureaucracy. Finally, bureaucracies are relatively stable compared to the legislative power, which is much more transitory—every two years a number of Congress members are replaced (Peters, 1978, 16-38). Thus, governmental agencies are not powerless before Congress in trying to obtain what they desire the most: resources and statutory autonomy.

Other Government Agencies: Rivals and Allies

Once legislation leaves Congress and is signed by the president, it befalls to bureaucracies to interpret the letter of the law. They write the fine print that translates the legislated word into guidelines. Although a bureau does not have the structural power of Congress over other bureaus, it does have the ability to make jurisdictional claims for itself that impinge on other bureaus' claims. Such impingement is done through the act of interpreting a new law and prescribing the statutes and rules that guide implementation in ways that favor the interests of one's bureau over those of other agencies. Because there is hardly a policy space that does not involve at least a few agencies, such bureaucratic struggles are common. For these reasons, much of the energy of an agency is consumed building and maintaining relations with other agencies. Thus among the most important relationships for any government agency are those with other agencies sharing a policy space with it. As Kaufman (1981) found, any given bureau is impinged upon by at least a few others. The number of points of tangency among agencies is often striking. Downs pictured this observation in a diagram of territorial zones,

Although many of the interactions among agencies are highly routinized and non-conflictual, there are many circumstances that can force an agency to reevaluate its relationship with another agency. Of interest in this study are those circumstances in which there is an attempt, witting or unwitting, to redistribute "bureaucratic power" within a policy space, particularly in terms of resources and autonomy. These circumstances can be occasioned by any number of factors, not the least of which is the desire of the executive to change a policy space (e.g., through reorganization) or the actions of the legislative branch (through legislation, authorization and appropriation processes, or a number of other tools); but sometimes, a change in the prevailing circumstances within a policy space is initiated not by an agency's political masters but by another agency—e.g., one reinterpreting a mandate in its favor. In any case, all agencies "affected" by the change in the environment must

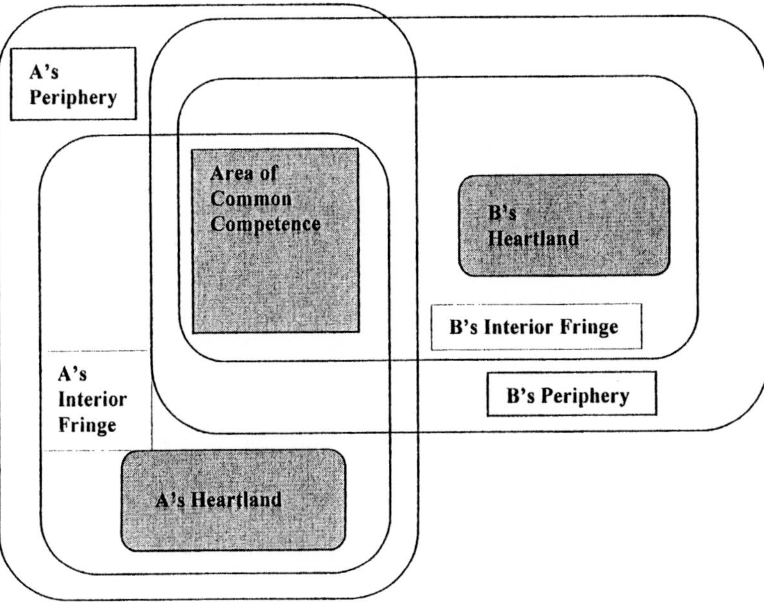

Figure 1.2 Overlapping jurisdictions (Adapted from Anthony Downs, *Inside Bureaucracy*).

ganization) or the actions of the legislative branch (through legislation, authorization and appropriation processes, or a number of other tools); but sometimes, a change in the prevailing circumstances within a policy space is initiated not by an agency's political masters but by another agency—e.g., one reinterpreting a mandate in its favor. In any case, all agencies "affected" by the change in the environment must respond by reassessing their organizational position in the overall policy space in which they operate. While routinized inter-agency operations are interesting, our model zooms in on the less stable and less congenial moments in relations among agencies—those that force agencies to reassess their bureaucratic power position vis-à-vis other agencies within their policy space. Incidentally, this study is not the first to focus on inter-agency environments. Eugene Bardach's (1998) work on getting agencies to work together posits that the inter-agency process involves,

> . . . at a minimum, leveraging personnel and financial resources for collaborative purposes, designing and managing an effective operating system, reaching and maintaining consensus on basic goals and on trade-offs among relevant sub-goals,

politics of bureaucracy must, consequently, be more revealing at precisely the more conflictive points of contact.

Other Actors in the Environment: Why They May Matter Less

What about the other actors in the environment of an agency? Do they matter for the purposes of bureaucratic politics? Are they important at all as catalysts of political behavior in governmental organizations? Of course they matter. In this study, however, these actors are held "frozen" for the purposes of parsimony. Although the literature on bureaucracies is full of examples on why an agency's clients and regulated interests are central to bureaucratic politics,[27] this work focuses on an agency's political masters and on the rival and allied agencies that share its policy space. These relationships are assumed to be singularly significant in the environment of an agency from a bureaucratic politics perspective. These two actors provide sufficient instances to draw important conclusions about the politics of bureaucracy. What enables us to keep the other actors in an agency's environment "frozen" is that most other actors act through an agency's political masters if they desire to alter an agency's decisions, neutralize its actions or hurt it. The public and the media, for example, can put pressure on a government agency regarding the effectiveness of its performance or its failures and successes, but if they desire to fundamentally alter the structure of the policy space of an agency—e.g., its resources and organizational autonomy—they must generally act through its masters, Congress or the executive. The public and the media do not legislate the statutory authority of an agency, fund it, or oversee it with the imposing power of Congress or the executive. Also, public pressure or media criticism cannot directly punish an agency for its fundamental preferences regarding resources or organizational autonomy. Only Congress or the executive can. Similarly, the suppliers of an agency have an equally low leverage to alter the structure of an agency's policy space. They can lobby for or against an agency or seek redress before Congress or the executive, but their influence over the resource and organizational autonomy of an agency is always filtered through the sieve of Congress and the executive. In regard to an agency's beneficiaries and sufferers as well as its regulatees, these cannot fundamentally alter an agency's policy space without having to move Congress or the executive (or even the courts) to act on their complaints or petitions. Moreover, this process takes a long time and it seldom has the pressing or threatening urgency over an agency that a congressional act, an executive order, or the claims of a competitor or rival have. The influence these "other" agents in the environment of an agency have over its resource and autonomy claims are encapsulated in the relationship between an agency and its political masters and between an agency and its fellow dwellers in any given policy space.

A Typology of Conflict among Government Agencies

Our focus on the relationships between an agency and its masters and among agencies in a single policy space suggests a typology of possible situations faced by a bureau when someone threatens its resources and autonomy. If what triggers the political behavior of an agency is a change in the prevailing distribution of bureaucratic power—resources and autonomy, then there must be specific types of responses that describe nearly all situations faced by a bureau at any given point in time. Three factors matter in this regard: 1) the type of change; 2) who initiates the change; and 3) the object of change. In regard to the first, changes in the power distribution of a policy space can occur without an increase in the absolute amount of power contained in that space—a zero-sum game for the government agencies involved. Change can also occur with an accompanying increase to the absolute amount of power contained in that space—e.g., more resources appropriated for the policy, expanded jurisdictions, etc.—a "grow-the-pie" scenario. The first situation is likely to cause *offensive/defensive* political behavior; the second scenario will cause *competitive* political behavior. In regard to the second factor (who initiates the change), a change of power distribution in a given policy space is either initiated by an agency's political masters (politicians) or by other agencies (rivals and competitors) that seek opportunities to expand their own claims over the policy space. Who initiates a change is therefore another determinant of the types of actions that a governmental agency can and may take to counter change. But regardless of who initiates change, once it has begun bureaus are compelled to reassess how change affects their share of resources and their autonomy. Then, they must act. For some agencies, change represents opportunities to acquire more resources or to increase their level of autonomy. For others, the change implies having to defend their existing resources or organizational autonomy. Both of these actions are considered political behavior. An actor that initiates a revision of the status quo with the potential to affect bureaucratic power within a policy space will be called a "revisionist" actor. An actor that prefers the current state of affairs within the policy space will be called "a status quo actor." Status quo actors view nearly all change as a challenge. Finally, the object of change also matters. Change in a given policy space may imply a change in material resources—either a redistribution or an increase/decrease—or a change in the jurisdictional boundaries within the policy space—a gain or a loss in organizational autonomy. Depending on the object of change—resources or autonomy or both—the conflict may be either allocational or functional or both. Given these three variables, the resulting possible scenarios are the following:

		Autonomy	
		Status Quo Actor (Politician/Other Agencies)	Revisionist Actor (Politician/Other Agency)
Resources	Status Quo Actor (Politician/Other Agencies)	No Conflict	Functional Conflict
	Revisionist Actor (Politician/Other Agencies)	Allocational Conflict	Allocational and Functional Conflict

Figure 1.3 Typology of bureaucratic conflict.

"No conflict" is indicated in the box showing that no one is attempting a revision of the status quo. "Functional conflict" is indicated when either a politician or an agency within the policy space attempts to revise the status quo in terms of statutory autonomy. There is "allocational conflict" when either a politician or an agency attempts to revise the status quo in terms of resources. Finally, both "functional and allocational conflict" ensue when a politician or an agency attempts to revise the status quo to redistribute autonomy and resources.[28] Competitive political behavior (not typologized in figure 3) by governmental organizations is triggered by an increase in resources or jurisdictional power for the group of agencies in a policy space, without attempts to revise the prevailing distribution. Now, a further distinction must be made regarding who initiates the redistribution of bureaucratic power. When the revision is initiated by a political master (Congress or the executive), changes that increase an agency's jurisdiction over a set of tasks or its budget, whether they do so at the expense of another agency's resources or autonomy or not, will be well received by the benefiting agency. Immediate and forceful resistance by an affected agency, however, should be expected. Our cases will focus on situations that represent a competitive or a conflictive situation.

Assuming Organizational Unity of Action and Rationality

Our models seek to explain bureaucratic behavior assuming "unity of action," that is, that the actions of the members of a governmental organization, as Lipsky (1980,

p. 13) put it, "when taken in concert...add up to agency behavior." Now, clearly there is always some slippage between the personal goals and behavior of individual bureaucrats and the organizational goals and behavior of the agency, but this slippage is seldom enough to throw off the assumption that bureaus seek to maximize their resources and autonomy. Moreover, organizations through various structures of incentives and disincentives easily overcome this slippage. This assumption of unity of action is also justified by the fact that most bureaucrats appear to cooperate with and contribute to an organization's goals regarding its resources and organizational autonomy. Individual dissent (whistle blowing) on these goals appears to be rare and public scandal by individual dissent on the organizational goals of an agency is even rarer. Moreover, individual bureaucrats may disagree with a particular policy but they seldom mistake this disagreement with the goals of the organization in terms of its resources and autonomy.

Similarly, the model assumes that governmental organizations are rational entities: that they employ the most efficient means to achieve their organizational goals. These are entities with purposive lives and concrete interests and goals. While bureaucratic actors suffer from the same limitations to their cognitive capacity as any other actor in any other circumstance of life, the assumption is that the members of an agency make the most rational decisions in the pursuit of the goals of the organization, even, of course, when they are imperfectly informed.[29] This assumption is crucial for any model of bureaucratic politics.

Factors that Explain Agency Behavior: Politics

The basic elements that explain the political behavior of a bureau come from this postulate: governmental organizations seek to expand their material resources and enhance their organizational autonomy and, if under attack, to defend these desirable goods. This drive alone is a necessary and sufficient condition to cause *political* behavior in government agencies. When this primordial desire is accompanied by a challenge to the status quo in the distribution of bureaucratic power within a policy space, political behavior is heightened. It is the desire to acquire more material resources and greater autonomy intensified by a change in the environment that ultimately drives the more interesting political behavior of bureaus. But, if the desire to increase resources and the desire to enhance organizational autonomy are the *drivers* of political behavior, particularly under "revisionist" circumstances, what shapes and colors the political courses of action that agencies take in a given circumstance?

The course of action that government agencies take is shaped and colored by the responses to these questions: 1) What agencies are involved? 2) What is the relative influence of each agency? 3) What are the agencies' available channels of action? Let us specify each of these. As for the first, to understand political behavior in a given scenario it is necessary to consider the government agencies involved. The specific governmental organizations involved in a given scenario are largely determined by the content of the revisionist initiative. A list of the organizations involved helps us to know which organizations stand to benefit and which ones are affected as we contemplate the change at hand in the distribution of resources and autonomy in a policy space. Determining who "wins" and who "loses" helps us discern the position of each agency regarding the matter at hand—principally who is on the offensive and who is on the defensive. Establishing what agencies are involved also allows the identification of potential organizational alliances and helps measure the level of "conflict." The intensity of the conflict is directly proportional to the size of the win or loss implied for each agency in the policy space. Previous bureaucratic rivalries may also intensify the conflict—history matters.

The relative influence of each agency also matters. Influence is measured by 1) the agency's position and standing vis-à-vis its rivals and competitors and 2) its position and standing in the eyes of its political masters. As Allison suggests, organizational power is a function of the leverage associated with standing—but an agency's effectiveness and willingness to make use of this leverage is also crucial. Clearly not every agency has the same level of influence to make its organizational interests heard and felt. U.S. Customs, for example, was the primary interdiction law enforcement agency and its influence over interdiction decision-making was huge. It not only provided Congress with a large part of the information on the subject but it also cultivated enormous influence on Capitol Hill by serving the needs of a number of senators and House members and their staff. In addition, Customs was a large, prestigious agency with solid support from its department. This "standing" gave it advantages to make aggressive moves or fend off encroachments on its area of competence within the anti-narcotics policy space.

Finally, the channels of action available to an agency determine much of the structure of a political game by circumscribing the maneuvers available to an agency and those unavailable to it. Channels of action can be formal and informal. A formal channel of action would be, for example, the ability of an agency to appeal to its departmental executive for protection from moves by rivals and competitors or political masters—through established, systematic procedures to appeal or fend off those moves. An informal channel of action would be, for example, the ability of an agency to negotiate an "opposing alliance" with other affected agencies to oppose the designs of a revisionist actor. The result of negotiations with potential friends/allies (and with rivals/competitors) is often expressed in "Memoranda of Agreement" or "Memoranda of Understanding." Such instruments are not uncommon among government agencies.

There is an additional *contextual* factor that might be useful to consider because it adds to the level of conflict—the history of the relationships among the agencies involved. Some governmental organizations have natural allies while others have natural competitors. If the conflict occurs between two natural allies, the likelihood of a negotiated—and even cordial—compromise is high. If it occurs between two natural competitors, the conflict can be more intense; negotiations, if possible, can be more difficult; and outside—even forced—intervention by third actors might be required. The DEA and the FBI, for example, have long histories of rivalry. DEA has traditionally viewed the FBI as an outright threat to its survival. When the FBI has tried to absorb DEA, the latter has fought it off in a panic mode. The history of the relationship precludes much cooperation between the two agencies and heightens conflict between them. Other agencies, such as the U.S. Coast Guard and the U.S. Navy are natural allies. Cooperation in the war on drugs between the two organizations flowed rather smoothly. In many ways, the Navy accommodated the Coast Guard to help it fulfill its commitments to the war on drugs without getting into it any deeper than most Navy personnel really wanted. The Coast Guard benefited enormously from such arrangement. These organizations appeared to complement each other's tasks in the drug war by virtue of the medium in which they operate. The result was that the U.S. Coast Guard made the Navy look good in the eyes of the politicians that care about the war on drugs and vice versa and the U.S. Coast Guard took advantage of the new resources to grow and prosper. This was a mutually convenient relationship.

The *Political* Behavior of Organizations

Having defined the forces that give origin to and shape bureaucratic political behavior, how do we classify the relevant behaviors of an organization? What should we expect to see when organizational *political* behavior occurs? Before answering this question, we need to clarify an assumption made here regarding bureaucratic behavior. A government agency is a nonprofit organization created by political authorities to provide a good or service. Agencies are functionally specialized, financed by periodic congressional appropriations. They are composed of individuals appointed, retained and promoted mainly on the basis of their performance. They are managed hierarchically and have complex structures of authority. Most relationships within the agency, with other agencies, and most of the activities of the bureau are prescribed in written regulations (Niskanen, 1971). Having said this, *organizational political behavior* can be defined as the set of actions, strategically calculated, that an organization carries out to expand or defend its resources and autonomy. This definition suggests two types of political behavior: offensive and defensive. An offensive posture by a governmental organization occurs when an agency seeks to take advantage of a perceived opportunity to increase its resources or autonomy. A defensive posture is one adopted by an agency that believes its material resources and autonomy are jeopardized by an offending agency's moves—or the actions of a political master. Segregating organizational political behavior into an offensive and a defensive set of actions leads to this question: What are the actions that embody an offensive or a defensive set of actions given the constraints and opportunities the American political system affords an agency? An offending agency may, for example, interpret a new legislation to its advantage—e.g., in a way that excludes other agencies from a set of tasks previously shared. It may also lobby Congress for a particular mission or a stake in a mission shared with or already in the hands of another agency. An "offending" agency may also seek to expel another agency from a set of shared tasks by employing tactics such as withholding information, avoiding joint tasks, failing to share assets, etc. It may also seek statutory changes in existing laws in order to acquire greater resources. It may seek to bring the support of its political masters to bear on a jurisdictional dispute with another agency in order to resolve the dispute in its favor. Actions such as these are indicative of *offensive* political behavior.

Defensive behavior occurs when the resources or autonomy of an agency come under threat. In a jurisdictional dispute, a defending agency may seek the aid of its congressional allies or it may look to build an alliance with other agencies that also feel threatened by the revisionist designs of an actor. It may employ rhetoric that would portray any change within the policy space as being to the detriment of national policy. It may seek to shore up its autonomy by appealing to the public or the media or to members of Congress for support. These types of actions in reaction to a revisionist actor would be considered *defensive* political behavior.

Predicting Agency Behavior: Politics

If we consider the content (resources or jurisdictional authority) or the direction (increase or decrease) of change in a policy space, we can predict agencies will engage in various kinds of political behavior. Competition for a greater share of the additional resources is such behavior. Avoiding shared jurisdiction over a set of tasks is another. If they must share the jurisdiction with another bureau, agencies will seek opportunities to limit their dependence on other agencies or, eventually seek opportunities to decrease the shared overlap. When an agency attempts to reduce the overlap in the tasks shared with another agency, it will have to do so at the expense of the other agency and therefore provoke resistance—another type of political behavior. The natural reaction of the affected agency will be to seek the political support of its departmental leaders and elected politicians to avoid being shut out of that set of tasks. Also, agencies will, over the long haul, try to secure greater resources that will help improve their functional performance because this improvement helps secure their current jurisdictional authority over a set of tasks. When under attack, agencies will seek to build alliances to fend off competitors and rivals and might pay back by helping an ally to consolidate a prominent role in the policy space. This will depend partly on whether the agency perceives the ally as a threat or not. Agencies will try to acquire jurisdiction over sets of activities that they consider relevant to the agency's core sets of tasks. This can be referred to as "creeping imperialism." When this is done to the detriment of another agency, resistance should be expected. As a corollary, in case of general budgetary reductions, an agency will seek missions to help contain these reductions. Insecure agencies, e.g., agencies whose survival has been threatened in the past, will seek to achieve equality with the agency that threatened them and will try to demonstrate rhetorically their indispensability for the conduct of national policy on the pertinent issue. Agencies will use rhetoric designed to convince their political masters of the necessity of their contribution to the overall national policy. Equally, agencies will avoid new tasks they do not desire by portraying them as distracting from the "real" work of the bureau. Also, agencies will seek concrete, favorable ways to show their contribution to the overall success (but not the failure) of a policy. They will try to diminish the importance of potentially damaging information by portraying it as temporary problems or inconsequential glitches or irrelevant. Agencies should be expected to "compete" for credit on the achievements of a national policy. Bureaucrats will seek to satisfy the needs of the various congressional organs that fund and oversee them and cultivate "patrons" among congressional members and even among powerful congressional staff who will offer political cover when adverse changes occur within a policy space. When inter-agency teams are formed, the primary commitment of the members of the team will be to represent their agency's interests; only secondarily will they think of the overall national policy. These—and others—are some of the expected kinds of political behavior that one is likely to see in the bureaucratic politics game in nearly any one policy space.

Organizational Culture

The concept of organizational culture has produced abundant controversy. There are fundamental disagreements on the definition of culture, the mechanisms by which it influences the behavior of an organization, and how it should be observed and measured. On the one hand, organizational culture has been hailed as the source of new and inventive thinking about organizations and, on the other hand, it has been criticized as an intellectual dead-end, a fad without scientific theoretical foundations, far from mainstream organizational research. This book does not intend to resolve these disagreements. Instead, it simply intends to assess whether organizational culture can help explain the behavior of government agencies.

The Genesis of Organizational Culture

Organizational cultures do not emerge ex nihilo. The emergence of an organizational culture is a complex phenomenon that requires time. It starts with the social function that an organization is created to perform. That social function stems from a public need: to police the streets, to provide welfare for the poor, to guard the borders, to clean the environment, to stem the flow of illegal drugs, etc. All government agencies are created by legislative fiat to respond to a perceived public need. From the legislative fiat creating the agency, its founders derive an explicit "mission" or social function for the agency. This mission is the statement that embodies the way the organization responds to the public need it was created to alleviate. The mission of an organization is the subjective operationalization of the mandate received from its political masters (creators). Generally, the mission of an organization is displayed prominently in the publications of the organization, its personnel manuals, its web sites, and other places. This mission is the primary guide to discern what an organization does, but it is insufficient to discern the culture of an organization. For that we must delve further into the tasks that the organization performs—including its training and socialization systems. If the explicit mission follows the legislative mandate, the tasks a governmental organization performs follow from its mission. From the organization's mission statement, the members of an organization determine the specific tasks that need to be performed to carry out the mission. These tasks do not emerge spontaneously from the organization's mission. Instead, there is a somewhat lengthy process through which the members of an organization learn, discover and develop certain tasks central to the mission. The organization's members also develop over time a hierarchy of tasks that indicates which of these is central and which of these is less important or can be considered a secondary task. All the organization's tasks eventually become routinized activities.

If we follow the thread, it becomes clear that the organizational tasks generate another link in the process of the emergence of an organizational culture. Over time, through carrying out these tasks, the members of an agency establish and consolidate the norms and practices that help it execute its tasks with at least a modicum of success. These norms and practices are fundamental to an organization. They become the tangible guide to an organization's members' day-to-day activities. Finally, an organization's norms and practices engender a set of basic attitudes and assumptions acquired by its members through the training and socialization through which an agency puts its members. This is reinforced by the day-to-day tasks. This set of attitudes and basic assumptions are the "good instincts" that underlie and support a sense of "rightness of action" among the members. It gives its members a sense of what is impermissible or "wrong." This set of basic attitudes and assumptions enables a street policeman, for example, to view the exchange of a mysterious package between two people at a street corner with greater attention and a good dose of suspicion than a simple passer-by would. We can picture the emergence of an organizational culture in the following way:

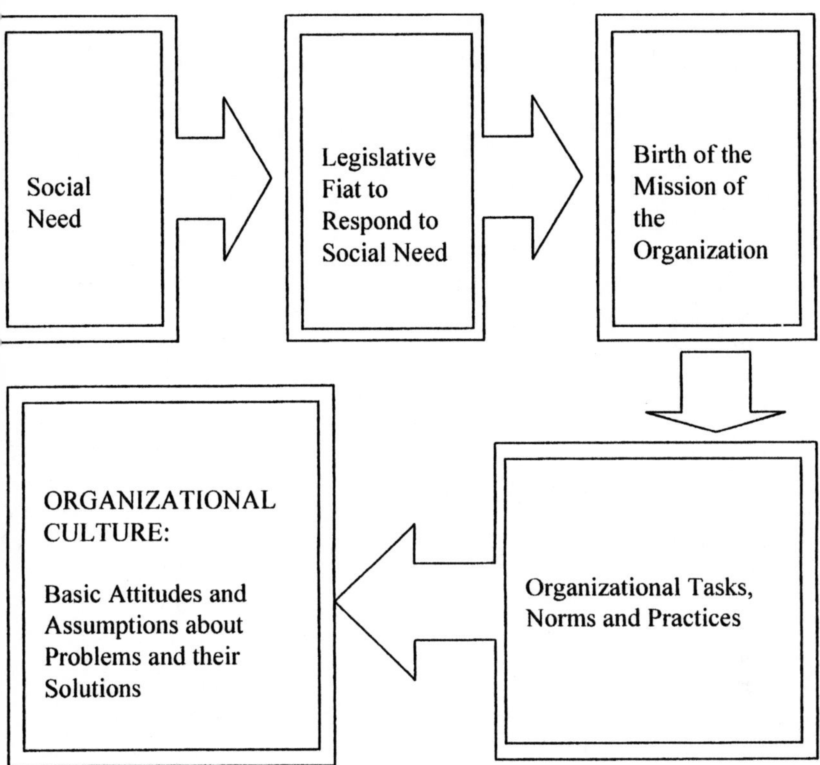

Figure 1.4 The progression in the emergence of an organizational culture.

There is disagreement among scholars regarding the "content" of culture, but there is a general agreement that culture has a "patterned," consistent way to its constituent elements. These elements are often represented in symbols—logos, signs, gadgets, rituals, etc. These symbols, however, are not the content of culture that is of interest here. Instead, our interest is on the subjective, underlying basic attitudes and assumptions that buttress the motivations behind action by an organization's members. The subjective nature of organizational culture is what leads us to ask: where exactly in this "genealogy" does organizational culture reside? What is culture more specifically?

Defining Organizational Culture

All organizations develop a culture. "Culture is to an organization what personality is to an individual" (Wilson, 1989, p. 91). But, what is personality in an individual? What is culture in an organization? Culture is a consistent and persistent pattern of basic attitudes and assumptions behind action manifest in the norms and practices of the members of an organization that have been invented, discovered, or developed over time as the group learns to cope with the issues and problems that arise from trying to carry out its mission. These basic attitudes and assumptions must be proven and have worked well enough to be considered valid and effective by the members of the organization. They are taught to new members as the correct way to perceive, think, and feel in relation to those problems and their solutions.[30] This definition enables the purist scholar of organizational culture to include elements as concrete as the artifacts of an organization—for their representational value—and to rely primarily on the subjective manifestations of culture—such as the common values held by the members of an organization by virtue of belonging to it—for causal explanations of behavior. The artifacts remain secondary; the internalized elements are where causal relations reside. This definition also enables us to do two things: 1) discern the effects of culture on an organization and 2) determine where these effects can be observed and measured. This definition implies the existence of a mechanism by which culture influences the behavior of the members of an agency. This mechanism is the internalization of the basic attitudes and assumptions by the members through a process of socialization and then the application of these basic attitudes and assumptions to problems and solutions. To understand this, it behooves us to turn our attention to determining the effects of culture on an organization and then to establishing how these effects can be measured.

The Effect of Culture on Organizational Behavior

We must now turn to establishing a causal relation between organizational culture and organizational behavior. To get to the root of the cause-and-effect of culture on organizational behavior, we must focus on the primary functions of culture in an organization. First, culture helps an organization achieve internal integration and coherence—it gives the organization a sense of unity. A well established organizational culture provides the members of the organization with stability and predictability. It sets the parameters of comfort within the organization and lessens the anxiety of the unknown. Individuals in organizations feel at greater ease when there are commonly held assumptions and behavioral patterns because these not only tell them how to behave but tell them what to expect from the organization's fellow members. In this comfort lies the sense of "family" and commonality that the members of an organization feel toward one another. More importantly, these "feelings of commonality" have specific effects on an organization. They help establish organization-wide consensuses. Such consensuses enable the organization to override the desires of specific individuals by appealing to transcendent, more powerful unity-creating metaphors that can gain the enthusiastic commitment of the organization's members. They also provide consistency of action by encouraging processes strongly underpinned by common meanings and a normative order. Symbolic consistency is also provided when certain ceremonial actions are conducted in order to hold high what is valued and what is not—to distinguish the "sacred" from the "profane." Content consistency is provided through the creation of programs that reinforce each other into a coherent whole. Culture excludes confusion and ambiguity by providing a "guide" to what is acceptable and rewarded and what is unacceptable and censured. These feelings of commonality help interpret the metaphorical argot and emblems of an organization. Culture helps alleviate anxiety, control the uncertain, bring predictability to the environment, and clarify the ambiguous. The result is organizational coherence and minimal dissent.[31]

Second, culture guides the external adaptation of an organization to its environment. It becomes the sensing organ through which external information is filtered, interpreted and processed. Culture has a "differentiational" function. Culture helps the members of an organization to determine not only what belongs within but also what belongs without. Culture sets the boundaries where the organization ends and where it begins; where the "external" world is and where the "internal" world resides. It clarifies any "inconsistent" elements making their way into the organization and any "incompatible" influences facing the organization. This "differentiational" function of culture is central to this work. It bears much of the explanatory responsibility for a model that attempts to explain organizational behavior. It does so because the culture of an organization helps its members deal with external influences by guiding them to the islands of clarity of what is acceptable and unacceptable. It helps make judgments on the "rightness" or "appropriateness" of an organization's actions. It creates a logic of appropriateness in the minds of the organization's members. When change in the environment of the organization occurs, the members of an organization appeal to their sense of congruence and assonance (differentiation) to shape their attitudinal disposition toward change. The response to any stimulus is closely guided by that logic of appropriateness. It is in this sense that culture shapes the behavior of the members of the organization—the addition of whose behavior is equal to the behavior of the organization.

In sum, this study tests whether culture has any effects on the response of an organization toward external stimuli. It tests whether the "patterned and enduring differences among systems of coordinated action...lead those systems to respond in different ways to the same stimuli." The goal is to see whether "when faced with changed environmental conditions, some organizations persist in traditional ways of behaving" (Wilson, 1989, p. 93). If so, culture matters. If not so, culture is then largely irrelevant to the study of organizational behavior.

Observing and Measuring the Effects of Organizational Culture

Focusing on the functions of internal integration and external adaptation of the culture of an organization allows us to observe and measure culture *at work* in concrete ways. However, while much of the literature focuses on the "internal integration" function of organizational culture, this work emphasizes the "external adaptation" role of culture in organizations—the response to environmental stimuli. This is because we are interested in the environment—the policy space—within which an organization operates and within which it must respond to problems. This helps us get to the root of our concern: organizational behavior. Thus, to determine the effects of culture on the behavior of an organization we must observe the responses of its members to changes in the circumstances of a policy space. Observing how an organization's members respond to such changes should offer patterns of action that are consistent and coherent across the organization. This focus enables us to see the tangible effects of culture in situations of interaction between the members of an organization and the external stimuli that they must acknowledge and deal with. If we define the "content" of culture in an organization as the basic attitudes and assumptions of its members, then we should be able to predict their reaction to an external stimulus.

A Word about the Pathologies of Organizational Cultures...

Not all cultures are healthy cultures. Some act in detriment of the organization's ability to adapt in the face of rapid or abrupt changes. Sometimes an organization's members internalize the basic attitudes and assumptions in such a way that the developed affection for the "ways of doing things" in the organization blunts all sense of good judgment regarding the true nature of the environment where the organization operates and the need to adapt and respond to changes in that environment. If the culture impairs the ability of the organization to adapt to change, the organization will find itself increasingly isolated, unable to fulfill its mission and eventually at risk of being punished or dismantled by its political masters or in peril of being challenged on its mission and task by a more effective competitor. An ultimate price is paid when the organization is simply unable to adapt and change; it may even die.

...and a Word about Subcultures

Introducing the concept of differentiation as a mechanism to respond to external adaptation pressures enables us to make some inroads into the topic of subcultures, a fact of organizational life. Organizational culture scholars agree that organizations have one or more cultures. When there is more than one, each is a subculture. Subcultures are important because in a given environment an agency does not always decide or can decisively oppose the imposition of new mandates by its political masters. Thus, by focusing on the subject of subcultures we have one more opportunity to draw important conclusions about agency behavior. For example, ambiguity, if it *must* occur and be tolerated within an agency, will make the members relegate the ambiguous element to the periphery. Ambiguous and dissonant elements within an organization often become subcultures. They constitute isolated units standing as the "odd man out."

The concept of subcultures is also useful because it can help us understand the hierarchy of tasks inside an agency. If the organization must prioritize its tasks according to the distance of each task from the core mission of the organization, some tasks will be assigned a subculture status; they might be recognized as important and may even be necessary but they will not command the level of commitment and the affection of the members of the organization in the same way. Accounting and administration, for example, must be done at the Drug Enforcement Administration, but these will never have the glamour and affection of street-drug busting or drug trafficker arrests as fundamental tasks in the organization. The Navy will never consider flying spy planes in Colombia for the purposes of gathering information for the war on drugs as fundamental to the organization as flying stealth bombers or more glamorous aircraft. Spying for the drug war will always be a subculture. It will experience discrimination and be easily pushed aside. It will never be well funded or lobbied for and will be subcontracted whenever possible. The members of the Navy flying those spy planes will never achieve the status and admiration of all in the same way as the pilots who fly bombers and other dearly cherished aircraft. Promotions within the organizations will be unlikely and few.

Factors that Explain Agency Behavior: Culture

In being more specific about explaining the *cultural* behavior of government agencies, the factors by which organizational behavior can be predicted are the answers to these questions: 1) What is the social function that the organization was created to fulfill? 3) What is the mission of the organization? 3) What are the organization's tasks through which it seeks to fulfill its mission? What are the organization's "central" and "secondary tasks"? 4) What are the norms and practices that the organization has invented, discovered, or developed over time? 5) What attitudes and basic assumptions underlie these norms and practices? Let us take up each of these questions.

What are the agency's social function and mission? Every agency was created with a specific public need in mind. By fiat, the policy intent of the legislation gives rise to the social function of an organization. This social function is captured in the explicit mission of an organization. The Drug Enforcement Administration, for example, was created to fulfill a specific function. In its web site, the DEA states that,

> The mission of the Drug Enforcement Administration (DEA) is to enforce the controlled substances laws and regulations of the United States and bring to the criminal and civil justice system of the United States, or any other competent jurisdiction, those organizations and principal members of organizations, involved in the growing, manufacture, or distribution of controlled substances appearing in or destined for illicit traffic in the United States; and to recommend and support non-enforcement programs aimed at reducing the availability of illicit controlled substances on the domestic and international markets.[32]

Because the explanatory power of organizational culture begins with an organization's mission, the mission statement should serve as a "guide" to the members of the organization who may want to determine whether a "new mission"—say, one assigned to the agency post facto by another legislative fiat—is perceived to be assonant or dissonant with the stated, well-known and accepted mission up to that time. When faced with a change in circumstances in the environment—e.g., the "assignment" of a new social function, the members of an organization are likely to know instinctively how distant from the original mission of the agency is the new assignment. They know this because they tend to ask themselves what this implies for the very nature of the organization as they know it. The answer that the members of an organization give to the question "what does this change mean for the organization?" should reveal a connection between what an organization's employees think and how they behave.

What are the organization's "central tasks"? What are its "secondary tasks"? For more explanatory power we have to delve into the more specific activities of the agency, the tasks through which it purports to fulfill its mission. Over time, organizations invent, discover, or develop specific tasks that enable them to carry their mission with at least some success. The DEA web site and other documents, for example, state that its organizational tasks include:

- Investigation and preparation for the prosecution of major violators of controlled substance laws operating at interstate and international levels.
- Investigation and preparation for prosecution of criminals and drug gangs who perpetrate violence in our communities and terrorize citizens through fear and intimidation.
- Management of a national drug intelligence program in cooperation with federal, state, local, and foreign officials to collect, analyze, and disseminate strategic and operational drug intelligence information.
- Seizure and forfeiture of assets derived from, traceable to, or intended to be used for illicit drug trafficking.

- Enforcement of the provisions of the Controlled Substances Act as they pertain to the manufacture, distribution, and dispensing of legally produced controlled substances.
- Coordination and cooperation with federal, state and local law enforcement officials on mutual drug enforcement efforts and enhancement of such efforts through exploitation of potential interstate and international investigations beyond local or limited federal jurisdictions and resources.
- Coordination and cooperation with federal, state, and local agencies, and with foreign governments, in programs designed to reduce the availability of illicit abuse-type drugs on the United States market through non-enforcement methods such as crop eradication, crop substitution, and training of foreign officials.
- Responsibility, under the policy guidance of the Secretary of State and U.S. Ambassadors, for all programs associated with drug law enforcement counterparts in foreign countries.
- Liaison with the United Nations, Interpol, and other organizations on matters relating to international drug control programs.[33]

From these *general* tasks more *specific* tasks are derived. These specific tasks give rise to individual jobs. From the intelligence clause, for example, DEA built a considerable capacity for collecting, analyzing, and distributing intelligence information. Intelligence collectors, analysts, and distributors must be hired. But even as the mission turns into general tasks and these turn into specific tasks, what remains constant is that these tasks are directly connected to the explicit mission of the organization. Like the mission, the tasks an organization performs are also subjected to a "differentiational" process by the members of the organization. At the very concrete level, it is possible that a street-level DEA agent refuses to chase a criminal whose action was the vandalizing of a postal mail box—even if the agent witnessed the crime. Though his job is law enforcement, the agent discriminates among the types of laws that his organization enforces (although one would presume that he would be moved to do something nevertheless).[34] Thus much of the explanatory burden of organizational culture lies in a phenomenon that could be labeled "a hierarchy of tasks." An organization makes a clear distinction among organizational tasks. Some tasks are directly related to its mission while others are less central to it. It can be said that some tasks carry out the mission while others tasks merely "support" those central tasks. The latter are considered auxiliary or secondary tasks. Thus, in an organization there are various categories of tasks: those that are directly and those that are indirectly connected with the mission of an organization. "Indirectly" connected tasks would be, for example, administrative jobs. This classification leads to the discovery of what an agency values as directly contributing to its success and what it values only as an auxiliary activity, perhaps even a dispensable one in times of budgetary cuts.[35] When faced with an external change in circumstances, an agency applies a "differentiation" criterion to figure out what can be changed and what cannot be changed,[36] what is important and what is not important. Downs' concept of a bureau's territorial domain can help us understand this. The boundaries between the central tasks and the secondary tasks of an organization are never neatly set; there is always some ambiguity as to where some boundaries begin and where other boundaries end. The members of an organization, however, use their "good instincts" to identify those activities that they consider centrally valuable and others which they consider secondary or even tertiary to the mission of the organization. The interior territory of a bureau is known as the "core." Employees identify the tasks that belong in this core and their "attitude" is most protective or "territorial" around these core tasks. The territory that includes secondary or auxiliary tasks is known as the "periphery." The members of an organization may not consider these tasks as important and may behave less territorially about them. But as we move further and further out from the core, the territory can be labeled as "fringes" and the areas completely outside the organization's (extended) territory can be labeled "no-man's land."[37] One simple example can help us illustrate what this means. The vandalizing of a postal mail box may, for a DEA agent, be just the kind of crime that falls in no man's land—at the very least not in *his* land. Often the attitude toward the tasks that fall on the fringes is indifference and maybe outright rejection. An agency will resist changes that include a transformation of its core tasks the strongest. Its resistance should ease as the intrusion moves away from the core. This distinction between attitudes toward the core tasks and the secondary tasks also enables us also to predict that as a task is further removed from the core, it should be more likely to suffer neglect by the organization—or at least not be valued as highly. In sum, organizations develop territorial sensitivities because its members develop a hierarchy of affectivity toward what they do. This affectivity—and corresponding sensitivity—decreases as the bureau's territoriality progresses from core to periphery to fringes to no-man's land.

What are the norms and practices that the organization has invented, discovered, or developed over time? What are the fundamental attitudes and basic assumptions that underlie and support those norms and practices? Norms specify the behavioral expectations by defining what is the right or wrong way of responding to situations. All organizations develop these behavioral expectations. Although norms are generally unwritten precepts, their power to provide the member of an organization with a strong sense of expectations is important. The widely accepted practices of an organization are an important source of guidance for what are the correct ways of doing things within the organization. Both norms and practices have to do with the expected behavior of the members of an organization. DEA may train its agents to enforce drug laws in specific ways that are neither required nor implied in its overall mission or may be different from other agencies that enforce the same antinarcotics statutes. DEA, for example, relies heavily on undercover techniques and employs buy-and-bust tactics to enforce drug laws, something the FBI does not favor to enforce the same statutes. DEA has simply developed the practice of doing so. Overtime, the members of an agency develop a trust in and even affective feelings toward the practices of the agency. As with the previously specified variables, a change in the practices of an organization, say, at DEA because a hypothetical Supreme Court ruling that buy-and-bust tactics are unconstitutional, would bring great turmoil to its members. Because the members of an agency develop a cognitive, affective and evaluative attachment to "the way the organization does things," one should expect a great deal of resistance to a change in the environment that directly challenges such practices and, conversely, a warm welcome to the external stimuli that reinforce their value.[38]

The attitudes that the members of an organization adopt as they are socialized are crucial in explaining the behavior of organizations, as are the basic metaphysical and moral assumptions they make about the nature of human relationships and the nature of their organization. The basic attitudes and assumptions are at the root of the way the members of an organization view their role in society and the utility of the social function their mandate defines. They contribute to the hierarchy of affection toward the mission and the tasks of the organization and ultimately serve as a code for behavior. They do so by integrating the personal stakes of bureaucrats into the stakes of the organization through a process of training and socialization through which individuals get "acculturated." An organization performs its social function by dividing it into tasks; bundles of tasks make up jobs; and jobs made up careers. Individual bureaucrats' careers are not isolated from their work identities and roles. Bureaucrats take on the role, build an identity around their careers, carry these after 5:00 PM, and often modify their entire behavior to reflect the ethos of the organization as a whole. Attitudes carry over beyond working hours. Cops are vigilant even when they are off-duty. A diplomat does not cease to be a diplomat off the State Department's or the Embassy's premises. A soldier carries with him a role and identity wherever he or she goes.[39] Our organizational culture model predicts that bureaucrats build stakes in the organization's identity. These stakes become the work of preserving the role and the identity of the organization because these define his or her own role and identity to a large extent. Bureaucrats simplify the world by producing mental schemes about what the organization is about and what it is not about. Such role-taking and identification enables a bureaucrat to handle decision making, respond to external stimuli, and navigate the organization's political environment. Culture is a modifier of behavior because it is ultimately a definer of identities.

Together, the mission of an organization, the hierarchy of tasks stemming from that mission, the norms and practices of the organization, and the basic attitudes and assumptions of its members carry the explanatory burden of organizational culture. Observing and tracing these elements, it should be possible to predict how an agency will respond to changes in the policy space it inhabits.

The Cultural Behavior of Organizations

How do we identify the relevant actions of an agency that constitute cultural behavior? How should we expect an agency to "behave" when placed under the microscope of organizational culture? Is it possible to establish a list of "cultural" organizational responses to change in the policy environment? It should be possible to observe the culturally based behavior of an agency when there is a change in the policy space that implies a transformation, in whole or in part, of the nature of the mission and tasks of the organization or to challenge the norms and practices of the organization, and requires adjustment of the basic attitudes and assumptions of the members of an organization. In this case, the culture of an agency would call for *resistance to change* as the most likely organizational response. The mechanism by which the impact of these changes is assessed and by which it is judged are the "good instincts" of an agency's members regarding the nature of the organization and the "correct" way of handling things.

Second, if an organization faces a change in which it is "assigned" a new mission that it cannot reject, it is possible that it will appeal to its existing norms and practices, as well as its basic attitudes and assumptions, to carry it out. For an organization that only has hammers, everything new will look like a nail. Although this does not preclude the possibility that an organization will learn over time the more efficient ways to perform that task, the initial reaction is likely to be to treat the "problem" with the same instruments invented, discovered, or developed over time. But the new mission can also become a subculture or a neglected area within the organization. In an inter-agency environment, what others do will be judged and valued according to its dissonance or assonance, in theory and practice, with what one's agency does and values. A diplomat is likely to find some of the practices of "cops" or "soldiers" unacceptable behavior from the perspective of his agency.

The exact response/behavior of an agency depends on the type of external stimuli that arrive at its doormat. But depending on the situation, it can be one of resistance to change; appeals to internally invented, discovered or developed tools to deal with a new or unforeseen problem; or compartmentalization, stagnation, or neglect of an unavoidable but unwanted mission. Or it could be a combination of these responses. In general, bureaucracies take a hard look at any change in their environment that threatens its sense of self and the "way the organization does things." An agency will look at all such changes against that very sense of self and take a stand according to the compatibility or assonance of the possible change in respect to that sense of self.

The U.S. anti-narcotics policy space is peculiar because the boundaries of the policy space have never been keenly defined. Over time more and more agencies and bureaucrats and more and more resources were committed to the policy. Congress in particular was responsible for making dozens of agencies responsible for one part or another of the overall anti-narcotics policy. The budget also expanded considerably over the 80s and 90s. The type and number of anti-narcotics activities also rose dramatically. Dozens of agencies became involved in eradication, interdiction, or investigations. Bureau after bureau had to cope with the new mandates from Congress in the anti-drug fray. They were left to deal with a role that many of them did not even want. Bureaus had to readjust their norms and practices to accommodate the anti-drug mission. In some cases, they also had to transform their organizations to accommodate the new set of tasks. Attitudes and basic assumptions too had to change in order to make room for the attitudes demanded by having to "fight" a drug war.

Some of the more specific responses by government agencies follow. Some agencies accepted additional resources when these enhanced its existing mission. When they did so, some attempted to redirect them to strengthen the existing core tasks. When resources were reduced, some agencies sacrificed the more peripheral tasks first and protected the central mission and tasks of the organization. Some agencies accepted only missions that directly strengthened the agency's core mission and central tasks or derived directly from these and resisted or rejected those they considered secondary to the agency's social function. When the new mission and its tasks were unavoidable, some agencies compartmentalized them or outright neglected them. Other agencies, faced with the inevitability of a new set of organizational tasks that they did not want, appealed to their well known invented, discovered, or developed tools to carry them out. Other agencies employed rhetoric that portrayed an undesired change in its environment as detracting from performing well in their current social mission. Agencies facing cuts in their budgets did not seek "incompatible" missions to contain the budgetary erosions. Those that did ensured that any new missions were directly "plugged" into their existing mission and tasks; they had to look very much like what the agency already did. When agencies received new budgetary resources for an unwanted mission, they spent the added funds to support their existing tasks. These and other similar responses were quite consistent with predictions based on organizational culture as an influence on the behavior of organizations.

The Scope of this Study

The Actors within the U.S. Anti-Narcotics Policy Space

Anti-narcotics policy tends to flow from the halls of Congress and the White House to the corridors of bureaucracy and then on to three principal types of organizations at work in the anti-narcotics policy space: law enforcement agencies (cops), the military (soldiers), and the diplomatic corps (diplomats). Among cops, this study will focus on the most important agencies operating in the drug war between 1989 and 1993: the Drug Enforcement Administration (DEA); the U.S. Customs Service (USCS); the U.S. Coast Guard (USCG); and the Federal Bureau of Investigation (FBI); with occasional references to others. Within soldiers, there were two principal groups: the Pentagon and the forward deployed commands. The forward deployed commands included the Southern Command (SOUTHCOM); the Atlantic Command (LANTCOM); the Pacific Command (PACOM); the Forces Command (FORSCOM); and the North American Aerospace Command (NORAD). Diplomats included the Department of State and, within it, the Bureau of International Narcotics Matters (INM), and the Department of State's "embassy teams," headed by the ambassador and staffed mostly by Department of State Foreign Service officers (FSOs) and the attachés of various other U.S. agencies. Each of these organizations is a central partaker of the anti-narcotics policy space through legislation, statutory authority, and organizational interest.[40]

Then there are the "sovereigns"—the executive, Congress. While the Courts are also a master of bureaucracies, our study is primarily focused on a bureau's *political* masters. The President exercises the greatest influence through such powers as appointment or dismissal of personnel and the prerogatives to initiate changes in a bureau's functions. Congress has a "structural significance" through its legislative role that defines a bureau's legal status, its budget, and the "how and when" a bureau acts.[41]

Bureaus, though, are not mere puppets controlled by the executive and Congress. Bureaus recognize they are and have the functional means through which the intentional purpose of the executive or Congress is achieved. Thus, bureaus cultivate relations with their masters so that material support and the boundaries of policy space meet a bureau's preferences.

While the Courts are a constitutional "sovereign," they have historically acquiesced to the executives and Legislatures innate senses of jurisprudence to define legislation. Sometimes, though, the Courts have become quite active in certain areas of policy by telling bureaucracies what to do.[42] Thus, the role of the courts in the study of bureaucratic organizational behavior is somewhat nebulous and undefined. The intuitive knowledge that courts matter less in bureaucratic politics and organizational culture than do an agency's political masters permits us to hold the role of the courts "constant" and to focus instead on the role of two other clusters of actors in a bureau's environment: its political masters and its fellow dwellers in a policy space.

Why the Inter-Agency Environment?

This study focuses on the inter-governmental environment. This choice requires some justification. In regard to bureaucratic politics, the inter-governmental organization environment allows us several important advantages. Observing agencies working *together* in a policy space enables us to draw conclusions regarding their *political* behavior. For example, do governmental organizations *compete* directly for greater resources (allocation conflict) or greater jurisdiction (functional conflict)? Do they prefer to create or to seize opportunities to acquire resources or enhance their autonomy without provoking conflicts? Questions like these can be addressed in an area where all agencies are, at some level, functional rivals—as in the anti-narcotics policy space. The choice of an inter-governmental organization environment goes directly to the question of whether governmental agencies behave eminently politically or prefer to stay away from politics.

From the perspective of organizational culture, the inter-governmental agency environment enables us to maximize our leverage in testing the effects of culture on an agency. Focusing on the inter-government agency environment helps center on the contrasting ways in which different agencies deal with the same problem. Putting agencies under the microscope simultaneously before the same problem enables us to test the very definition of culture that Wilson (1989, p. 93) provides: "organizational culture consists of those patterned and enduring differences among systems of coordinated action that lead those systems to respond in different ways to the same stimuli."

The Cases

The cases are then governmental organizations. We focus on cops, soldiers, and diplomats. Cops or law enforcement organizations (LEAs) are among the oldest agencies dealing with illegal narcotics. Over time, they have developed organizational interests both in terms of their resources and their autonomy and they have developed distinctive organizational cultures. Both, LEAs' political interests and their organizational cultures were challenged between the years of 1989 and 1993, when all of them had to make adjustments to accommodate new actors, new technologies, increasing budgets, and an even more fragmented anti-narcotics policy with the arrival of the military to the anti-narcotics policy space. A changing anti-narcotics policy space and the existence of both organizational interests and distinctive organizational cultures within this space can help measure the effects of bureaucratic politics and organizational culture on LEA behavior.

The military is among the last governmental organizations to enter the anti-narcotics policy space. At the time, the military faced substantial budgetary cuts and many of its institutional interests were being put to the test on account of these cutbacks. In addition, it was entering a completely new terrain—law enforcement—something not at all part of the history or culture of the military. During the period under consideration, the military too had organizational interests and a sufficiently powerful culture to enable us to test our models.

Although diplomats are not new to anti-narcotics, their importance increased in the 1989-1993 period of the Bush Administration because efforts and funding in the international area of U.S. anti-narcotics policy grew. In the midst of this growth, diplomats' interests in terms of statutory authority over the international drug war were challenged by other agencies. The organizational interests of the State Department and its embassies were threatened. Similarly, the culture of diplomacy constitutes a very different type of culture from the culture of LEAs or the military. How did diplomats accommodate the needs and culture of law enforcement? LEAs pushed and pulled on diplomatic authorities to enhance their autonomy—often at the expense of diplomatic lines of authority abroad. In addition, when the military entered the fray, diplomats had to accommodate the stubborn independence of the military now operating well within the "territorial" authority of ambassadors and the State Department. These are good conditions to test our theories.

Notes

1. The concept of *policy space* as used by Anthony Downs in *Inside Bureaucracy.*

2. To this day, at the core of U.S. anti-narcotics policy is a complex bureaucratic web. Dozens of federal bureaus claim some kind of jurisdictional authority over the issue of illegal drugs.

3. An excellent case for the study of agencies in an inter-agency environment is made by Eugene Bardach in *Getting Agencies to Work Together: The Practice and Theory of Managerial Craftsmanship* (Washington, DC: Brookings Institution, 1998).

4. Systemic explanations of governmental behavior rely on the analysis of issue networks, interest groups, the structure of the executive and legislative branches, and the role of coalitions. Psychological perspectives focus on personalities. Rational models of governmental behavior assume that individuals and organizations are capable of putting aside their differences in favor of some common and well-understood good—the rational choice.

5. See also Roger Hilsman, *To Move a Nation* (Garden City: Doubleday and Company, 1967).

6. Some exceptions to this are studies that use bureaucratic politics to examine some important cases. See Juliet Kaarbo, "Power Politics in Foreign Policy: The Influence of Bureaucratic Minorities," *European Journal of International Relations* 4 (1998): 67-97; B. Ripley, "Cognition, Culture, and Bureaucratic Politics", in L. Neack, J. A. K. Hey, and P. J. Haney, eds., *Foreign Policy Analysis* (Englewood Cliffs, NJ: Prentice-Hall, 1995); S. Smith, "Policy Preferences and Bureaucratic Position: The Case of the American Hostage Rescue Mission," *International Affairs* 61 (1985): 9-25; and J. Valenta, "The Bureaucratic Politics Paradigm and the Soviet Invasion of Czechoslovakia," *Political Science Quarterly* 94 (1979): 55-76. Another notable example, albeit a disconfirming one, is Rhodes, "Do Bureaucratic Politics Matter?" *World Politics* 47:1 (October 1994): 1-41.

7. For a collection of empirical studies which test various bureaucratic politics hypotheses in various scenarios see David C. Kozak and James M. Keagle, *Bureaucratic Politics and National Security: Theory and Practice* (Boulder: Lynne Rienner Publishers, 1988).

8. The relationship between positivism and culture as a research program is complicated. Some culturalists, though skeptical of positivism, have embraced a positivist method-

ology, arguing for the necessity of clear and systematic causal relations and the construction of testable hypotheses derived from tidy theories. In sum, some culturalists seek to compete with other explanatory paradigms (rational choice, structuralists, etc.) on a common methodological turf.

For the argument that all knowledge is scientific see Ian Bullock, Oliver Stallybrass, and Stephen Trombley, eds., *The Harper Dictionary of Modern Thought*, rev. ed. (New York: Harper and Row, 1988), 669.

9. See Robert K. Merton, "Bureaucratic Structure and Personality," *Social Forces* 17 (1940): 560-568. Later (in 1949), Merton would write a seminal work in the study of "cultural structures." See *Social Theory and Social Structure*, 1968 Edition (New York: The Free Press, 1968), particularly Part II, "Studies in Social and Cultural Structure": 175-490.

10. See Herbert A. Simon, "Decision-Making and Administrative Organization," *Public Administration Review* 4 (1944): 16-25.

11. The concept of organizational culture, however, was not unknown before Allison and Halperin applied it to the study of policy making in the field of foreign policy. James G. March and Herbert A. Simon, for example, refer in their work to "organizational identity" and to "cultural pressures to participate" within an organization. Their theory, however, is a more comprehensive theory of organizational behavior and does not give a prominent place to organizational culture as a central determinant of organizational behavior.

12. In Wilson's definition of culture one can sense some of the tensions between cultural studies and positivism. The scientific requirements of positivism dictate that a researcher focus on similar behavior across organizations and find those variables that make actors act the same way even when faced with different external stimuli. Culturalists, on the other hand, begin by focusing on the differences among organizations that make these same organizations behave differently given the same external stimuli.

13. But Wilson is not specific enough in this regard. Some organizations, for example, make it a point to embrace innovation. Of course, the kinds of innovation they embrace may be selected carefully, but innovation is neither unacceptable nor foreign to their very essence. Large software corporations and the US Air Force, for example, have a tendency to want innovations and newer technology that enhance their cutting edge image or their performance.

14. For a comprehensive and thorough collection of sociological essays exploring the concept of culture in general and, in Chapter 5, the concept of organizational culture, see Diana Crane, *Sociology of Culture: Emerging Theoretical Perspectives* (Oxford, UK: Blackwell, 1994).

15. For some serious critiques and observations on the limitations of culture as explanation see David J. Elkins and Richard E. B. Simeon, "A Cause in Search of Its Effect, Or What Does Political Culture Explain?," *Comparative Politics* 11: 2 (January 1979): 127-145. Ole Elgström, "National Culture and International Relations," *Cooperation and Conflict* 29: 3 (September 1994): 289-301. Robert Brightman, "Forget Culture: Replacement, Transcendence, Relexification," *Cultural Anthropology* 10:4 (1995): 509-546.

16. See Carol Pateman, "Political Culture, Political Structure, and Political Change," *British Journal of Political Science* 1: 3 (July 1971); and David D. Laitin, "The Civic Culture at 30," *American Political Science Review* 89:1 (March 1995).

17. See David D. Laitin, *Hegemony and Culture: Politics and Religious Change among the Yaruba* (Chicago: Chicago University Press, 1986); and Aaron Wildavsky, "Choosing Preferences by Constructing Institutions," *American Political Science Review*

81:1 (March 1987).

18. See Clifford Geertz, *The Interpretation of Cultures* (New York: Harper, 1973).

19. See the substantial collection of essays put together by David C. Kozak and James M. Keagle, *Bureaucratic Politics and National Security: Theory and Practice* (Boulder: Lynne Rienner Publishers, 1988). Often, the authors in this volume seem to have in common only the label "bureaucratic politics."

20. For a thorough assessment of Niskanen's simpler model, with its emphasis on material resources, see André Blais and Stéphane Dion, eds., *The Budget Maximizing Bureaucrat: Appraisals and Evidence* (Pittsburgh, PA: University of Pittsburgh Press, 1991).

21. Niskanen, *Bureaucracy and Representative Government*; 38. Niskanen's model argues that "it is not necessary that a bureaucrat's utility be strongly dependent on every one of the variables which increase with a budget, but only that it is positively and continuously associated with the level of the budget." The word budget is used by Niskanen in a general sense to mean resources.

22. For a discussion of the mechanisms of bureaucratic control and, by implication, why a bureaucratic agency can be expected to dislike oversight, see Cornelius M. Kerwin, *How Government Agencies Write Law and Make Policy* (Washington, DC: Congressional Quarterly Press, 1994), 215-270.

23. The definition of politics employed in this study adheres closely to Harold Lasswell's definition: "Who Gets What, When, and How." Politics is the tug of action between two or more actors to see who gets what, when, and how. See Harold D. Lasswell, *Who Gets What, When, and How* (New York: McGraw-Hill, 1938).

24. This study views governmental organizations as relatively independent units rather than as harmonious clusters operating within the confines of their departments.

25. William T. Gormley has argued that legislative freelancing oversight has increased considerably since the 1970s. Gormley writes that "Individual legislators, responding to constituency pressures or to their own personal agendas, proceeded to tell bureaucrats what to do, what not to do, and what would happen if they did or didn't do as they were told." A little later Gormley adds that "From a bureaucrat's perspective, the freelancing legislator is a menacing figure who inspires fear, though not necessarily respect." See William T. Gormley, *Taming the Bureaucracy: Muscles, Prayers, and Other Strategies* (Princeton, NJ: Princeton University Press, 1989), 195.

26. Legislators have an awesome arsenal which can be used either in favor of or against a bureaucratic organization. This arsenal includes legislation, appropriations, hearings, investigations, personal interventions, confirmations, and "friendly advice," often ignored at the agency's executive's peril. See Herbert Kaufman, *The Administrative Behavior of Washington Bureau Chiefs* (Washington, D.C.: Brookings Institution, 1981), 164.

27. The literature in the field of political science in this regard is vast. There is capture theory, interest group pluralism theory, corporatism, and many other theories and frameworks that show that the other actors in an agency's environment matter considerably.

28. Conflict is understood as a situation of friction between bureaus originating in an attempt to alter the status quo within the relevant policy space by one actor in detriment of the organizational resources or autonomy of a bureau.

29. A discussion of the fundamental problems of assuming rationality is beyond the scope of this study. However, for a discussion of why organizations sometimes can be smarter than the individuals who compose them, see Jonathan Bendor and Thomas

Hammond, "Rethinking Allison's Models," *American Political Science Review* 86:2 (June 1992): 312-313.

30. This definition is based on, but different from, the definition given by Edgar H. Schein in his work "Organizational Culture." See Edgar H. Schein, "Organizational Culture," *American Psychologist* 45:2 (February 1990): 109-119.

31. For a more thorough discussion of the "integrative perspective" of organizational culture see Joanne Martin, *Cultures in Organizations* (New York: Oxford University Press, 1992), 45-70.

32. DEA Mission Statement <http://www.usdoj.gov/dea/agency/mission.htm> (July 31, 2000).

33. DEA Mission Statement <http://www.usdoj.gov/dea/agency/mission.htm> (July 31, 2000).

34. In a very extreme case, a street-level DEA agent witnessing this very kind of crime might not consider it important at all, at least not so when compared to a "dope crime." But let not a postal police officer know that this crime is not important because he would thoroughly disagree.

35. In the case of many private (and increasingly some public) organizations, one should expect secondary tasks to be more readily contracted out.

36. It is important to mention that this study assumes a fundamental commitment to the organization as is, that is, its members build an "emotional" bond to the organization for what it is and, all things being equal would prefer no change.

37. See *Diagram of Territorial Zones* in Downs, *Inside Bureaucracy*, 214.

38. These three important elements of human interaction (cognitive, affective, and evaluative) were discussed extensively much earlier by Sidney Verba and Gabriel Almond in *The Civic Culture: Political Attitudes and Democracy in Five Countries* (Princeton, NJ: Princeton University Press, 1963). For a concrete case of how the members of an organization develop these cognitive, affective, and evaluative orientations toward the organization they belong to see W. Jack Duncan, "Organizational Culture: 'Getting a Fix' on an Elusive Concept," *The Academy of Management EXECUTIVE* III:3 (1989): 229-236.

39. In *The Ropes to Skip and the Ropes to Know*, R. R. Ritti and G. R. Funkhouser argue that each member, upon arriving in an organization, faces the problem of gaining "entry into the men's hut," that is, gaining access to the basic organizational secrets. Sometimes this occurs through a rite of passage. The process involves an assessment of the individual as able to assimilate the values of the organization and embody what the organization is about. Individuals eventually internalize norms and values in a process known as acculturation (socialization and indoctrination) and the organizational or professional ethic becomes part of the member's identity. In fact, so ingrained are these that sometimes some serious "unfreezing" or "unlearning" is required to initiate change. See R. R. Ritti and G. R. Funkhouser, *The Ropes to Skip and the Ropes to Know: Studies in Organizational Behavior* (Columbus, OH: Grid, 1977). See also Michael Diamond, *The Unconscious Life of Organizations: Interpreting Organizational Identity* (Westport, CT: Quorum Books, 1993), 57-91.

40. Since our period of study, these structures have been reorganized, often considerably, or their names changed. Neither is significant for the purposes of our analysis.

41. For a history of the increase, types, and qualitative characteristics of congressional oversight over bureaucracies since the 1970s, see William T. Gormley, *Taming the Bureaucracy: Muscles, Prayers, and Other Strategies* (Princeton, NJ: Princeton University Press,

1989), 194-223.

42. For a more thorough discussion of these issues see Kenneth J. Meier, *Politics and the Bureaucracy: Policymaking in the Fourth Branch of Government*, 3rd Ed. (Belmont, CA: Wadsworth Publishing Company, 1993), 162-167.

Chapter 2
Cops

This chapter explores the organizational behavior of drug federal law enforcement agencies (LEAs). How did bureaucratic politics and organizational culture influence LEA behavior in the drug war between 1989 and 1993? To answer this question, in the first part, this chapter applies bureaucratic politics to LEA behavior and then proceeds, in a second part, to apply organizational culture to their behavior in the hope of discerning whether politics and culture are good explanations of agency behavior.

Bureaucratic Politics: Law Enforcement Organizations

LEAs are at the center of the anti-narcotics policy space. LEA bureaucrats are the primary agents for the combat of illegal drugs. They perform multiple tasks to keep illegal drugs out of the country and off the streets. At home, LEA agents, or "cops," investigate criminals; make arrests; seize drugs and drug-related property and evidence; gather drug-related intelligence; intercept drug-smuggling aircraft, vessels, and vehicles; inspect persons and containers crossing the border; build cases for prosecution; and so on. Abroad, LEA agents train foreign police forces; collaborate with foreign police entities in investigations; build informant networks; cultivate liaisons; help bust drug-producing labs; etc. At the base of these LEA activities against illegal drugs lies a quilt of crisscrossing organizational interests and a multitude of debates and disagreements over various aspects of the drug war. The nature of the anti-narcotics policy space is therefore ideal to study the agency behavior of LEAs. At every turn, LEA bureaucrats had to maneuver to defend the interests of the agency to which they belong and make judgments and political calculations about the well-being of their organization, even as they were trying to plan and implement overall U.S. anti-drug policy.

Four of the most influential LEAs in the drug war are DEA, FBI, U.S. Customs, and the U.S. Coast Guard. Each of them plays an important role in the drug war. The agencies manage two very important aspects of the drug war: investigations and interdiction efforts. Customs is dedicated to border interdiction as well as interdiction abroad. The U.S. Coast Guard is engaged in maritime interdiction. DEA and FBI conduct anti-drug activities in the area of investigations, with DEA having a considerable presence abroad (ten percent of its work force in 1992). Finally, all of these agencies grew during the period of our study, and at least part of that growth can be attributed to the increasing drug war budget. This chapter focuses on these four major LEAs

For the purposes of comparison throughout this study, the following numbers are helpful. The tables show the total annual FTE (full-time equivalent) employees' salaries of each LEA under study and their annual budget for fiscal years 1989, 1990, 1991, and 1992.[1]

Table 2.1 The growth of law enforcement agencies in the drug war

Budget (in 000s)	FY1989	FY1990	FY1991	FY1992
DEA	$534,450	$548,709	$696,000	$730,000
FBI	$1,439,100	$1,684,444	$1,699,000	$1,971,000
U.S. Customs	$1,508,833	$1,641,648	$1,742,000	$1,969,000
U.S. Coast Guard	$2,929,263	$3,093,690	$3,265,000	$3,419,000

The following pages analyze the extent to which bureaucratic politics influenced the fundamental behavior of LEA organizations between 1989 and 1993.

Drug Interdiction: Why Agencies Do Not Like to Depend

Agencies inherently dislike areas of shared competence with other agencies. The anti-narcotics area dictates that almost every responsibility is shared with one or more bureaus. The universal bureaucratic desire for exclusive jurisdiction and the reality of overlapping jurisdictions in the drug war provokes jurisdictional clashes among LEAs. Some important clashes have occurred between U.S. Customs and the

U.S. Coast Guard in the area of drug interdiction, for example. In the clashes between these two agencies, Customs has shown a solid determination to protect, defend, and even expand its exclusive jurisdiction over drug interdiction responsibilities.

Before the involvement of the military in the war on drugs, through the Defense Authorization Act of 1989, the main agencies responsible for drug trafficking interdiction (understood as the detection, monitoring, and interception of illegal drug-carrying aircraft, sea vessels, or land vehicles) were the U.S. Customs Service and the U.S. Coast Guard.[2] For much of the 1980s, there was no explicit comprehensive agreement between the two agencies to coordinate their efforts to detect, monitor, and intercept drug-trafficking aircraft or vessels. The lack of a coordination agreement between the two agencies resulted in a duplication of efforts at various levels of the interdiction process. Often, the agencies directed their own surveillance equipment at the same geographical point. Frequently Customs and the Coast Guard detected the same drug-smuggling aircraft or vessel and each agency employed its own equipment to monitor it *en route*. Sometimes, agents from both bureaus found themselves in pursuit of the same smuggling aircraft or vessel and not a few times agents from Customs and the Coast Guard came close to bitter confrontations over what one side perceived as encroachment by the other side on the performance of its responsibilities.[3]

By 1987, disputes between the two agencies had reached a peak. The fight had escalated to the point at which the Secretaries of Transportation and Treasury decided to compel Customs Commissioner, William Von Raab, and the Commandant of the Coast Guard, Admiral P. A. Yost, to go to the table to negotiate an agreement over the sharing of all responsibilities for drug interdiction. The negotiations between the agencies involved a review of the various tasks and the specification of the role of each agency in drug interdiction. The result of the negotiations was written on a memorandum of understanding (MOU) that delineated the interdiction jurisdictional parameters of the two agencies. The MOU (1987) established that the agencies "shared much of the responsibility for the enforcement of Federal statutes related to the interdiction of contraband drugs." According to the MOU, Customs would be the "lead agency to identify and prevent the illegal transportation of restricted and prohibited drugs across land border[s]." The Coast Guard would be the "lead agency in the interdiction of illegal drugs in the Maritime Area from the shoreline seaward." Air interdiction would be the responsibility of both agencies. To share air interdiction responsibilities, the negotiators created two communications, command and control centers (C^3I Centers), A SW Center and a SE Center. Customs was to chair the SW Center permanently; and both agencies would chair the SE Center on a two-year rotation basis. The staff for the centers would be provided on a 50-50 basis. The 11 May 1987 MOU was agreed to and signed by Adm. Yost and Commissioner Von Raab.

The centers were built and they had begun to function more or less smoothly by 1988 when Congress passed the 1989 Defense Authorization Act (September 1988) making DOD the "lead agency" for detection and monitoring (collectively known as surveillance) in all drug interdiction efforts. Whereas the MOU between Customs and the Coast Guard had divided the responsibilities for interdiction geographically, Congress pulled the rug out from under their feet and divided interdiction functionally. Detection and monitoring were to be done by the military; the actual physical interception of aircraft and vessels was to be done by LEA elements, even if they were aboard military vessels.[4] In addition, Congress was not very specific in regard to what LEAs were to lead the interception game during interdiction operations. Sometimes interdiction teams were composed of members from various agencies, such as Customs, Coast Guard, and DEA. But whether the division of responsibilities was done geographically, as in the MOU, or functionally, as in the 1989 Defense Authorization Act, the stage was set for functional conflict between the agencies.

Indeed, the new law prompted U.S. Customs to move quickly to declare that its Counsel "had determined that [the 11] May 1987 MOU incorporated language which conflict[ed] with the 1989 National Defense Authorization Act" because according to that Act, "DoD shall serve as the single lead agency of the Federal Government for the detection and monitoring of aerial and maritime transit of illegal drugs into the United States."[5] On 17 April 1989, Customs reneged on the MOU between the two agencies. Members of the Coast Guard felt that Customs, which already had full control of the SW Center, was now trying to expel the Coast Guard from the SE Center, effectively reducing the interdiction role of the Coast Guard to a minimum. Adm. Yost wrote a memorandum to the Secretary and the Deputy Secretary of the Department of Transportation regarding "U.S. Customs Service Attempt to Abrogate Air Interdiction Agreement." Adm. Yost complained that Customs wanted permanent command of the SE Center, much as it had acquired nearly total command of the SW Center, effectively expelling the Coast Guard from all interdiction activities by land and almost all by air. After making his complaint and explaining his position on the matter, Adm. Yost wrote by hand on the margins of the memo the word: "Help!" But help was insufficient. The MOU was abrogated and Customs was free to build its own air interdiction empire.

The behavior of U.S. Customs is consistent with the idea that agencies dislike areas of common competence with other agencies and will seize opportunities to eliminate the overlap. When Congress revised the jurisdictional boundaries on interdiction by making DOD the lead agency for surveillance, Customs viewed this as an opportunity not only to renege on a previous agreement but also to assert jurisdictional supremacy among LEAs over air interdiction. The U.S. Coast Guard would be relegated to maritime interdiction and maybe later U.S. customs could challenge the U.S. Coast Guard even on that medium. Customs adopted an aggressive posture and tried to assert sole jurisdiction over an activity (interdiction) that it viewed as entirely within its mission (to guard the borders).[6] Naturally, this posture reawakened the functional conflict that had pestered Customs-Coast Guard relations through most of the 1980s.

The response of the Coast Guard was expectedly defensive. When Customs moved to revise the air interdiction jurisdictional lines, the Coast Guard attempted to protect and defend its stake over air interdiction. When Customs was unmoved on the matter, the Coast Guard appealed to its political patrons and allies to help it fend off what they viewed as an act of aggression by U.S. Customs. Adm. Yost appealed to his bosses to intervene in the conflict between the two agencies and even took his complaint to Congress in a 9 June 1989 hearing before the Permanent Committee on Investigations of the Committee on Governmental Affairs. Nevertheless, the Coast Guard lost this battle and its role on air interdiction was curtailed further. Customs took control of both the SE and SW centers with only minimal Coast Guard participation. Adm. Yost's willingness to use whatever influence and channels of action were available to him was not enough.

A shrewd political understanding of "opportunity" allowed Customs to assert a higher level of autonomy over air interdiction. Its astute perception of the political nature of the anti-narcotics policy space was confirmed when Customs began in 1989 to court DOD and the military Southern Command (SOUTHCOM) in order to ensure the emergence of a Customs-military partnership that would favor Customs over other LEAs. In the eventual Customs-military cooperation partnership on air interdiction, the Coast Guard was largely excluded. This move gave Customs a leading role on air interdiction, alongside the military. This move toward dependence on the military, however, suggests that agencies do not necessarily view every other agency as a competitor. Agencies view some organizations as direct competitors and others as potential allies—or useful partners to enhance one's performance or complement one's activities. The military was not a direct competitor to Customs but an agency that could legally and functionally facilitate Customs' *interdiction* work. Customs viewed the entrance of the military in the drug war as an opportunity rather than a threat. This perception enabled Customs to adopt a shrewd strategy that allowed it to capitalize on the military's participation in the drug war for its own credit.

Customs' organizational behavior is entirely consistent with bureaucratic politics. Organizations value autonomy. When an opportunity to eliminate functional overlaps with other agencies comes, agencies are expected to use the opportunity to do so. Moreover, the military enhanced Customs' capabilities rather than competed with it; naturally Customs did not hesitate to initiate a partnership with the military to use its contribution to enhance Customs' performance and record, a highly desired good. The response of the Coast Guard is equally compatible with bureaucratic politics—a "defensive" position. When the Coast Guard felt pushed out of all air interdiction efforts, it naturally adopted a defensive posture. Unfortunately, the Coast Guard did not enjoy the clout that Customs did in order to prevail. Its "defense" resources (both formal and informal) were considerably small and, consequently, it lost the battle. Despite its willingness to defend, it lacked powerful political allies to set Customs back.

Interdiction and U.S. Customs: Bureaucracies and Empire-Building

The U.S. Customs Service was one of the federal agencies that managed to capitalize from the increasing prominence of the drug war among elected officials both at the White House and on Capitol Hill. Not only did Customs take advantage of the reshuffling in the anti-narcotics policy space—generated by the 1989 Defense Authorization Act—to acquire greater jurisdictional control over air interdiction—enhancing its autonomy in the process—but Customs officials also moved aggressively to increase the level of resources available to Customs for the performance of its tasks. Customs sought to complement its jurisdictional gains with a steady increase in its interdiction-related assets. The following quotation is taken from the remarks made to Congress (1988, p. 3) by Robert Asack, Deputy Assistant Commissioner for Enforcement, Aviation Operations, U.S. Customs Service. Mr. Asack's remarks, though taken from a 1988 seminar, are a representation of the many dozens of statements by Customs officials on Capitol Hill,

> I have spent a significant amount of my career in the role of, or working for air interdiction for Customs, and clearly the thing that we lack today, or tomorrow for that matter, is resources. Where we need resources the most, however, is in the area of interdiction. . . . So, if we wanted to do something immediately about the drug war, we should vastly increase our detection probability.

By 1989, a very important organizational goal at Customs had become to enhance its Air Interdiction Division assets. The agency acquired a sophisticated air wing that included a fleet of powerful Customs P3AEW, a four-engine turbo prop aircraft with a 360-degree radar-dome; a series of planes known as "Slicks;" a fleet of C550 Citation aircraft for tracking, interception, marine surveillance, and enforcement support; a fleet of C-12 marine surveillance aircraft; "Black Hawk" apprehension helicopters (UH-60); light enforcement helicopters (AS-350); and some Australian-built aircraft known as Nomads (or Nightstalkers), ideally suited for maritime work and equipped with FLIR (forward-looking infrared radars). Customs procured a variety of civilian and military ground-based radars, tethered aerostat radars, airborne reconnaissance aircraft and other sensors to conduct interdiction operations along the entire southern tier of the U.S., Puerto Rico, and the Caribbean. In addition, Customs acquired the privilege of using Howard Air Force Base (AFB) in Panama as a major Customs air stage. Regular access to Howard AFB made it easier for

Customs pilots to fly well outside the U.S. territory. Then Customs branched out to Honduras, Peru, and Colombia (and, much later, Ecuador). Customs also opened a new air branch in Puerto Rico.[7] With these sophisticated aircraft and new installations, Customs expanded significantly its interdiction role outside the U.S. borders. Commissioner Hallett viewed Customs not as a domestic agency guarding the borders—its obvious statutory mission—but as an *international* agency guarding U.S. interests at home and abroad.[8] This kind of international deployment by an LEA was unprecedented. Customs' original mission did not imply that Customs was an "international" agency at all; rather it suggested that Customs was formed as an agency with a domestic mission: to ensure that all goods and services entering and leaving the United States do so according to U.S. laws. By staking out a role in the anti-narcotics policy field as a major interdiction agency, Customs, instead of playing a passive role, that is, instead of waiting for these goods to move through the border and applying the law there and then, moved to play a more active and aggressive role of enforcing anti-narcotics laws abroad.[9]

As already hinted, besides substantially increasing its air interdiction assets, Customs sought to acquire an even more prominent role in maritime interdiction as well. It fortified its Maritime Interdiction Division.[10] Customs began to acquire a substantial marine fleet that included blue water vessels, interceptor vessels, utility vessels, and patrol vessels. It also increased the number of aircraft capable of operating jointly with sea vessels for interdiction operations on the seas. There were several reasons why building U.S. Customs' Maritime Division was not a reasonable decision. Customs personnel were not trained to conduct maritime interdiction operations as well as Coast Guard's personnel were. They did not master the art of maintaining and operating the equipment for maritime interdiction, including water-based radar systems and go-fast interceptor vessels. The Coast Guard not only had the necessary expertise but it already had the facilities and the know-how to simply train more people for maritime interdiction. Customs had none of these. Finally, Customs boarding authority was limited to the 12-mile contiguous zone; the Coast Guard's was not. Nevertheless, by legislative appropriation, the decision was made to continue to beef up Customs' Maritime Division. This decision by Congress was closely tied to what many perceived to be a very cozy relationship between Customs and some members of Congress, particularly Sen. DeConcini (AZ). Customs officials proved to be very skillful at extracting resources from Capitol Hill. Much as they had managed to acquire substantial resources for Customs' air interdiction division, they had now managed to place Customs at a competitive level in maritime interdiction. It was largely irrelevant that from the perspective of overall national policy effectiveness it would have made more sense to favor the Coast Guard in maritime interdiction. By 1993 Customs had achieved nearly sole jurisdiction on land interdiction; had become the major LEA player in air interdiction efforts (alongside the military); and held concurrent jurisdiction with the Coast Guard on coastal waters of the U.S. up to 12 miles offshore. Between 1988 and 1993, U.S.

Customs managed to leave its competitors in the dust and to consolidate itself as the primary interdiction LEA.

The fundamental premises of bureaucratic politics are confirmed in the case of U.S. Customs. If organizations are driven by a desire for greater resources, Customs is the epitome of that desire. Customs' behavior in the anti-narcotics space was aggressive—or "offensive" in our behavioral categories. Having weakened its major rival in the area of drug interdiction (the Coast Guard), Customs was relatively free to take advantage of the opportunity to grow. Customs' resource growth helped it anchor its jurisdictional power over interdiction. Finally, Customs had the right kind of allies on Capitol Hill. These alliances enabled it to make greater acquisitions of resources and to fend off functional competitors.

Bureaucratic Alliances: Oil and Water Do Mix

Most LEAs viewed the 1989 Defense Authorization Act that made DOD the "lead agency for detection and monitoring" as a threat—the proverbial "800-pound gorilla." Although there were conflicts over military aircraft availability for law enforcement missions, Customs very soon began to change its mind about the role that the military could play in interdiction efforts. In spite of its increasingly prominent role in U.S. interdiction efforts, Customs began to view the military as a force complementary to its own efforts. After all, the military would bear many of the costs for detection and monitoring (surveillance) but they could not make seizures and arrests. But Customs could. So, Customs began to see this substantial change in the anti-narcotics policy space—the entry of the military into the anti-narcotics policy space—as an opportunity to increase its own autonomy and resource use in the drug war. Again, the military was not and could not be an LEA—it could, at most, serve as an effective support for the enhancement of law enforcement efforts. Customs top bureaucrats immediately started looking for ways in which they could use the military to enhance Customs' position in the anti-narcotics policy space. After moving to renege on Customs' interdiction agreement with the Coast Guard, Commissioner Von Raab and particularly his successor Commissioner Carol Hallett began to cultivate close cooperation arrangements with DOD's Southern Command (SOUTHCOM). Starting in 1990, Commissioner Hallett cultivated a close relationship with SOUTHCOM's CINC Gen. George Joulwan. This relationship resulted in a high level of cooperation between the military and U.S. Customs. Although it could be argued that the positive personal rapport between Joulwan and Hallett was the glue that held their bureaucratic alliance together, this argument is neutralized by two important factors: 1) there was no opposition to SOUTHCOM-Customs cooperation anywhere within any of the two organizations; and 2) this cooperation endured well after both Joulwan and Hallett had left their respective organizations.

The complementary relationship between the two agencies appeared to transcend the personalities of their managers. This shows that agencies seek to form alliances that benefit them as a whole, regardless of the personalities of their top officials—a premise consistent with bureaucratic politics.

The SOUTHCOM-Customs "bureaucratic alliance" paid off when a 1990 proposal emerged within the Pentagon to reorganize the deployed commands and transfer jurisdiction of the West coast of South America (and the interdiction operations therein) from SOUTHCOM's control to the control of the Atlantic Command (LANTCOM). Under this plan, interdiction operations on the West coast of South America would be placed under LANTCOM's anti-drug Joint Task Force (JTF). Customs immediately saw this move as a threat to the agency's turf. The transfer was viewed as a setback for Customs because while SOUTHCOM had accommodated Customs' imperialistic ambitions, there was a degree of uncertainty in having to start again to cultivate a similarly favorable relationship with LANTCOM's CINC. In fact, Hallett believed that the change would have eliminated Howard Air Force Base as a staging area for Custom's air wing altogether. Thus Hallett recruited Gen. Joulwan's support under the justification that such a move would have gutted all interdiction efforts in the area. Hallett and Joulwan set out to defeat the Pentagon's proposal. As Hallett pointed out in an interview,

> There was a major, I say major . . . a very significant battle ensued over jurisdiction. And General Joulwan and I [Hallett] appealed to Colin Powell to leave it as it was. Everyone else, all of the other agencies, and everyone else in the military, pushed for it to be taken from SOUTHCOM and put into LANTCOM. . . . Ultimately Colin Powell agreed that it should stay as it was. That was a huge victory because it would have totally changed the support. Howard Air Force Base might have evaporated in terms of being a staging location [for U.S. Customs].

When Pentagon officials moved to reorganize the geographic division of the forward deployed forces, Customs felt threatened. Predictably, Customs moved to protect and defend its stake. Hallett portrayed the proposed jurisdictional change not as a setback to the interests of her agency but as a "setback to the overall anti-drug efforts." This reasoning suggests that government agencies often confuse the national interest with the interest of the agency. It also confirms our hypothesis that top leaders in an organization will use rhetoric designed to convince its political masters and others that the solution that favors their agency is the best for national policy. This is further supported by the fact that while Hallett (or Joulwan) never meant to undermine the overall effectiveness of the policy by opposing the plan, she had no solid basis for believing that the shift would have been bad for the drug war in South America. She could not have been sure that the drug war would not have been better served by having LANTCOM control the west coast of South America rather than SOUTHCOM and Customs. But Hallett simply did what she thought she was supposed to do: to protect and defend her agency's turf when it came under threat or at the very least, the status quo. Customs' behavior also confirms the hypothesis that government agencies dislike losing the ground gained, and it suggests that agencies dislike the uncertainty of sudden change. Bureaucratic agencies are likely to oppose change in order to avoid risking the loss of the turf already accrued, regardless of the sound or unsound nature of the present policy for the overall national goals of policy makers. Rhetorically, bureaucrats appear to portray such changes as being in detriment of the goals of the nation, rather than as a setback to their agency's interests.

Customs' alliance with the military paid off even more handsomely when the Gulf War broke out. After President Bush made the determination not to let Saddam Hussein's aggression against Kuwait stand, the military began readying for a possible war against Iraq. For SOUTHCOM this meant a drastic reduction in the assets dedicated to the war on drugs. Whereas LANTCOM and PACOM (Pacific Command) had created Joint Task Forces (JTFs) with dedicated assets to deal with the war on drugs, SOUTHCOM's CINC at that time, Gen. Maxwell Thurman, had decided to handle the drug war as part of SOUTHCOM's day-to-day operations. Consequently, LANTCOM and PACOM's dedicated assets were not seriously affected by the requirements of the Gulf War, while SOUTHCOM's assets, which were not dedicated assets, were called to serve the Persian Gulf War effort. Gen. Joulwan recalled that "everything got ripped off for Desert Storm," particularly the highly valued AWACS.

With the drug war under assault by the Pentagon's Gulf War priorities, Customs moved quickly to fill the vacuum. In a calculated decision, Customs placed much of its powerful air wing at the "disposal" of SOUTHCOM's CINC. Soon, Customs officers and military personnel flew Customs planes together in South and Central America and the Caribbean on anti-drug missions. The following remark by SOUTHCOM's CINC, Gen. Joulwan, is illustrative:

> When I could not get AWACS [because] they got ripped off for Desert Storm, I got Customs' P3 Domes and Slicks, and we worked that area.

The Customs-SOUTHCOM partnership enabled Customs to seal its stake in U.S. air interdiction efforts. It also enabled Customs to get a step ahead in the credit game by being the first LEA present during a surveillance and interception operation by the military. Customs' agents had the first shot at a "drug bust" and were able to claim credit first. Customs' relationship with the military illustrates once again how so much of what government agencies do in a highly political policy space obeys the "law of opportunity" rather than indiscriminate empire-building. Moreover, Customs' reputation for forcefully making use of such opportunities is well known and it contributes to its organizational success. And clearly, willingness to use one's leverage for organizational purposes appears to be as important as having it. Customs was not only able to; it was also willing. These observations are entirely congruent with our bureaucratic politics model, which argues that organizations do not seek to expand chaotically but rather channel their growth guided by opportunities along the way. This conclusion represents a refinement over simpler bureaucratic politics models that argue that agencies will simply seek greater resources because these represent greater prestige, perks, and other amenities.[11] The logic of opportunity is much more effective in explaining how organizations expand and grow.

Drug Investigations: The Recovery of an Agency Empire

Customs' emergence as a key player in the drug war in the late 1980s represented a major turnaround from the organization's diminished role after the 1973 Reorganization Plan No. 2 that created the Drug Enforcement Administration (DEA). Customs emerged from the Reorganization Plan No. 2 "in a disheveled, demoralized, and threatened state. It had lost 700 of its elite narcotics agents and support personnel to the new Drug Enforcement Administration" (Rachal, 1982, p. 112). In spite of this organizational nadir, Customs managed to retain its jurisdiction over narcotics interdiction on land borders. Also, its Office of Investigations (OI), nearly wiped out by the reorganization, was not closed but was reduced to a few dozen agents. With this setback, Customs set out to conduct an organizational overhaul. Customs' officials were determined to showcase the organization as an effective drug interdiction agency along the border. They could do so because 1) DEA was not by its own definition a border agency—only a small portion of its operations took place along the border; and 2) Customs was ideally situated to detect and intercept drugs smuggled along the border. DEA agents were aware of the advantages of Customs as an *interdiction* agency along the border, and they were happy to let that be; but they insisted that *investigations* operations on narcotics cases were the exclusive jurisdiction of DEA, according to the spirit and the letter of Reorganization Plan No. 2. By DEA estimates, Customs was required to turn over all investigations to DEA special agents soon after drug smuggling was detected and intercepted along the border.

Predictably, Customs agents disagreed with DEA's claims to sole and exclusive jurisdiction over narcotics investigations. Customs had kept OI open after the reorganization. Customs OI agents did not agree with opening an investigation file after a "border bust" and then turning it over to a DEA narcotics agents. Customs special agents wanted to conduct their own investigations. DEA and Customs often clashed over this subject during the 1980s. By 1989 the rivalry had reached a peak. Each agency had its own reasoning for claiming jurisdiction over narcotics investigations on drug busts along the border. By virtue of its investigations mission, DEA argued that when Customs agents found contraband or illegal drugs, DEA should be summoned to take over the investigation. DEA was, after all, the primary agency for narcotics investigations; the agency built cases for prosecution and "milked" them for their narcotics intelligence value. Customs, according to DEA, was the "detecting" agency; DEA was the "investigating" agency. OI Custom's agents disagreed and often pursued investigations beyond the initial discovery and reporting of the case. They too wanted to claim credit for the work, collect intelligence, and build their own cases for prosecution. Because of this disagreement, Customs and DEA agents sometimes engaged in choleric squabbles over who should follow up an investigation, even as detained smugglers waited in the room next door to be processed. Those years, John Hensley (1999 interview) stated,

> There was a stove pipe effect in terms of the way the agencies were working. DEA was working its side of the street; we were working our side of the street. . . . There was jealousy there and DEA was not cooperating. [According to DEA] Customs had a role in the smuggling but not in the domestic case. . . . DEA would define the law extremely narrowly; and Customs would try to define it broadly. And so those would constantly come into conflict. And that affected really all of the other pieces as Customs tried to solve the narcotics problem. . . . And they were not passing intelligence to us.

Being kept out of investigations at that time, argued Commissioner Hallett (1999 interview), is "one of the reasons that...instead of being one hundred percent successful, you might only be eighty percent successful." Customs desired a greater investigative role in anti-drug matters even after the case moved from the border into bureaucratic halls and the courts. From DEA's perspective, once an investigation moved away from the border inspection post, it became its case.

The irritating incidents between U.S. Customs and DEA agents obliged the parties to come to the negotiating table. The negotiations, which took place between December 1989 and February 1990, produced an agreement between the two agencies that established that Customs agents could pursue drug-related investigations autonomously of the DEA four miles into U.S. territory alongside the U.S.-Mexico border. The agreement gave one thousand Customs special agents "cross-over jurisdiction" on investigations. They were now free to conduct their own investigations without having to receive authorization by DEA on a case by case basis. The resulting MOU also stated that DEA would share investigations intelligence with Customs. "From that point on," said John Hensley (1999), "January 1990, they [DEA] couldn't shut us down...but old dogs don't like to learn new tricks. So, DEA field guys still wanted to 'supervise Customs.' That was the hardest hurdle for them to get over." Because DEA field agents tried to "ignore" the agreement, DEA and Customs top bureaucrats had to create a mediation mechanism called HRT—Headquarters Review Team—which met regularly for breakfast at 6:30 or 7:00 AM in order to smooth out particularly contentious cases. The HRT managed to resolve nearly 98% of the conflicts. The remainder would move up to the Commissioner's and the Administrator's desks.[12]

The jurisdictional conflict between DEA and Customs raises several important considerations from a bureaucratic politics perspective. First, agencies attempt to establish sole or at least largely exclusive jurisdiction over a set of tasks. Agencies facing direct competitors over the same set of tasks are extremely protective of their turf. DEA's "defensive" posture before Customs' assertiveness is thus expected from a bureaucratic politics standpoint. And again, from a historical perspective, this case is important because it shows that, even though Customs lost its investigations empire to DEA in the 1973 Reorganization Plan, it kept its Investigation Office (IO) open, perhaps with the hope that it would eventually find an opportunity to "recover" its jurisdiction over anti-drug investigations. Incidentally, this confirms the earlier hypothesis regarding the fact that agencies seek windows of opportunities to push for their preferences. For Customs, that opportunity showed up in the Bush Administration; and its managers took good advantage of it. Our advocacy of a logic of opportunity as the preferred organizational means to grow is strengthened by this evidence.

Second, having the backing of the spirit and even the letter of the law does not guarantee success at the negotiating table. Terence Burke, interim Administrator of DEA at that time, proved ineffective at defending DEA's organizational interests at the table. The favorable remark about Mr. Burke by John Hensley may reflect Customs' satisfaction to DEA's caving in to Customs demands on the area of narcotics investigations. He "was a real gentleman to work with," said John Hensley (1999 interview) of Customs. DEA neither possessed the leverage of Customs nor the willingness or effectiveness in using whatever leverage it had to assert its supremacy over domestic drug investigations. Consequently, the area of investigations in the drug war is shared by DEA and Customs (in addition to the FBI and a myriad of other agencies at all three governmental levels). In any event, the statistics show that in the late 1980s and through most of the 1990s the investigation operations and drug convictions by Customs grew quite considerably.

DEA and Interdiction: Testing the Limits of an Agency's Mission

In the spring of 1992, DEA Administrator Robert C. Bonner and his team met at the DEA headquarters in Arlington, VA. The group drafted a plan, which called for building a DEA-based air wing. The aircraft was to come from the aircraft already owned by U.S. Customs, the U.S. Coast Guard, the National Guard, and the International Narcotics Matters (INM) Bureau of the State Department. Bonner's plan also required that the Department of Defense transfer to DEA control a fleet of (the coveted) Black Hawk helicopters.[13] This was an unprecedented move because there had been up to then an understanding that DEA did not play a role in U.S. interdiction efforts, except, sometimes, at the end of the process, where prosecution of the captured drug smugglers was to take place. That other agencies took this move to mean that DEA was claiming a role in the area of drug interdiction is not surprising. The official justification for the move was that DEA agents were frustrated because they were aware of drug trafficking activities going on, principally in Central America, and no one was doing anything about that. DEA felt it had to step in to fill in the action void, but it did not have the assets. A transfer of assets would enable it to "do something about it." Although the plan contained no clear reference to a DEA role in interdiction efforts, the plan was a daring attempt to assume just such a role. In making asset-related demands, already a bold move, likely to bring about an allocational conflict, DEA should have realized that these would inevitably bring a challenge to the jurisdictional claims of other agencies over air interdiction, given the proposed use of these very assets. Thus, from the perspective of our bureaucratic politics model, Bonner's plan is interesting because the move engendered both allocational and jurisdictional conflicts. DEA had never played a significant role in air interdiction efforts because it was more of an investigating agency, but DEA's officials now wanted to bring DEA to bear in that area of the drug war because they feared that the drug war was "being lost" in Central America. However, without adequate air assets, DEA could not conduct interdiction activities. Up to then, DEA's air wing consisted mostly of small, confiscated aircraft used mostly for transportation of DEA agents to various places within the U.S. and abroad. Whenever DEA required more sophisticated air assets for a particular mission (e.g., Black Hawk helicopters), it depended on the cooperation of other agencies, including Customs, the Coast Guard, INM (DOS), and DOD. DEA sometimes had trouble securing the cooperation of these agencies for its operations—which should have warned DEA about the unwillingness of other agencies to surrender their air assets to the agency.

DEA's plan was initially handled with a great deal of secrecy—perhaps with the intuitive understanding that it was a controversial plan. Bonner first consulted with Attorney General William Barr, his boss. Barr had no objections to it. He even considered the plan a good idea for the Justice Department as a whole because he viewed the issue of drugs primarily as the job of the Justice Department (Interview with William Barr, 1999). Backed by Attorney General Barr and armed with a plan under his arm, Bonner went to the National Security Council in The White House—straight to the horse's mouth. In a classic end-run, at the White House, Bonner managed to get the assent of President George Bush and the National Security Advisor, Brent Scowcroft, for his plan. [14] When Bonner thought that he had mustered enough support up and down the political ladder of the executive, he let the plan be known by other agencies.

Predictably, the plan provoked fierce opposition from every agency involved in narcotics interdiction operations. DEA failed to realize that the interdiction area of the drug war was an intensely contested area with heavy-weights like U.S. Customs, the Coast Guard and, starting in 1989, the Department of Defense. These agencies quickly moved to protect and defend their assets. The plan's presumed asset transfer requirements were particularly intolerable for the agencies in the air interdiction area. Some thought that DEA's plan was a ploy to take credit for air interdiction efforts but let others "foot the bill" (Interview with Olson, 1997). The "affected" agencies made their opposition to the plan clear. Some in the Department of State's INM predicted disaster for the plan. The head of the State Department's INM, Mel Levitsky (Interview, 1999), did not think that anyone would willingly surrender any assets, much less any jurisdiction, to the DEA.

Having failed to convince a single bureau to hand over any assets to DEA, Bonner set out to lobby the State Department for the transfer of at least some of its helicopters to DEA. DOS strongly opposed even this dramatically discounted request. Bonner believed that DOS's B-212 helicopters "were not quite as effective [as the Black Hawks]," but "could help some" (Interview, 1999). INM used those helicopters to carry out crop eradication operations in Central and South America—and they were sometimes used to support DEA operations such as transport of personnel, but always at the discretion of DOS personnel. But as far as DEA was concerned opium poppy eradication was not as important as the operations that DEA could carry out if it had the use of the B-212 helicopters. The U.S. Embassy in Guatemala through the Narcotics Affairs Section (NAS) operated some of the helicopters. NAS strongly opposed the equipment transfer. NAS's objections were taken to Mel Levitsky at INM. Levitsky initially denied the helicopters to the DEA but, after some negotiations, agreed to make the B-212 helicopters in Guatemala available to the DEA when NAS was not using them for crop eradication purposes. The Foreign Service officers in charge of NAS-Guatemala, however, made sure that the helicopters were never available to DEA. Finally, DEA tried to push this initiative through Congress. Bonner "spoke with several members of Congress" but, he said, "I've forgotten who right now, but, [they] blocked it, so it didn't happen."[15] Senator Mitch McConnell was one of the members of Congress who strongly opposed DEA's plan and was key in neutralizing DEA's lobbying on Capitol Hill.

That Bonner intended to carve away at other agencies' assets and their jealously guarded stakes in air interdiction was unacceptable to the players with strong interests already in place. These actors reacted in defense of their organizational interests. Several of them sought support in Congress against DEA's plan and some finally appealed to President Bush himself. The President, who had at first assented to Bonner's plan, now adopted a neutral position and gave the equivalent of a "you boys work it out among yourselves" (Interview with Olson, 1997). And this they did. The plan was scrapped and the DEA had to remain within the boundaries of its usual role in the war on drugs—where it had virtually nothing to do with air interdiction efforts.[16] DEA simply lacked the ability to bring about its preferences because it lacked real support from its political masters; did not possess the effectiveness to sell its plan to anyone else in the anti-narcotics space; and provoked an almost unanimous bureaucratic alliance against its designs. In the end, DEA managed to borrow some of the less-liked B-212 helicopters for transport of personnel.

From the perspective of bureaucratic politics, the case of DEA's plan is revealing. In an inter-agency environment, much of what an agency can accomplish can be understood in the following formula: there is an inverse relationship between the number of actors in a policy space and what an agency can accomplish in its desire to enlarge its stake in it. The greater the number of actors, the greater the combined resistance to an agency's designs is. Moreover, an additional lesson is that when an agency provokes a conflict that involves both reshuffling of assets *and* of jurisdictional power (allocational and functional conflicts), it should expect even fiercer resistance. Naturally, the ambitious plan by DEA could not have provoked more resistance. Finally, it is worth noting that even though allocational conflicts among agencies are rare, they do happen, as this case illustrates. Jurisdictional (or functional) conflicts are more common.

DEA and FBI: The Struggle for Agency Equality

This story begins with the considerable jurisdictional overlap between the FBI and the DEA. DEA was created as the primary agency in the enforcement of illegal drug-related crimes. It has only one overarching statute to enforce. While the FBI's law enforcement jurisdiction extends to many more types of crimes (it covers many more statutes), the agency is also responsible for organized crime. Since most illegal drugs are produced, transported, and sold by organized criminal entities, the FBI considers drug trafficking a significant part of its mission. Its major effort is invested in going after drug traffickers and drug trafficking organizations. To seal this jurisdictional claim, the FBI received explicit statutory authority to conduct drug investigations under Title 21 on January 28, 1982.

> Acting on recommendations from the Department of Justice, DEA and the FBI, the Attorney General gave the FBI concurrent jurisdiction with DEA over federal drug laws and mandated the FBI to focus on complex conspiracy investigations (*Enforcement*, 1995).

Thus, the FBI and the DEA jurisdictional powers overlap considerably. An important consequence of this enormous overlap has been that the FBI considers DEA a very specialized and therefore a redundant agency. Their positions in the policy space pit the two organizations as direct competitors. Conflicts between the two agencies are now chronic. This situation has come close to threatening DEA's very survival. On several occasions in the past, FBI directors have proposed to absorb the DEA into the FBI's organized crime division (*FBI and DEA*, 1993). DEA administrators have had to go on the defensive and try to demonstrate that drug crimes are a different type of crime and deserve separate treatment. DEA officials argue that drugs are a matter of national security, a different phenomenon from organized crime, and deserve special attention—attention which they would not receive at the FBI. Drugs, they contend, require the existence of a specialized agency to deal with them (interview with Lawn, 1999). Thus, while FBI agents view the DEA as a redundant agency whose job can be done by the FBI, DEA agents view illegal drugs as a category unto itself deserving of their own category.[17] Consequently, like a jealous younger sibling of the FBI, for most of the 1980s, the DEA strove to raise the status of the agency and increase its resources as a strategy to avoid capture by the FBI. In general, the objective was to get the DEA name to evoke as much respect and sense of awe as the label FBI does and to create a sense of inevitable necessity for the agency in society. The ultimate goal was achieving at least *equality* with the FBI (Lawn interview, 1999). David Westrate's (interview, 1999) comment is illustrative,

> Now, did we have an inferiority complex at DEA? We did, in terms of always being, always seemingly being up for grabs. And, any time the FBI felt like it wanted to make a merger proposal, it did. And it didn't matter how much of an impact it had on morale and all this energy it took to fight it or any of that stuff.

Historically, the FBI has had the upper hand in resources, personnel, and prestige. The FBI is an older and generally a highly respected institution. Its resources are vast; the criminal statutes it covers many. This has translated into a sense of pride and status. An FBI agent believes that to solve a crime he must do it by shrewd deduction, scientific inquiry, and artful surmise. Most FBI agents do detective work wearing white shirts and ties and proudly wear the agency's symbols. In contrast, by the late 1980s, the DEA had not yet been able to achieve the prestigious status of the FBI or its resources. Its agents were viewed as unkempt, door-busting grunts in jeans and cowboy shirts. These elements had as a consequence the development of a certain "organizational insecurity" at DEA.

Exacerbating this deeply seated dispute is the fact that the two organizations have historically developed very different investigative styles. As James Q. Wilson's work argues, DEA agents are primarily instigators. They actively seek their cases. This leads them to behave differently from FBI agents who are not "instigators." FBI agents are "investigators;" they do not go out and look for criminals by conducting drug buy-and-busts or go undercover to develop informants that might lead to drug busts. Instead, FBI agents are more akin to "white collar workers." They dress in suits and ties and are generally clean shaven people. DEA agents, on the other hand, wear beards and mustaches, dress in jeans and boots or tennis shoes, and use street language in their daily activities. FBI investigators prefer not to make immediate arrests, unless a crime has been committed right before their eyes. Instead, investigators are interested in solving crimes through the steady building of a case for prosecution. DEA agents tend to copy a rough street style of behavior to inspire confidence and "instigate" the commission of a crime so that they can move in and arrest the perpetrators.[18] Because of these differences, DEA's advocates, within and without the agency, have argued that the FBI's investigative style is not well suited to dealing with illegal drugs and its resulting crime.

The tension between the two agencies regarding their "professionalism" has continuously been a source of worries for DEA administrators. Administrator Lawn tried to change this by "professionalizing" his agents. He complained to his personnel that they were not appropriately dressed; that Levi jeans and cowboy boots were ruining their image and the agency's credibility and reputation. Lawn began to require that everyone at DEA headquarters dress in suit and tie and leave the boots behind. He also established a physical fitness program. All of this was required, he said, "to develop self-respect in the organization." He also insisted that the DEA train its new recruits in Quantico, VA, where the FBI trained its agents. He was very concerned that they receive the same kind and quality of training as everyone in the FBI. But Lawn was also afraid that training DEA agents at FBI headquarters would put ideas among FBI people that this could be a first step toward folding the DEA into the FBI. The next goal then became to set up exclusive DEA training facilities in Quantico. These facilities, however, had to be comparable to those of the FBI, though completely independent. And Lawn was not wrong. When FBI top level officials tried but failed to fold the DEA into the FBI in the late 1980s, they realized that it was going to be very hard to do so and decided to give the DEA "two weeks to get your agents out of Quantico. Find another place to train." Lawn then proceeded to search for a piece of land "proximate to FBI [training] headquarters" on which to build DEA's training headquarters. He found 55 acres which he obtained from the Marine Corps for $1. The DEA now had its own training headquarters in Quantico, VA, comparable to the FBI's, close to the FBI location, but independent from the FBI.[19]

In an agency as vulnerable as DEA, the administrator has to constantly be on the look out for competitors (U.S. Customs) or even predators (FBI). The fractious nature of the anti-drug policy space only adds to DEA's vulnerability because its potential competitors are many. Too many agencies claim jurisdiction over illegal drugs on account of some part of their mission. For DEA, combating drugs is its only mission. Lawn resented competition and argued that the DEA should be given ultimate responsibility for all drug efforts.[20] Lawn told Sen. Joseph Biden (D-DE) that there was already a drug czar and that was the Attorney General. Under this scenario DEA would be, of course, the sole agency responsible for overall coordination of all anti-drug efforts. He thought that if a new drug emerged—similar to crack in the mid 1980s—it was the DEA administrator who would be called to testify before Congress and who would be held responsible, and not the FBI or Customs, in spite of the fact that they shared the burden for fighting it according to Congressional designs. Lawn testified before Senator Biden and opposed the creation of the Office of National Drug Control Policy (ONDCP). But Senator Biden had sought to create this new agency since 1982 and was not willing to give it up now that it was so close at hand. Now the DEA would have a new competitor. Lawn's successor, Bonner, also expressed his opinion that the ONDCP was redundant. "I think it could be the proverbial fifth wheel," he said. He argued that DEA stands for "Drug Enforcement *Administration*; not *Agency*, but *Administration*," therefore, it should be the center of all coordination for the war on drugs, not just another agency in the mix (1999 interview).

DEA administrators also tried to reconceive DEA as an *international* agency. Lawn and Bonner preferred to view the agency no longer as a purely domestic LEA, but as an international LEA. Under Lawn and Bonner's time the number of DEA agents operating abroad increased considerably reaching ten percent by 1990. Lawn also tried to insert the agency in a prestigious lineage. He argued that General McArthur himself, during the occupation of Japan after WWII, saw drug enforcement as an important mission and took some drug law enforcement people with himself. Thus, DEA, even before it was born, was an *international* agency. But, having personnel abroad did not come without conflict for the DEA. The fact that the DEA had so many agents abroad complicated relations with the State Department, which assertively proclaims ultimate oversight authority over any operations carried abroad by any U.S. agency, no matter what the issues is. Ambassadors and FSOs abroad insisted that DEA do absolutely nothing that had not been authorized by the DOS embassy team first. DOS personnel at embassies abroad showed themselves more than willing to protect this principle aggressively. At home or abroad, DEA's potential ambitions were kept in check. DEA's "aggressive stands" were thoroughly resisted.

The relationship between DEA and FBI is one largely characterized by an uneven distribution of jurisdictional power. Although both are law enforcement agencies and there is a considerable overlap on the issue of drugs, the FBI is an agency with a much broader law enforcement mandate that includes drug trafficking. The more inclusive investigative mandate of the FBI has caused the agency to view DEA's role in law enforcement as redundant and attempted, three times, to absorb the agency. At DEA, the FBI's aggressive style has caused the agency to feel relatively threatened. The response of DEA has been a naturally political response. DEA's *defensive* strategy has involved several tactical maneuvers. The first consists of making the argument that drugs are a "special" problem and deserve special attention, e.g., a dedicated agency. DEA has also tried to turn FBI's advantages on their head by arguing that the problem of drugs would not receive due attention in an agency with as broad a mandate as the FBI's. In effect, the issue of illegal drugs would get lost in a larger bureaucracy such as the FBI's. Second, DEA tried to shed its reputation as a "door-busting" agency of "cowboys" by seeking to match the FBI's training and techniques. DEA also sought to acquire the same prestige and reputation of the FBI's professionalism. Third, DEA sought refuge in the fact that Congress does consider drugs a special problem deserving of special attention. DEA has not only capitalized on this view of Congress to lobby Congress successfully against any potential reorganization that may threaten its very survival or policy mandate. In effect, DEA has used successfully the leverage granted to the agency by the prevailing views in Congress to fend off aggressive moves by the FBI that threaten DEA's autonomy. This three-pronged strategy has served DEA well to preserve its supremacy over investigations in the drug war—although Customs too poses a threat. Its posture within the anti-narcotics policy space, though defensive, has been helped by the enormous importance that Congress places on the issue of illegal drugs. Finally, it is worth mentioning that the FBI's much broader jurisdiction appears to make it a much more "secure" agency, whereas DEA's very narrow jurisdiction makes it much more vulnerable to capture.[21]

Bureaucracies and the Structure of Credit Taking

In the competitive environment of the anti-narcotics policy space, LEAs are under intense pressure to "produce results," that is, to demonstrate a tangible effect on illegal drug production, trafficking, and consumption. But results in the drug war are not easy to measure. Not only is it hard to observe the procedural performance of anti-narcotics agents, but LEAs are also trying to have an impact in an area in which they have, at most, educated guesses as to the real extent of the "problem."[22] While the "stats" of an agency do show what the agency has accomplished in a relatively tangible way, the "real" effect on the overall illegal drug fight is hard to know.[23] In spite of this, LEAs still face constant pressure to produce "results" and demonstrate their impact on the overall drug trade. The result is that the "stats" (e.g., number of drugs busts, arrests, drug seizures, convictions, etc.) have acquired a phenomenal importance for LEAs.[24] It is the only way for an agency to make an argument for its effectiveness against drugs, independently of the fact that an increase in the quantity of drugs intercepted could represent a success, if a higher proportion of the traffic has been seized, or a failure, if the overall traffic is up and is the real cause of the increased seizures.

The pressure to show results comes from the political principle of accountability that prevails in the U.S. political system. The role that Congress plays as an important life-line of an agency contributes enormously to this pressure on LEAs regarding the "stats." The political urgency of elected politicians to show results is passed on to LEAs. This pressure, combined with the difficulty of knowing to what extent illegal drugs are being successfully combated, has made LEAs rely on specific result-measuring procedures that they can control. LEAs have resorted to justifying their very existence based on the statistics regarding the number of tons of drugs seized, the number of arrests made, the number of successful convictions, the number of assets confiscated, and the total amount of cash captured from drug rings.

These numbers are flaunted as proof of the success of the agency or a demonstration of its vital place in the war on drugs. Taking credit for an operation has become a major preoccupation for LEAs. Yet even comparisons of seizures by one agency or another can be misleading, as they may reflect changes in trafficking patterns as well as changes in relative effectiveness of the agencies.

To be sure, the numbers do have their intrinsic importance. Not only do agencies show an impact on drug production, trade and consumption through the "stats," but the absence of quantitative data would make it difficult for agencies to know what their agents were doing; and it would make it difficult to assign personnel, calculate budgets, etc. Allocation would be nearly impossible. More importantly, without the stats, it would be impossible for an agency to go to Capitol Hill to argue for more resources or greater jurisdiction. Thus, while agencies try to hide the fact that it is extremely hard to calculate the relationship between their statistics and the reality of drug production, trafficking, and consumption, they openly flaunt their "stats" as a measure of their success.

At the more practical level, the issue plays itself out whenever there is a joint drug bust. After a drug seizure or arrest, for example, LEA officials from the agencies participating in the bust scramble to call their own press conferences and issue their own releases announcing the success of the operation and touting their agency's role in it. Fierce competition for the numbers is common. Often, agencies' personnel quarrel over who gets what credit for what operation. One effect of this is the duplication of statistics. It became hard to know the exact overlap in the numbers of any two agencies. The problem escalated to the point at which the Drug Czar's office (ONDCP) began weeding out duplicate seizures in agencies' claims. In 1991, for example, the ONDCP reported that while the combined seizure claims of U.S. Customs, DEA, IRS, Coast Guard, and FBI, were almost 360,000 pounds of cocaine, the actual figure was closer to 229,000 pounds. When asked about the seizure claims by Customs, John Hensley, Customs Assistant Commissioner, said that his agency's figures were "probably pretty accurate." If drugs busts were counted more than once, he said, his agency was not the culprit.[25]

To stop the double reporting, the FDIN (federal drug identification number) system was created. The FDIN system filtered reports from all agencies to ensure that double-reporting was eliminated in order to gain a more accurate picture of the overall illegal drug enforcement accomplishments. Unfortunately, this system was set up so as to give credit to the first agency to call in the report. This only exacerbated the competition among agencies. U.S. Customs was particularly aggressive at the credit taking game. Customs officials went as far as equipping their field agents with cell phones intended not to improve communications with headquarters or among agents in the field but to allow Customs agents to be the first ones to call in a bust to the FDIN system in order that Customs get the credit.

Finally, the annual publications of anti-narcotics LEA agencies as well as most of their elaborate budget requests and presentations before congressional committees include flashy charts and ostentatious numbers that presumably show the importance of the agency's impact on the war on drugs. Charts and graphs touting progress, with sizeable upward trends, were quite common.

There is disagreement over the effects of competition among bureaus. Anthony Downs argued that this type of conflict is largely responsible for governmental growth because pressure to fund all these agencies, even when efforts are duplicated, results in increasingly larger budgets given that the goal of each agency is to maximize its budget. Robert Goodin (1975) argued that this competition has the more benign effect of allowing agencies to preserve their share of a pie and gain cooperation of other agencies, through compromise, for a better overall national policy. It could also be argued that bureaucratic competition has a place as a means of allocating resources among competing policies. But, regardless of the purpose that bureaucratic competition serves, in the anti-narcotics policy space it is intense and pervasive and the politics behind it fierce. Given the dependence of the overall system on the stats game, agencies find creative ways of laying claims to and presenting the numbers in such a way that they favor their organizational interests. The behavior of LEAs in regard to credit taking is distinctively political behavior. The statistics represent an important lifeline for an agency. Poor statistics can bring about harsh criticism from an organization's political bosses and perhaps the threat of reorganization or a redistribution of resources that may result in detriment of the agency. Because the uncertainty of such a scenario is not agreeable to a bureau, governmental organizations are likely to produce the rosiest scenarios possible to deflect criticism and avert revisions of the policy space that may affect the agency's resources or autonomy.

Political Dynamics between LEAs and Capitol Hill

No study of bureaucratic politics is complete without a discussion of congressional-bureaucratic relations. As Patricia Rachal has argued, to understand the politics of bureaucracy, it is necessary to understand the structure and dynamics of Congress and how these shape, proscribe, and provide opportunities for the political behavior of governmental organizations. The structure and dynamics of Congress not only influence the political behavior of government agencies toward Congress and of Congress toward government agencies but they also influence the political behavior of these agencies toward one another. Over a policy such as anti-narcotics there may be as many views as there are congressional committees or even members of Congress. Agencies are well aware of the cleavages in Congress on any one policy area and they can often take advantage of these to reap many benefits. Conversely, congressional members benefit from cultivating various relationships with certain agencies. Agencies curry favor with Congress members, and their staff, by providing services that cannot be found elsewhere; tending to a Congress member's constituency expediently and with dispatch; providing Congress members the opportunity to claim credit for securing some benefit for his/her constituency; going to great pains to spare a Congress member's district from program cutbacks or elimination of services; and providing expert information for a legislator who may want to enhance his/her reputation as policy expert or may be eager to improve his or her performance in legislative proceedings. For all these reasons, all agencies understand that it is in their best interest to cultivate strong personal and supportive relationships with members of Congress, particularly those that have budgetary or oversight authority over the agency.[26] The cultivation of supportive and protective relationships between Congress and government agencies is an evident practice in the war on drugs. In anti-narcotics policy, these relationships are shaped by two important factors: 1) structural factors; and 2) personal factors. U.S. Customs and DEA are good examples of the dynamics between Congress and the bureaucracy in this regard.

First, part of the favor that Customs enjoys on the Hill is "structural" (in a legal sense) given that the agency enforces some 400 to 450 statutes, including drugs, whereas agencies such as DEA have a much narrower focus. By virtue of the number of statutes that Customs handles, it is more likely to have the ability to cultivate more allies on the Hill. DEA, on the other hand, is more likely to satisfy fewer Congress members while being more closely scrutinized by many more—an uncomfortable position for any agency. As DEA Administrator Bonner (1999 interview) put it,

> I think Customs has always played the political game fairly well. It has the Treasury behind it. It has a way of, let's say, responding more immediately to politicians' needs...Senator DeConcini, he might as well have been the head of Customs, as far as I was concerned. The very first time that I was interviewing, going around the Senate Judiciary Committee.... Senator DeConcini, who was going to confirm me [as head of DEA], the very first question he was asking was how I was going to give concurrent jurisdiction to the Customs Service [over drugs], and I made no commitments whatsoever to him.

In other words, Customs simply has more buttons to push. There are many representatives who do not particularly care one way or the other on the issue of drugs. But every Congress member cares about one issue or another handled by Customs authority. Someone, Hensley (1999 interview) argued,

> . . . may have a farm state and they have unfair competition from Mexican tomatoes. It may be that they are a textile state and they have big competition from Chinese textiles. It may be that they are a tobacco state, and they do not like Turkish tobacco. It may be a bank, and we do the Bank Secrecy Act. So, Customs touches more buttons than any other agency. If some congressman has a pet bill in terms of keeping turtle wax out of the United States, or keeping peanuts out, or enforcing

> copyright violations, or child pornography, whatever their particular hot button is, we probably enforce it.

Thus the "structural" scenario on Capitol Hill favors Customs over DEA because Customs possesses the means to "satisfy" more politicians than DEA. In addition, Customs is particularly adept at taking advantage of its wider statutory authority. This is equivalent to having formal channels of action available and being willing to use them. Consequently, Customs has reaped handsome benefits. Overall, throughout the late 1980s and early 1990s, Customs officials continuously made the case for increasing budgets, particularly in the area of interdiction and they generally obtained them.

Another important "structural" element in congressional-bureaucratic relations is the issue of congressional committees. U.S. Customs is responsive to many more committees than DEA is. It has the opportunity to cultivate many more relationships, with various groups and subgroups within Congress, and the means to satisfy more members in various committees. DEA, on the other hand, is more likely to be criticized by many members of Congress, partly because it has little to offer to many of its oversight committees in terms of a real quid pro quo. In effect, DEA is an agency that is easy to chastise in order to express a commitment to the drug war. It's vulnerable to receive blame for failure but it does not easily receive credit for success. Custom's wide mandate and its effectiveness in avoiding being cornered as a single-issue agency have helped it escape some of the harsh criticism that DEA can draw from Congress.

As it is apparent, personal patronage from the political masters of an agency matters considerably. In Senator DeConcini, Customs had a personal ally who made its work a lot easier and who stepped in to defend Customs whenever the agency was engaged in a dispute or came under criticism from another agency.[27] DEA lacked the same kind of patronage, although some Congress members and Senators did show some interest in the agency. But even so, DEA was just not as adept as Customs at "working the Hill." Even if they had been willing to use this clout, the organization's own managers were not as skillful at cultivating DEA's relationships in Congress—a factor probably exacerbated by the "structural" factor that DEA has less to offer to Congress members, given its considerably narrower mandate. Customs Commissioners, on the other hand, have been extremely skillful at cultivating political relations with Congress members as well as with the heads of other agencies.[28] Of Carol Hallett, John Hensley (1999 interview), Assistant Commissioner for Law Enforcement, said,

> Carol Hallett is a practiced politician. . . . Carol understood the bigger picture and politics that everyone got a piece of it for some reason. And if you know why they have a piece and you address their needs, you're going to win. And that is the way she worked. She took care of the Hill; she took care of ONDCP; she took care of the White House; she took care of the Treasury; she made calls in with Justice; she

> engineered her position every time. She worked the phones better than anyone I have ever seen in my life.

When comparing these two agencies and their relationship to Congress, it is possible to see that "structural" power matters in Congress-agency relations and to notice that the personal interest of a member of Congress can be exploited for an agency in favor of its organizational interests. But these sources of influence must be accompanied by the willingness to use them and must be channeled by astute agency officials who can effectively utilize them. DEA, weak on both counts, cannot expect to occupy the place that Customs has carved for itself in the war on drugs—even though it is the primary anti-drug agency in the U.S. government!

Some Conclusions on LEA Political Behavior

Rarely have American political elites agreed on how to conceive the issue of illegal drugs. Over the course of the twentieth century, the "problem" of drugs has been defined and redefined. A prominent conception of the issue in the nineteenth century and the beginning of the twentieth century was as a health problem. This conception gave way to a view of illegal drugs as a criminal issue. Finally, since the 1980s, illegal drugs have been viewed as a national security concern.[29] And these conceptions have not necessarily been mutually exclusive. Congress, for example, has often viewed the problem as a combination of these issues. Nevertheless, the evolution of the conception of the issue brought an explosive growth to the anti-narcotics policy space. This growth was particularly intense during the George Bush administration. By 1993, over sixty federal agencies, including the military, were involved in the enforcement of U.S. counter-drug laws.[30] The federal counter-drug budget grew substantially every year between 1988 and 1993, from $4.7 billion in FY88, to $6.7 billion in FY89, $9.8 billion in FY90, $11 billion in FY91, $12 billion in FY92, and $12.3 billion in FY93.[31] The activities of the sixty-some bureaucratic agencies involved in enforcing counter-drug laws include both national and international components.[32] Finally, the policy space came to be characterized by a series of overlapping jurisdictions, duplication of tasks, conflicting arrangements for sharing information and resources, complex multi-agency and inter-organizational efforts and multilayered programs. In this scenario, the potential points of conflict among LEAs multiplied. The counter-drug policy space became a perilous spread of fragmented power and authority for any agency to navigate.[33]

The explosive growth of the anti-narcotics policy space between 1989 and 1993 produced a highly competitive environment in which each governmental agency's decision making process was conditioned by what other governmental agencies did. The interactive nature of the anti-narcotics policy space caused LEAs to behave in an increasingly political manner. LEAs attempted to capture part of the increasing resources being allocated by Congress for the war on drugs and, sometimes, agencies attempted to acquire assets directly from the stocks of other agencies. Some agencies also attempted to redraw the jurisdictional boundaries within the anti-narcotics policy space, often in a desire to enhance the agency's autonomy. The attempt by one agency to acquire a greater budget, more assets, or more personnel, moved other agencies to do the same or to defend their own. This led to allocational conflicts among them. The attempt by an agency to assert greater or sole jurisdiction over a set of tasks provoked others to protect their jurisdictional authority. This was at the root of many functional conflicts among them. Both allocational and functional conflicts were common among LEAs and between LEAs and other governmental agencies during the period under examination.

But, as it will become evident, federal agencies' did not attempt to revise the distribution of bureaucratic power in the anti-narcotics policy space indiscriminately. While most models of bureaucratic behavior insist on finding stable patterns of behavior that transcend time-bound elements, an examination of LEA behavior in the anti-narcotics policy space leads us to consider one important time-bound factor: opportunity. The LEAs under consideration did not "play politics" indiscriminately of time and place. Instead, each agency "struck" when the conditions for success were perceived as favorable—although this perception did not necessarily guarantee success. The political process had to be played out and the result was not necessarily what anybody wanted.

What are the strengths and weaknesses of bureaucratic politics in explaining the behavior of LEAs in the war on drugs? The preconditions of our model are present in the case of LEAs. The policy space is fragmented and competitive. All agencies analyzed exhibit the desire to increase their organizational resources and statutory autonomy. In addition, there are enough points of conflict among them, allocational and functional, that enable us to observe whether the behavior of LEAs follows a political approach. And indeed it does. Resistance was almost invariably the response of the agencies that stood to "lose" something in the process. This resistance took the form of appeals to Congress or the executive; the building of coalitions with other "affected" agencies; the use of rhetoric to portray the proposed change as being detrimental to national policy—rather than the interests of the agency; and the oft-inevitable negotiations between organizations. But success in bringing about one's preferences at the negotiating table or in resisting a given change in the power distribution of the policy space was determined by the relative power of the actors involved; the channels of action for each of the agencies involved; and the history between the agencies involved. An added word on the last two variables, however, is merited.

The channels of action open to an agency, whether to initiate a revision of the bureaucratic power distribution or to resist it, proved to be more ad hoc and less regularized than most studies on bureaucratic politics make it seem. The course of action that an agency followed was one of "opportunity." The "aggressive" agencies engaged in revising when they perceived an opportunity to bring about their organizational preferences. The "defending" agencies succeeded to the extent that they mustered clout with their political masters, built bureaucratic coalitions, and made use of both formal and informal channels of influence. While the concept of "opportunity" is quite vague and perhaps excessively sui generis, the cases studied suggest that agencies do operate with an eye to the most opportune moment for action. They follow logic of opportunity.

Interestingly, the "history" between two agencies also mattered. For example, whenever FBI and DEA came into contact, the long-simmering resentment of DEA and the FBI's constant threat to it were ever present. As David Westrate (2000 interview) said, DEA was not going to do "things the way the FBI did them" because down the road a couple of years [they] "would just throw the switch and all this ground work was done" for the FBI to absorb DEA. It also mattered between Customs and DEA. The suspicion between the two agencies went as far back as the 1973 Reorganization Plan that created DEA out of the Bureau of Narcotics and Dangerous Drugs and most of Customs Investigative Office agents. This suspicion worked itself out during negotiations regarding Customs' desired "cross-over jurisdiction" to pursue drug-related investigations beyond the border.

Finally, our analysis makes it evident that the managerial styles and capabilities of the officials of the various agencies mattered. In spite of the fact that most bureaucratic politics models would want to dispense with "personality" factors—including this one, it is evident that personality variables mattered. Hallett, for example, had high inter-personal skills that surpassed the skills that Lawn and Bonner ever had to push their agency's agenda. This variable also mattered because it enabled Customs to capitalize on many more and greater opportunities to grow, build coalitions (e.g, with SOUTHCOM's Joulwan), and prosper than DEA. It would thus appear that when one compares the behavior of agencies in a highly competitive environment such as the anti-narcotics law enforcement, who occupies the top positions does matter. This is an important point of vindication for Graham T. Allison's model of bureaucratic politics. Allison relies heavily on personality variables and has been soundly criticized for mixing up organizational-level with personal-level variables to explain bureaucratic behavior. Nevertheless, this study has found that personal variables do appear to matter—a vindication of Graham Allison's original model.

Organizational Culture: Law Enforcement Organizations

The behavior of organizations does not emerge from a vacuum. All organizational behavior has both external and internal behavior motivators. Among the internal motivators of behavior, organizational culture is a widely debated concept. This is because of the fact that culture, in and of itself, is a vague and abstract concept. It is not only difficult to define it but it is also difficult to establish the many thin but strong mechanisms by which culture influences the overall behavior of an organization. Nevertheless, culture is not less real than say, personality is to an individual. Culture establishes boundaries that, when violated, provoke reactions, no matter how vestigial and antiquated these boundaries may be. It is the culture of an organization that often guides its members' patterns and ways of thinking about a problem and the solutions to it.

Taking into consideration the difficulties in viewing culture as a source of organizational behavior, the remainder of this chapter sets out to discern the effects of organizational culture on the behavior of LEAs in the anti-narcotics policy space.

DEA: Putting People First

Between 1989 and 1993, the Drug Enforcement Administration (DEA) increased its budget and personnel considerably.[34] DEA's presence abroad also grew steadily and reached ten percent of its work force by 1990 when Robert Bonner became DEA administrator. Although DEA was not originally intended to have an international component, its presence abroad grew as a natural extension of the foundational belief of the organization that *people* break the law and, therefore, people must be targeted for arrest and prosecution. If the law-breakers live and operate abroad, they must be targeted abroad. In addition, this sharp focus on people has given DEA a way of distinguishing the "real work" of the organization from "garbage work." DEA's focus on "people as law-breakers," can help explain why DEA has remained, for the most part, disengaged from certain facets of the war on drugs—facets which other agencies have readily embraced—or why in general DEA agents exhibit a relatively low degree of confidence in the effectiveness of strategies other than arresting key individuals and dismantling criminal organizations.[35]

Although DEA has faced perilous moments in its existence—including several reorganizations, various scandals, a shift from one department to another, and at least three serious threats of a merger with the FBI, the fundamental belief that *people* are its target, the priority of the tasks the organization performs, and the crime-fighting methods it employs have hardly changed at all. Criminal and general investigations consume most of the DEA's resources. In addition, half of all its personnel are composed of street-level "investigators"—or, as Wilson put it, "instigators." This group constitutes by far the majority within the organization and has remained steady at that level. The "investigative mind set" dominates the air within the organization. This mind set originates in the "mission" or "distinctive competence" of DEA.[36] Among DEA agents, the highest valued member is one who possesses the right skills to build a network of informants, is quite effective at doing undercover work, and ultimately manages to conduct a successful drug bust and "puts the crooks in jail." These agents are the ones who receive the "honors" that peers give in the form of "a hall reputation." The job, said Stephen H. Green (2000 interview) of DEA, continues to be "to identify the traffickers and their organizations, to take away their resources, but above all, to take away their freedom."

Throughout the period under examination, the number of operations designed to target individual traffickers and their drug trafficking organizations through investigative work, undercover techniques, and the building of networks of informants grew considerably both at home and abroad. DEA's primary strategy was to cripple or dismantle the trafficking organizations and to arrest and prosecute their members. This focus is derived directly from what DEA considers its foundational mission as a law enforcement agency. As Bonner (1999 interview) put it, "I think we have to treat it [drugs] as a law enforcement issue and take law enforcement approaches to devise and develop ways to essentially crush, dismantle organizations and their structures." Later, his successor, Thomas A. Constantine would say much the same thing,

> The serious prosecution and incarceration of the top Colombian drug lords is our primary goal. . . . DEA will continue to work with the Government [of Colombia] to provide intelligence, information, and evidence which will lead to the full range of judicial measures available" (*International Narcotics*, 1994, p. 35).

Consequently, large portions of the increasing resources of DEA at the time were dedicated to hire and train investigators as well as to organize and carry out operations that targeted drug trafficking organizations and their members. The statements cited would not be as interesting except for the fact that the overall U.S. government approach to the drug war goes well beyond investigations and extends to eradication efforts, interdiction strategies, and international treaties on money laundering, extradition treaties, etc. Yet, DEA has remained outside most eradication and interdiction efforts and has not been as forceful on money laundering efforts.[37] Its primary focus remains targeting individuals in organizations—the investigative and prosecuting segments of the drug war.

The following segment relates one of the operations of which DEA is highly proud; it is the kind of operation which tends to raise the morale among agents. Though the operation occurred in 1992, as of 2000 DEA still proudly displayed it in its web page as an example of the type of operation that will "make a dent" on illegal drugs. The narration contains all the highly valued elements of a DEA agent's perfect operation,

> Operation Dinero, a joint DEA/IRS (Internal Revenue Service) operation, was launched by the DEA's Atlanta Division in 1992. In this investigation, the U.S. Government successfully operated a financial institution in Anguilla for the purpose of targeting the financial networks of international drug organizations. In ad-

> dition, a number of undercover corporations were established in different jurisdictions as multi-service "front" businesses designed to supply money laundering services such as loans, cashier's checks, wire transfers, and peso exchanges, or to establish holding companies or shell corporations for the trafficking groups. Believing these services were legitimate, the Cali mafia engaged the bank to sell three paintings, a Picasso, a Rubens, and a Reynolds. These paintings, estimated to have a combined value of $15 million, were seized by the DEA and IRS in 1994. The operation resulted in 116 arrests in the United States, Spain, Italy, and Canada and the seizure of nine tons of cocaine, and the seizure of more than $90 million in cash and other property. The two-year joint enforcement operation was coordinated by the DEA, IRS, INS, FBI, and international law enforcement counterparts in the United Kingdom, Canada, Italy, and Spain.[38]

In addition to the "cult" of investigation, DEA has sought to develop strong intelligence capabilities. Much of the intelligence the DEA procures, however, is tied to classical investigative work—it comes from informants. Informants are a vital part of DEA's operations. It is the way the agency maintains a close eye on drug traffickers and their organizations. It is the way the agency follows the thread down to the final "bust." The informant networks on drug trafficking built by DEA are considerable. As Wilson put it,

> DEA agents rarely receive any complaints from organizations or individuals that credibly allege a serious law infraction; instead, the narcotics agents must create their own workload by inducing individuals to reveal information they would prefer to keep confidential or to engage in transactions they, if fully informed and free to behave autonomously, would avoid.[39]

Intelligence that emerges from satellites or spy planes is by far less important to DEA. As a DEA agent remarked, the guy on the ground, with the connections, can serve as great or even greater purpose than the plane or the satellite above (Green, 2000 interview). It is noteworthy also that DEA has not aggressively pursued high technology for its intelligence operations—unlike Customs, which is continually seeking the newest technologies. DEA does not have the "domes" or aerostats or other technologies that Customs has acquired. It appears that high-tech intelligence, though not unwelcome, is simply not that popular at DEA. This makes sense if we view this high technology as somewhat opposed to the investigative work of people rather than machines and if we note that most of this technology is designed to conduct operations for interdiction, an area in which DEA has exhibited a low degree of interest. In other words, the highest anti-drug technology does not reinforce or serve the preestablished notions of DEA's work in the anti-narcotics policy space.

As a testimony of what is more highly valued at DEA, a cocaine seizure made in Sylmar, California, in 1989, is still held up by DEA agents as an example of how the drug war is fought. Part of the awe toward this operation is related to the fact that in terms of sheer numbers the bust was the largest victory DEA ever had. The drug seizure consisted of 47,554 lbs. of cocaine seized in a house in Sylmar, CA, on 29 September 1989. But besides the numbers, it was the careful, calculated and patient investigation. DEA agents worked through informants. They prepared the case with months of anticipation. They surveyed and monitored the place constantly. Finally, they conducted the kind of raid that DEA agents admire the most—undercover agents moved in on the property and seized the drugs and arrested a whole network of drug traffickers. Stephen H. Green (2000 interview) praised that event as the "kind of thing that the government should do to eradicate the scourge of drugs."

It is not only what DEA agents do and love to do that is revealing, but also what they dislike to do and seldom choose as a course of action. There is within DEA, for example, a certain degree of contempt for crop eradication and for drug interdiction as well as for treatment and education programs, even though these constitute important components of the overall national strategy to combat illegal drugs. This is not to say that DEA does not participate at some level in any of these activities; indeed they support many of them with intelligence information. But these tasks are not as highly regarded by DEA agents as is investigative work. DEA's relative lack of confidence in the effectiveness of crop eradication is captured in Bonner's (1999 interview) words,

> In terms of crop eradication, we had voluntary programs, nothing, by the way, that ever had any impact whatsoever in Peru, where about seventy percent of the coca was grown. I don't think [it] had any significant impact in Bolivia, although there was a voluntary program which *campesinos* were paid to destroy and stop growing coca in areas of the Chapare. That was never a very effective program.

This level of disdain for crop eradication is not unlike the dislike that DEA agents feel for most interdiction initiatives. Of drug interdiction operations through the use of aerostats—initially a Customs operation and later a DOD-Customs joint operation, Jack Lawn (1999 interview) said,

> If only ten percent of that money spent for aerostats was put into PI/PE–purchase of information and purchase of evidence—paying persons within those organizations to make it worth their while to risk their lives to provide information for us, [it would have been] much more valuable. The person on site who develops the information is always of much greater value than issues like balloons or aerostats."

Similarly, Stephen Green of DEA said that interdiction was ineffective because the drug traffickers "are simply forced to find other methods; they go around us." At DEA, confidence in the deterrent effects of interdiction was low—even after the military became involved in the war on drugs. Bonner argued that the military does not understand the nature of the business. Informants, he contended, know more than the man handling the [military] radar,

> Well, if you are bringing in the military, they tend to think in, let's say, military solutions to problems. Or . . . is it a border control problem?, which is the way Customs would tend to look at it. Frankly I must say a lot of the very superficial thinking in Congress tends to be, 'let's look at the border,' where actually, it's kind of laughable. It's so ludicrous that anybody who knows the issue, that you are actually going to view it as simply a border control problem; that somehow you're going to significantly staunch the flow of drugs in the United States. To me, it was very clear that the essence of the problem was attacking the major organizations in a very sophisticated way (Bonner, 1999 interview).

In a similar vein, DEA agents did not exhibit excitement or enthusiasm for domestic campaign ads. The organizational culture of the DEA goes a long way to explain this implicit rejection of these facets of the war on drugs. The logic is relatively clear: DEA was created as a law enforcement agency whose fundamental focus was and remains people who break the law. This focus influences the overall levels of confidence that DEA exhibits in specific strategies with investigative work being by far the highest priority as reflected in its budgetary and personnel priorities as well as in the attitudes and the words of DEA's agents and bureaucratic leaders.

The fact that the DEA stuck to its core conviction that it is people who must be targeted meant that their strategies sometimes clashed with the priorities of other agencies. The DEA had to change its modus operandi abroad to a large extent because its domestic modus operandi clashed directly with the Department of State's modus operandi. The strategies pursued within the United States, such as the "buy-and-bust" strategy, did not translate well to the international environment. DEA agents could not as easily go undercover and infiltrate an organization in another country. They did not fit easily among drug traffickers and their cartels. While the core tasks remained to gather intelligence on individuals and to arrest, extradite (when possible) and prosecute them, the geographical situation forced DEA agents to adjust to some new conditions. The jungles and rivers of Bolivia, Colombia, and Peru are rough and strenuous terrain. They are nothing like working the streets of Cleveland or New York. Many agents working abroad became convinced that they were waging a true "war." The "drug war" rhetoric as well as the rough conditions of the terrain in which they were working captured the imagination of many DEA agents stationed in South America. They began dressing in fatigues and conducting surveillance, lab-busting, and chases in jungle conditions. Many of these agents had a military background and some of them had been Green Berets. Some began to see little conflict between the quasi-military operations they were beginning to conduct starting in the mid-1980s and the more subtle investigative work of a law enforcer.

But the agents operating abroad underestimated the extent to which their investigative style, highly flexible and fast-paced, would be considered "rogue" or "paramilitary" by U.S. Foreign Service officers stationed in those countries. Indeed, DEA operators occasionally have some trouble adjusting to the requirements of diplomacy. Accustomed to operating in a decentralized fashion, getting into action on short notice and drawing resources quickly, including cash to conduct payments for information, DEA agents found themselves accountable to the Ambassador, under the very tight control of the Deputy Chief of Mission (DCM) and the Narcotics Affairs Section (NAS) in each embassy. They were frustrated because they could not conduct operations without the explicit approval of the Ambassador or his DCM and NAS. They could not easily draw any funds because all foreign expenditures are handled by the Embassy through Department of State's budget for law enforcement abroad. The "petty cash" concept for drug busts or information acquisition does not exist in the highly formal interactions of the State Department personnel. Moreover, all actions and activities by DEA agents had to be checked for potential diplomatic trouble. DEA agents' resistance to the style of the Foreign Service abroad finally gained them a reputation as "rogues" and prompted Foreign Service officers working at Embassies in South America to keep a very close eye on them. These restrictions turned out to be frustrating to many DEA agents who viewed FSOs as soft on drugs and drug traffickers.[40]

DEA agents' use of paramilitary tactics, their quasi-military fatigue uniforms, the use of helicopters to fly low in search of drug-related activity, and their overall aggressive attitude was disliked by State Department personnel. The tactics and the "look" irked State Department personnel because they saw potential diplomatic problems with the "door-busting rogues" of the DEA. "It looked like an invasion," some Embassy personnel complained. Mel Levitsky (1999 interview), chief of DOS International Narcotics Matters bureau at the time, stated that,

> . . . during the first trip I took out to the Huallaga Valley, Peru, [I realized that] they [DEA] had the wrong kind of people, helicopters . . . hanging around from helicopters [in fatigue] with no seat belts, with their legs hanging out and with a gun across their chest. They looked like Green Berets, which many had been. So, we changed that.

The frustration of some DEA agents with the State Department reached its peak when the five-year chief of the DEA bureau at the U.S. Embassy in Colombia, Joseph Toft, resigned in anger in 1994 and called a press conference where he revealed the content of secret DEA tapes that revealed Colombian President Ernesto Samper's dealings with the Cali Cartel during his political campaign. This press conference caused serious consternation within the U.S. Embassy. Joe Toft labeled Colombia a "narco-democracy." This name-calling strained relations between the State Department and the DEA. In effect, Toft had forced the hand of the less confrontational FSOs within the U.S. Embassy in Colombia, who now had to face publicly the fact that the very president of the country might be involved in the messy business of drugs. There had been a veritable cultural clash. And the State Department was not wrong. Relations between the U.S. and Colombia reached record lows after the press conference. By 1996, the U.S. "decertified" Colombia labeling it a country not cooperating with the war on drugs.

The clash between the DEA's fast-moving, independent-minded DEA agents abroad and the more circumspect modus operandi of State's FSOs was not trivial. If the overall "cop" mentality of the DEA was not altogether compatible with diplomacy, the paramilitary culture developing among DEA agents in South America was even less compatible with DOS's mind set. While the State Department personnel are charged with the establishment and maintenance of relationships with foreign governments, DEA agents often see the relationship as expendable if a serious blow can be dealt to a powerful drug trafficking organization or drug kingpin.[41]

DEA has a highly developed consciousness of what the organization is about. This consciousness has filtered well down the hierarchy. It shapes and proscribes what DEA agents find acceptable and unacceptable. Often, however, particularly in inter-agency environments, the culture of DEA shines through and contrasts sharply with the culture of other U.S. bureaus. Perhaps nowhere is this more evident, and culture more finely defined, than in DEA's relations with the State Department. It is more difficult to compare the differences between the culture of the military and the culture of law enforcement, specifically DEA, because these two groups of bureaucrats have stayed largely clear of each other. Future studies must look closely at how the military operates with LEAs in inter-agency environments.

A Tale of Two Cultures: U.S. Customs and its Subcultures

Sometimes within an organization certain "professions" stake out a dominant role. They form an elite corps and control certain assets, operations, and policies within the organization. The consequence is that one group of people is "in" and the rest are "out." Although organizations exhibit different kinds of such "splits," including professionals and non-professionals, superiors and subordinates, etc., sometimes those splits occur along cultural lines. Cultural splits are common when the architects of an organization lump several different social functions into a single organizational structure—although this "lumping" may not occur by intentional design. The result is generally that the organization is composed of several subcultures—sometimes even incompatible with one another.[42] The natural aftermath of this, according to our organizational culture model, is that one culture will be dominant over the others. The former will be at the center of the organization while the latter will suffer from neglect. Within Customs there are two clearly discernible subcultures, both of which deal with the issue of drugs. The first is the "inspection culture"; the second is the "interdiction culture." In examining these two subcultures, it is pertinent to ask whether the hypotheses derived from our organizational culture model hold.

The first mission of Customs was to ensure that all goods crossing the U.S. border do so according to U.S. laws. Customs has fulfilled this mission since the founding of the country. In the 1960s, however, President Nixon became extremely preoccupied with the drug threat. His strategy for combating illegal drugs, though primarily based on treatment and education, included a strong interdiction component. It is somewhat puzzling that Customs sought out an interdiction role in the 1960s and even more aggressively in the 1980s and 1990s because interdiction implied asset-heavy operations on land, air, and sea both at home and abroad. It is puzzling because this expansion overstepped the boundaries of Customs original mission. But even more puzzling is the fact that, though a late-comer, interdiction thrives as a culture within U.S. Customs, along with its more immediate and natural mission: inspection.[43] It is difficult to harmonize the interdiction mission with Customs' original mission—to ensure that all goods crossing the U.S. border do so in accordance with U.S. laws.[44] Why is it that interdiction does not suffer at all as a "secondary" mission, as would be predicted by organizational culture models?

Asking this question assumes that interdiction is considered a "secondary" mission at Customs. It is not. U.S. Customs has, in effect, managed to build not one but two dominant cultures within the agency. Customs, like other agencies, notably the military, has achieved the maintenance of more than one culture on an equal footing. How has Customs managed this? Largely by keeping them apart. The structure of the organization is such that the "interdiction wing" people hardly interact with the "inspection wing" people of the organization. Not only are they separated even geographically because the interdiction mission of Customs is not necessarily located along border posts, but the people that compose each group are recruited from different sources and their training is also different. Customs agents working for Customs Aviation Interdiction Program, for example, are recruited mostly because they already know how to fly.

> Customs air crews include highly trained law enforcement professionals who bring special skills to the fight against drug smuggling. Customs pilots, many of whom are former military [or civilian] aviators, must have logged over 1,500 hours of flight time before being hired. The Customs pilot is well versed in all aspects of tactical flying and operations.[45]

This statement was confirmed in a conversation with former Customs Commissioner Carol Hallett (1999 interview), who put it more clearly:

> Hallett: [Customs] has two different missions: one is trade and the other is drugs. And halfway in between, they also bring in a lot of revenue.
> Payan: Does that mean that Customs has two cultures?
> Hallett: Yeah, I think that the inspectors have a dual role. One is to look for illegal trade coming in—that would be textiles, etc. . . . They are also looking for drugs and money laundering violations. These agents do a lot more than just drugs. . . .

> These agents are trained to be agents. . . . With our air branch, our air wing, which is such an important part of the drug war, you hire pilots and then you train them to be agents. DEA did just the opposite. They hire agents and then train them to be pilots.

Border inspectors are focused on the original mission of Customs, a mission where drugs are one component among many. The interdiction mission is exclusively focused on illegal drugs. The harmonious existence of these subcultures is possible thanks to generous congressional appropriations for Customs, which have, so far, satisfied the needs of both subcultures. Abundant resources mitigate the potential for conflict within the agency because, as bureaucratic politics models would maintain, conflict is generally the result of disagreements over the distribution of the resources of an organization. When there is enough to satisfy everyone, conflict is unlikely and harmony within a bureau is more likely.

Thus, an analysis of U.S. Customs under the lens of our organizational culture model helps refine the model itself. Sometimes, when abundant resources exist, two or more cultures within a single organization will live in harmony and prosper. It is possible also that none of them will suffer neglect. The physical separation afforded by abundant resources also facilitates harmony.

These observations lead us to ask, what would happen to Customs if it faced a serious budgetary cut? What would go first if it had to set priorities? Though the case of U.S. Customs is not the right case the test this hypothesis, the U.S. Coast Guard is.

Budget Cuts and Secondary Missions: The Case of the U.S. Coast Guard

The Coast Guard is the lead federal agency for maritime drug interdiction and shares partial responsibility for air interdiction efforts with Customs. As such, the Coast Guard is a key player in combating the flow of illegal drugs to the United States. The Coast Guard's mission is to reduce the supply of drugs from the source by denying smugglers the use of air and maritime routes in the "Transit Zone," a six million square mile area, including the Caribbean, Gulf of Mexico and Eastern Pacific. While the Coast Guard has accepted drug law enforcement as a major part of its law enforcement mission, it decidedly did not follow the "imperialistic" path that Customs pursued in the area of drug interdiction. This, given the fact that the Coast Guard's original mission is not entirely incompatible with drug interdiction—certainly no more than Customs' original mission—is puzzling. The USCG's attitude stands in contrast to Customs' enthusiastic embrace of interdiction efforts.[46] This apparent lack of enthusiasm along with the fact that the Coast Guard did face severe budget cuts during the period of our investigation can help us test our hypotheses regarding "what goes first" when priorities among missions and tasks must be set. Indeed, an examination of the most important changes that occurred in the Coast Guard's interdiction mission permits us to say that it is plausible that organizational culture was a factor in the overall behavior of the Coast Guard in the area of interdiction when budget cuts came after 1990.

Although the case of the Coast Guard does allow us to test the hypotheses regarding what goes first when priorities must be set, it complicates matters in a different way. Discerning between culture and the influence of key individuals upon an organization is sometimes a difficult task. Though sometimes one negates the other, the Coast Guard is an example of an organization in which drug law enforcement is just one other activity among many law enforcement activities. This was true when Admiral P. A. Yost was the Commandant of the Coast Guard in the late 1980s and early 1990s. He had embraced the interdiction mission for the Coast Guard and institutionalized that mission as part of the day-to-day activities of the Coast Guard. But, in spite of his personal enthusiasm for the mission, drug law enforcement within the Coast Guard remained only one among the many responsibilities of the Coast Guard. Adm. Kime, Yost's immediate successor, was less concerned with drug law enforcement and turned his personal attention to the environment—a personal interest of his. Hence, personnel and budgetary priorities within the Coast Guard changed to reflect Adm. Kime's priorities. That Yost or Kime were able to personally impose their priorities on their organizations could also be a reflection of the fact that the USCG, given its enormously broad mission, is susceptible to capture by its own leaders. Further research on this point is required. But an emphasis on an organizational leader's personal preferences does not subtract from an organizational culture argument regarding the priorities of an agency. From an organizational standpoint, it is suggested that when an agency faces deep cuts in its overall budget, it is those activities that are valued less that go first. Looking at the deep cuts experienced by the Coast Guard from 1991 to 1995, it is clear that the Coast Guard did not retain the same level of commitment to drug law enforcement the that it had in 1990. The following chart suggests that, although Adm. Kime's priorities were with the environment and part of the reduction in drug-dedicated assets might be attributed to his priorities in areas other than drug interdiction, at least part of these reductions can be attributed to the lesser priority of drug law enforcement within the Coast Guard. Besides, dedicated assets continued to decline under Adm. Robert E. Kramek, even as he explicitly stated that drug interdiction continued to be a top priority for the Coast Guard. The reductions are quite dramatic, particularly in view of Customs' increase in interdiction assets in the same period.[47]

Table 2.2 Coast Guard interdiction force structures for FY 1990 and FY 1995

Dedicated Assets	FY 1990	FY 1995
HU-25C (F-16 Radar)	8	0
E-2C	4	0
EC-130V	1	0
HH-3F/HH-60J (OPBAT)	9	9
Dedicated Air Station	1	0
Sea Based Aerostat (SBA)	5	0
Land Based Aerostat (LBA)	2	0
Surface Effect Ship (SES)	3	0
C3I-East	1 Detachment	0
C3I-West	1 Detachment	0
Asset Resource Hours	**FY1990**	**FY1995**
Cutter	152,482	85,700
Aircraft	26,126	15,200
Coast Guard Drug Budget	$515.4 M	$293.6 M

The case of the Coast Guard is similar to the case of the military, where the drug budget went down from $1.2 billion in FY1992 to somewhat over $900 million after the severe budgetary cuts imposed on DOD by Congress in an effort to balance the budget of the mid-1990s. Both agencies responded to the overall budgetary cuts by restricting further their participation in the war on drugs. It was drugs what "went" first.

Finally, while Customs and the Coast Guard competed with each other in the anti-narcotics policy space, it is somewhat puzzling also that the Coast Guard did not view the Navy, after the 1989 Defense Authorization Act legislated the military into the drug war, as a threat to its drug activities. There was a remarkable level of cooperation between the Coast Guard and the Navy on the issue. Soon, the two organizations had worked an arrangement that enabled the Navy to say that it had fulfilled its mission in the drug war and enhanced the law enforcement capabilities in the area for the Coast Guard. The two organizations established a program called

Law Enforcement Detachment or LEDET. Organizational culture has also acted in several intriguing ways in the anti-narcotics policy space. To this day, LEDETs aboard U.S. Navy and foreign nation vessels perform the counter-drug mission. When not engaged in their primary mission, LEDETs are used to train or augment Navy and allied "Visit, Board, Search, and Seizure" (VBSS) teams performing international Maritime Interception Operations (MIO) in support of U.S. and international security policy; participate in interagency law enforcement operations with other federal, state, and local law enforcement authorities; deploy world-wide in support of port security and maritime counter-terrorist missions; provide law enforcement training to Coast Guard, federal, state, and local law enforcement units; serve as technical observers for the Coast Guard, the Navy, allied forces, and other law enforcement agencies; conduct law enforcement briefings to Coast Guard, Navy, and allied units; and augment and train other Coast Guard unit boarding teams while conducting law enforcement operations. What is remarkable about the LEDET program, reorganized and renamed Tactical Enforcement Team (TACLET) after 1993, is how "in sync" the Navy and the Coast Guard worked. This may be due to the fact that the Coast Guard, though part of the Department of Transportation, considers itself a military body. It may also be that the two agencies have a "sea" culture. Besides, involving the Coast Guard deeply in the Navy's anti-drug operations was a way for the Navy to fulfill its mission without having to get too deeply into it. The Coast Guard, for its part, was delighted to have its elements deployed in Navy ships, using the Navy's sophisticated equipment for surveillance operations. It was a match made in heaven.

Finally, and fully consistent with our organization culture model, is the fact that the Coast Guard's "sea" culture might have prevented it from fighting Customs more fiercely over jurisdiction in the air interdiction drug war. Clearly, Customs moved to expel the Coast Guard from nearly all air interdiction and the Coast Guard unquestionably retreated from the air interdiction area. This is puzzling because there were assets and resources to be had in the air interdiction area. If the Coast Guard had wanted to grow, the air interdiction area would have been the place to go. Yet, Coast Guard leaders and operatives opted for withdrawing from the air interdiction arena and allowing Customs to monopolize that facet of the drug war in an alliance with the military. This points to the fact that in the USCG, the drug law enforcement mission is only one component, but not a central one or not seen as anything of particular importance and therefore expendable.

LEAs and Organizational Culture

Organizational culture fares well in analyzing the behavior of law enforcement agencies. It appears to explain well DEA's reluctance to enter the interdiction, eradication, and prevention efforts in the drug war and its people's lack of confidence in the effectiveness of these counter-narcotics facets of the overall drug war. Similarly, an analysis of Customs' behavior through the organizational culture lens suggests that sometimes organizations are composed of two or more dominant cultures and that indeed two cultures can live relatively comfortably within the same organization. However, it also suggests two reasons for this. First, neither culture is subordinate to the other. They co-exist as separate and equal cultures—the operative word is "separate," of course. Second, an examination of Customs' organizational behavior suggests that these two cultures co-exist in relative harmony because there are abundant resources that permit both groups to satisfy their material needs without having to take from the other. In other words, redistribution conflicts have not ensued and therefore reprioritization of Customs' activities has not occurred. Such a conflict would enable us to see which activity would "go first" and therefore what is most valued within Customs. Which culture would stand to "lose" if drastic budget cuts were to force Customs to downsize is still to be seen.

The case of the Coast Guard partially reveals what the case of Customs cannot. What "goes first" when an agency that enforces multiple statutes is forced to face budget cuts that compel it to prioritize its activities and tasks? What is sacrificed is revealing. Drugs are only one of the many statutes the Coast Guard enforces and not the most important one. When the Coast Guard faced severe budget cuts in the early 1990s, it was forced to prioritize its tasks. The drug war clearly suffered. The downsizing of the Coast Guard's anti-drug assets was dramatic, even as there were resources to be had, particularly in the area of air interdiction. Coast Guard officials simply did not make the case before Congress. They simply let go of much of the drug war, implying that it was not viewed as central at all.

Finally, the case of the Coast Guard also suggests that when two agencies share a medium and develop similar cultures around that medium, e.g., the military culture and Navy symbolism that characterizes the Coast Guard, it is possible for these agencies to complement each other's missions. The LEDET arrangement enabled the Navy to fulfill its part of DOD's anti-narcotics bargain, without having to dwell on it, and the Coast Guard got to expose its personnel to the latest the Navy had to offer. But that they were able to do so was underpinned by the fact that their cultures were somewhat similar and complementary. This also worked because neither organization saw the other as a competitor. Their cultures were complementary and were not competing with each other because their priorities were different. What the Navy had—its assets for surveillance—complemented and enhanced the performance of the Coast Guard as an LEA. This is confirmed by the fact that a similar partnership between Customs and SOUTHCOM worked, but not the partnership between Customs and the Coast Guard on air interdiction. Here the two agencies competed directly with each other. Customs and the Coast Guard saw each other as competitors; their common "law enforcement" mission made them so. Incidentally, this reveals that our models might perhaps complement each other rather than compete with each other. Similar cultures (e.g., law enforcement) are not enough to "get long." There must also be the perception that operating jointly is advantageous to both agencies. If cooperation is perceived as a zero-sum game, as between Customs and the Coast Guard, in spite of apparently similar mission cultures, conflict is likely.

Conclusion

An examination of the behavior of our LEAs reveals that bureaucratic politics is a powerful motivator behind the behavior of LEAs in the drug war. Even under the narrower specifications of our model—considering only a bureau's political masters and its fellow-dwellers in a policy space—LEAs engaged heavily in politics. Some bureaus, such as U.S. Customs, actively pursued both greater budgets and greater autonomy. Customs went as far as taking advantage of various opportunities to expel the U.S. Coast Guard from the area of air interdiction—confirming the point that agencies abhor areas of common competence. But Customs was even more aggressive than this. It sought to recover its former prominence in the area of anti-narcotics investigations, even though it realized that DEA would not easily surrender its jurisdiction over drug investigations. But for Customs, it was a matter of a trade-off. Getting credit for drug war successes, e.g., arrests, seizures, and convictions, was far more important than having to share jurisdiction with DEA in the area of investigations.

The issue of who gets credit for a drug war success, however temporary, is an important one. LEAs were considerably competitive on this. LEAs sought to get credit for drug busts, seizures, arrests, and other "results" of anti-drug programs and operations. It was, in the end, the only way for an agency to demonstrate "progress" in a policy area where it is difficult to measure success. Competition for the "stats" went as far as causing confusion over national drug war statistics. On this, however, Congress is partially a culprit because it demands that agencies produce results. These demands only exacerbate competition among agencies.

Alliances among agencies were not uncommon in the drug war. Agency managers did try to recruit the support of allies, even that of other agencies' managers, to fend off aggressive moves by other agencies or by political masters who sought changes that encroached on the jurisdictional turf of a bureau. DEA, for example, provoked a formidable alliance against Judge Robert Bonner's plan to build an air wing for DEA from assets taken from other agencies and, consequently, to give DEA a role in the interdiction area. Either aspect of Judge Bonner's plan, the allocational aspect or the functional aspect, was not welcome among LEAs who were supposed to give up their assets or whose jurisdiction would be affected by DEA participation in air interdiction. In similar fashion, Customs sought support from other actors, including congressional actors, to prevent the Pentagon from handing the west coast of South America to PACOM and away from LANTCOM. In both cases, the agencies that stood to lose sought to garner support to oppose the changes they disliked. Incidentally, this appears to confirm the point that agencies will see potential losses with greater alarm than the measure of enthusiasm with which they see potential gains.

Finally, the case of DEA demonstrates an important lesson of bureaucratic politics. Agencies with very narrow mandates that can be easily absorbed by agencies with greater mandates, e.g., DEA being absorbed by the FBI, will develop a sense of insecurity. Fear of capture will be greater among narrower-mandate agencies. To prevent capture, an agency will seek to attain a sense of equality and convey to its political masters and the public that what the agency does cannot be done by any other agency or, if they were to be assigned the mission, it would be neglected. In that sense, agencies will likely try to develop specific niches—such as DEA on investigations—in which they can claim expertise and proficiency that no one else can provide.

Another important point is that not all agencies view each other as rivals. While some may simply not have anything to do with each other, others will actually view each other as complementary. Customs, for example, did not see the entrance of the military into the drug war as a threat. On the contrary, it saw the military as a great complementary force that enhanced its ability to carry out its mission and claim credit for drug war successes. Similarly, the Coast Guard viewed the Navy as an ally that enhanced its prestige and reputation. Both of these cases will be pursued further in Chapter 4.

In regard to our organizational culture model, each of these cases highlights ways in which organizational culture is at work shaping bureau behavior. DEA's case confirms the hypothesis that the preferences of an organization are determined by the ways which the organization discovers it can best carry out its mandate. For example, if DEA was created as an LEA, from very early on, it became clear to DEA's managers that because people break the law, people should be the focus of their enforcement efforts. Because DEA is focused on people as law breakers, it generally places little emphasis on other ways of combating drugs, including interdiction, education and prevention, and eradication. The U.S. Coast Guard's case confirms our hypothesis that in times of decreasing resources, agencies will seek to reduce first those tasks that are secondary to what the agency considers central. Because the Coast Guard never really considered drug law enforcement as primary to its work, it was one of the first elements to feel the budgetary cuts. Finally, the case of U.S. Customs confirms the hypothesis that sometimes agencies that have two or more subcultures will succeed in having these exist in harmony within the organization when they are kept separate, even physically separate, but it helps when there are enough resources to satisfy the needs of both subcultures, without one having to take from one for the other.

Notes

1. Numbers taken from *United States Budget* (Washington, DC: GPO, 1991, 1992, 1993, 1994).

2. In 1989 the National Defense Authorization Act made the military the "lead agency" for detection and monitoring, two of the three fundamental components of interdiction—the third being the actual physical interception of the drug trafficking vehicles. Prior to the 1989 Act, Customs and the Coast Guard shared the responsibility for detection, monitoring, and interception.

3. To be sure, on 28 January 1982, President Reagan had created a South Florida Task Force (SFTF), under the direction of Vice President George Bush, to coordinate the activities of all the agencies involved in interdiction efforts. Personnel from U.S. Customs, the U.S. Coast Guard, and some military, staffed the center, with some limited participation from the DEA and the FBI. SFTF was headed by Charles F. Rinkevich and was designed to smooth out inter-bureaucratic conflict between agencies. The soothing effects of the SFTF between U.S. Customs and the Coast Guard, however, did not last long. Soon the agencies were competing against each other again. See Charles M. Fuss, Jr., *Sea of Grass: The Maritime Drug War 1970-1990* (Annapolis, MD: Naval Institute Press, 1996); 92-93.

4. The Posse Comitatus Act (18 USC 1385) prohibits military personnel from executing local, state, or federal laws except as the Constitution or act of Congress authorizes. This precluded the military from making any property seizures or arrests during a drug interdiction operation.

5. *Information Memorandum for the Secretary of the Treasury*, written by Salvatore R. Martoche, Assistant Secretary for Enforcement of the U.S. Treasury Department to Secretary Brady (no date). The Memorandum from Martoche to Secretary Brady was written at the request of the Assistant Commissioner of U.S. Customs, Office of Enforcement, in a memo dated April 17, 1989.

6. Like other U.S. bureaucracies, U.S. Customs often appeals to history to highlight the importance of its mission. In a *U.S. Customs Update* issue published in 1992, the Service states that "The organization and mission of the 20th Century U.S. Customs Service can be traced back to the 1st Congress of 1789." *U.S. Customs Update 1992* (Washington, DC: Department of the Treasury, U.S. Customs Service); 2.

7. Interview with Carol Hallett, October 26, 1999. These points are important because it means that Customs intended to push further into the natural medium of the U.S. Coast Guard, maritime interdiction. This clearly represented "offensive" behavior.

8. For Customs, as for many other U.S. agencies, to be considered an *international* agency holds high value. The term "abroad" is used here on purpose because it implied a fundamental conflict with the State Department over jurisdiction. State never looked favorably on any agency operating abroad that did not like to subject itself to its jurisdictional power.

9. The original mission of U.S. Customs did not suggest the necessity of moving well beyond the U.S. borders to enforce the U.S. statutes under its charge. Over time, however, the U.S. Customs Service has reviewed its mission to allow itself at a minimum the implicit license to go well beyond U.S. borders. In 2001, Custom's mission was stated as follows:

"U.S. Customs assesses and collects customs duties, excise taxes, fees and penalties due on imported goods; prevents fraud and smuggling; controls carriers, persons and cargo entering and departing the United States and intercepts illegal high technology exports to proscribed destinations; cooperates with other federal agencies in suppressing the traffic in illicit narcotics and pornography; enforces reporting requirements of the Bank Secrecy Act; protects the American public by enforcing auto safety and emission control standards, flammable fabric restrictions, animal and plant quarantine requirements; and protects U.S. business and labor by enforcing regulations dealing with copyright, trademark, and quotas." This is obviously a broad mission open to many interpretations.

10. U.S. Customs had played a role in maritime interdiction since the mid-1970s at least. "By the mid-1970s U.S. Customs was cranking up its marine program to target drug smugglers." Fuss, *Sea of Grass*; 34. By 1989-1990, U.S. Customs was engaged in a turf battle with the U.S. Coast Guard to advance its jurisdictional control over the 12-mile U.S. territorial waters.

11. A similar theory is developed by John W. Kingdon in *Agendas, Alternatives, and Public Policies* (Glenview, IL: Scott, Foresman, and Company, 1984); pp. 210-215.

12. The HRT was composed of Customs' Director of Investigations (Domestic Operations), Director of Foreign Operations, and Director of Investigative Services and DEA's John Coleman, Stephen Green, and Doug Wineholt.

13. Personal interview with Mr. Doug Wineholt.

14. In an interview with Mr. Scowcroft, he did not have any recollections of having approved this plan. Interview with Brent Scowcroft, October 26, 1999.

15. Interview with Robert C. Bonner, October 5, 1999, and interview with Melvyn Levitsky, September 2, 1999. There is, of course, some disagreement with Bonner's view over the motivations of DOS personnel. DOS interviewees claimed, for example, that NAS narcotics affair units in embassies did make their helicopters available to DEA quite frequently for their own needs. DEA, however, had fallen well short of their stated plan and, consequently, they were likely to view the status quo ante as a defeat.

16. In an interview Mr. Bonner spoke about his plan. He insisted that he did not intend to step on other agencies' toes. Instead, he argued that DEA picked up intelligence that the Colombians were now using Guatemala as a transit base on their way to Mexico and then finally to the United States. He believed that if the military, "which wanted to be helpful and wanted to get involved," provided DEA with some Black Hawk helicopters stationed about one and half hours away in Honduras, and the State Department provided some of its B-212 aircraft, that they used in Guatemala, then DEA would be able to be more effective by anticipating the smugglers' moves and striking at the drug dealers in transit. Mr. Bonner did not believe that this type of action had anything to do with interdiction. In most experts' views, however, this is precisely what interdiction is. Interview with Robert Bonner, October 5, 1999.

17. The latest attempt to fold the DEA into the FBI came with a recommendation in 1993 by Vice President Al Gore's "National Public Review" that the DEA be folded into the FBI. This attempt was stomped by Attorney General Janet Reno, who did not believe this was a good idea, although she did give the FBI all powers to resolve operational disputes among all Justice Department agencies, including the DEA. Bonner stated that "designating the FBI director to adjudicate disputes between FBI and DEA is like 'trying to resolve disputes between IBM and Apple' by giving the job to the chairman of IBM." *The Washington*

Post, 31 October, 1993.

18. These points are made by James Q. Wilson in *The Investigators: Managing FBI and Narcotics Agents* (New York: Basic Books, Inc., Publishers, 1978), pp. 26 and 43-48.

19. This story was corroborated with an interview with John Walters, August 27, 1999.

20. Lawn was particularly worried that while many agencies share the responsibility for fighting the drug war, it was ultimately DEA who was "hauled up to the Hill" to be accountable for its overall success or failure. In other words, DEA was vulnerable to receive all the blame while at the same time it was not completely in charge of the mission. Interview with John C. Lawn, September 28, 1999.

21. This point has been argued before by Jonathan Macey. Macey contends that regulatory agencies with broad jurisdictions are less susceptible to capture than agencies with narrower jurisdictional mandates. See Jonathan Macey, "Organizational Design and Political Control of Administrative Agencies," in *The Journal of Law, Economics, and Organization*, Vol. 8, No. 1 (1992); pp. 93-110.

22. Wilson defines a craft agency as one where the procedural performance of the operators is hard to observe, but the results are not. He suggests that law enforcement agencies are craft agencies. But in the war on drugs, the "results" or "outcome" is hardly a good measure of success, given the nature of the drug business. See Wilson, *Bureaucracy*; pp. 165-168 and 201.

23. To illustrate the difficulties in knowing the "real" impact on drugs, consider the following example. The CIA and the DEA came up with wildly disparate calculations on the international narcotics trade in 1992. The CIA's estimate, some 770 tons of cocaine a year, was roughly twice the DEA's estimate. See *The Houston Chronicle*, June 28, 1992; A2. LEAs routinely come up with different estimates on the overall extent of the problem and their own impact on it.

24. To some extent, LEAs have always played the "numbers game." In the anti-narcotics policy space, however, the numbers game has become central to the overall interaction among LEAs and between LEAs and politicians. For a discussion of the "numbers game," see Wilson, *The Investigators*; Chapter 3, pp. 61-88 et al.

25. See *The Houston Chronicle*, June 28, 1992; A2.

26. See Rachal, Federal Narcotics Enforcement; p. 25.

27. To be sure, U.S. Customs had its critics and detractors on Capitol Hill as well. Rep. J. J. Pickle was a constant critic of U.S. Customs. But Rep. Pickle's criticisms of Customs were not sufficient to overwhelm the clout of Custom's allies on Capitol Hill.

28. Other scholars have explored the important role that personalities play in the life of an agency. See, for example, Herbert Kaufman, *The Administrative Behavior of Bureau Chiefs* (Washington, DC: Brookings Institution, 1981); David T. Stanley, Dean E. Mann, and Jameson W. Doig, *Men Who Govern: A Biographical Profile of Federal Political Executives* (Washington, DC: Brookings Institution, 1967); Jameson W. Doig, *The Assistant Secretaries: Problems and Processes of Appointments* (Washington, DC: Brookings Institution, 1965); and Eugene Lewis, *Public Entrepreneurship: Toward a Theory of Bureaucratic Political Power: The Organizational Lives of Hyman Rickover, J. Edgar Hoover, and Robert Moses* (Bloomington, IN: Indiana University Press, 1980).

29. For a history of the evolution of the U.S. government's conception of the production, trade, and use of psychotropic substances over the twentieth century, see John C. Wil-

liams, "Through the Past Darkly: The Politics and Policies of America's Drug War," in William O. Walker III, *Drug Control Policy: Essays in Historical and Comparative Perspective* (University Park, PA: Pennsylvania University Press, 1991), pp. 5-41.

30. In an interview, which took place in El Paso, Texas, I was invited to tour the facilities of El Paso Intelligence Center (EPIC), a major DEA intelligence coordinating center. The guide proudly showed me the sixty-some seals of the various federal bureaucracies involved in the drug war.

31. *National Drug Control Strategy Report*, The White House, Office of National Drug Control Policy, February 1994, pp. 186-187. The numbers have been rounded off to the higher value.

32. Only federal LEAs' efforts are examined in this study. State and local efforts are not examined and their budgets are not included.

33. That this is the case is not difficult to understand. DEA claims authority over any illegal drug related matters by virtue of its mission. The State Department claims jurisdiction over anything that concerns counter-drug efforts abroad. U.S. Customs and the U.S. Coast Guard by virtue of their mandate ensure that anything that crosses the U.S. border does so in compliance with U.S. laws. The FBI claims jurisdiction on account of its statutes regarding organized crime—and almost all illegal drug activity is highly organized.

34. Although the DEA grew steadily throughout the 1980s, it was between 1988 and 1993 that its growth shot up considerably, going from 5886 total employees in 1988 to 5923 in 1989, 6211 in 1990, 7013 in 1991, 7486 in 1992, and a decrease in 1993 to 7241 employees. The 1993 reduction reflects a general effort in the federal government to balance the budget by cutting back programs across the federal budget. Nevertheless, DEA's numbers remained high, reflecting the general high priority that Congress places in anti-narcotics policy—even if the architecture of the war on drugs that Congress has created may not be optimal to eliminate the "problem." For the figures, see http://trac.syr.edu/tracdea.

35. Some such areas are interdiction, eradication, and treatment efforts. It is indeed puzzling that these important components of the drug trade had not attracted the attention of the DEA to any considerable extent.

36. See Wilson, *Bureaucracy*; pp. 95-101. See also Philip Selznick, *Leadership in Administration* (Evanston, ILL: Row, Peterson, & Co., 1957), pp. 17, 42-56; and Morton H. Halperin *Bureaucratic Politics and Foreign Policy* (Washington, DC: Brookings Institution, 1974).

37. As David Westrate put it, DEA never took over the business of eradication because "that was a philosophical thing…because it's not law enforcement…It [consists in] managing a big aircraft fleet using pilots, either contract pilots or country pilots who are not enforcement guys. I think DEA is better off supporting it with intelligence and being a liaison as opposed to doing [eradication]. Interview with David Westrate, February 29, 2000. Eradication consists mostly of locating crops and destroying them.

38. http://www.usdoj.gov/dea/major/dinero.htm

39. Wilson, *The Investigators*, p. 57. For this reason, Wilson makes the argument that DEA agents are not truly investigators but rather that they are "instigators," agents who must go out and seek out criminals by engaging a person in a criminal act which they are ready and more than willing to commit. Then, an arrest is made or an informant is acquired.

40. The much more cautious, "do-not-rock-the-boat" approach of State Department diplomats and FSOs will be discussed at length in Chapter 5. In that chapter, attention will

be given to the clash between the two widely differing styles of the two cultures.

41. It is noteworthy that the "paramilitary" subculture of the DEA that developed in South America never went very far within the institution itself. In spite of the problems that this "extreme war-like look" of DEA agents caused between DEA and the State Department, DEA agents remained largely an investigative body. The small percentage of agents that took on a "war" outlook stayed in the minority and have seldom made it to the top levels of DEA. Joe Toft's tactics, in fact, showed that a penchant for paramilitary operations is, overall, not that welcome within DEA. Toft quit partly because the DEA itself was not willing to wage a war that looked like a real war. This is a noteworthy point given our own theory on subcultures within an organization.

42. In a classic example of a cultural split in an organization, Carl H. Builder elaborates on how the military has developed various subcultures and even within these subcultures, e.g, the Navy, there can develop several others. See Carl H. Builder, *The Masks of War: American Military Styles in Strategy and Analysis* (Baltimore: The Johns Hopkins University Press, 1989).

43. Established by Congress during the late 1960s in response to the growing number of airborne smugglers bringing drugs into the United States, the Customs Aviation Interdiction Program became operational in 1971. Its mission: to stem the flow of illicit drugs coming into the U.S. through the air and to assist other federal, state and local law enforcement agencies.

See http://www.customs.ustreas.gov/enforcem/air.htm.

44. On the other hand, some interviewees argued that extending the arm of the law beyond the U.S. borders, that is, to prevent illegal goods from reaching the U.S. before they come to the border, is a perfectly logical corollary of U.S. Customs' mission. In this study, I argue that nothing in the original mission of Customs allow us this freer interpretation of the geographical location where Customs is supposed to be performing the tasks around its mission.

45. See http://www.customs.ustreas.gov/enforcem/air.htm.

46. In its mission statement, the United States Coast Guard states that it is the nation's leading maritime law enforcement agency and has broad, multi-faceted jurisdictional authority. The Operational Law Enforcement Mission is directed primarily in the areas of boating safety, drug interdiction, living marine resources, alien migrant interdiction and responding to vessel incidents involving violent acts or other criminal activity. In addition, it enforces fisheries laws, commercial vessel regulation, and environment regulation, and conducts search and rescue operations. Like Customs, the number of statutes the Coast Guard enforces are multiple. Drug interdiction is but one component. See http://www.uscg.mil.

47. Taken from Coast Guard Interdiction Mission: Hearing before the Subcommittee on Coast Guard and Maritime Transportation of the Committee on Transportation and Infrastructure of the House of Representatives, 1 August, 1995, 104th Congress, First Session (Washington, DC: GPO, 1995); p. 25.

Chapter 3
Soldiers

This chapter explores the U.S. military's behavior in the drug war. Can bureaucratic politics help explain how the military handled its incorporation into the war on drugs? Can organizational culture help explain how the U.S. military behaved in it? The first section explores the *politically* determined behavior of the military in the war on drugs. The second section explores the *culturally* determined behavior of the military in the war on drugs.

Bureaucratic Politics: The Military

The bureaucrats involved in the U.S. drug war can generally be considered competent and dedicated people, who consider themselves rational decision makers, trying to accomplish the objectives of U.S. policy. Individual competence, dedication, rationality and good intentions, however, do not guarantee that the organization's overall behavior will exhibit the same competence, dedication, and rationality that any one bureaucrat or political master would like. Nor do they guarantee that the national policy goals will be accomplished. But according to bureaucratic politics, what is guaranteed is that a bureaucrat lodged in a particular policy space will watch after the interests of the organization to which he or she belongs. Bureaucrats will try to preserve the health of their organization, measured in terms of resources and autonomy. A healthy organizational level of resources and autonomy is pivotal for the psyche, if not the career benefits that come with belonging to a well-regarded organization. A bureaucrat maneuvering to protect and enhance the interests of his or her agency is the very essence of bureaucratic politics. There is no offhand reason to suspect that the military is exempt from working to enhance and defend the interests of the organization. They too develop such interests and navigate between the policy they are charged with and the interests of their agency. The following pages analyze the extent to which the behavior of the military in the war on drugs, as an organization, was influenced by fundamental political concerns with the health of the agency.

New Missions: To Accomplish or Not To Accomplish

Bureaucratic politics would posit that organizations faced with new missions that imply additional resources would take advantage of the opportunity to enhance their treasure and their jurisdictional power. Faced with such opportunity, agencies will seek to grow or to recover losses by growing where they can. To find out whether this holds or not, we have to consider the Pentagon and its most important military commands participating actively in the drug war. If bureaucratic politics is correct, the Pentagon and its forward deployed forces should readily have embraced the new anti-narcotics mission. Intuitively, it sounds reasonable to assume that the military should have taken on the new mission because of one additional factor: starting in 1990, the military underwent major budgetary cuts. Thus the military not only should have used the opportunity to grow from the drug war but also should have used the opportunity to contain the ongoing budgetary erosion by adopting the drug war as its own. Some authors have argued that this was the case: that in 1989, the Pentagon, which had adamantly opposed taking a role in anti-narcotics policy throughout the 1980s, changed its position regarding the war on drugs,

> . . . not just because of pressure from the President and Congress, but also for economic reasons. With the Soviet Union collapsing and becoming less of a threat to U.S. security, U.S. Secretary of Defense Cheney announced in November 1989 that the administration would be cutting the Department of Defense budget by $180 billion over five years. The announcement sent shock waves through the military, which could not but conclude that Congress would continue to reduce military expenditures, manpower, and operational commitments worldwide . . . The war on drugs was about to replace the Evil Empire as the bogeyman of U.S. foreign policy.[1]

The conclusion of this and other authors[2] is that Pentagon officials saw in the drug war the opportunity to make up for the budgetary losses announced in 1989.[3] The case looked perfect. The military was supposed to use the drug war to contain budget cuts. Moreover, the same argument that was made of the Pentagon was made of the forward deployed forces. A Pentagon interviewee, for example, argued that,

> . . . the CINCs probably had less of a mission [with the Soviet Union gone]. I guess you might say that the Latin American region did not have a big threat. The war on drugs gives them a real mission. Most of the assets that were assigned to SOUTHCOM were for counter-drugs. Most of their assets, riverine assets, air assets were for counter-drugs. SOUTHCOM had small headquarters. [In the Cold War] they had an engagement mission. They had to work with the countries. They had to develop relationships. But after Central America they were not going to fight a war; not that I know of.[4]

The implication here is that by 1989 SOUTHCOM was a resource-starved command with a receding mission and few reasons to justify resource acquisitions or even its existence. Thus, the war on drugs provided the Pentagon and its forward deployed forces with an opportunity to stop, at least in part, the resource hemorrhage by arguing for resource increases in the name of the drug war. This made sense if we consider that while the defense budget was shrinking, the drug war budget kept growing every year between 1989 and 1993.[5]

The evidence reviewed for this study does not suggest that Pentagon officials or the forward deployed forces and their Commanders-in-Chief (CINCs) either changed their unfavorable attitude toward the drug war or used drug war rhetoric to argue for budget and asset increases. Just as they had done throughout the 1980s, many Pentagon officials continued to argue against military involvement in the war on drugs. Even after the considerable defense cuts announced by Congress in November 1989, some Pentagon officials continued to argue against the "slippery slope" of involving the military in "law enforcement activities."[6] The overall drug budget at the Pentagon, even at its peak in 1992, never amounted to more than 0.4 percent of the overall defense budget. The money assigned by Congress for the Pentagon's drug war was not money the organization had requested at all, but money that Congress forced on it for that purpose. The ultimate incorporation of the Pentagon into the drug war appears to be more the product of haranguing and pressure by Congress members and the Executive than a military turnabout on account of the opportunity to stem the resource-letting announced in 1989. Bureaucratic politics fails to predict the behavior of the military vis-à-vis the drug war. The military simply did not want the mission, even if it implied an increase in resources.

This same conclusion can be drawn from examining the behavior of the Southern Command—SOUTHCOM—a key command for the drug war because it covered most of Latin America, except Mexico. Secretary of Defense Richard Cheney grudgingly issued a 19 September 1989 directive to all military CINCs to draw up plans to implement the Pentagon's drug war mission. After receiving this directive, Gen. Maxwell Thurman, SOUTHCOM's CINC, began to comply with the drug war mission, in spite of the fact that Thurman had exhibited the same profound dislike for the drug war that his predecessor, Gen. Frederick F. Woerner, Jr., had. Both Cheney and Thurman's actions appeared to be a turnaround of the military, which appeared to finally embrace the mission. But, does Thurman's apparent turnabout mean that SOUTHCOM was more willing than the Pentagon itself to use the new drug war mission to acquire the assets that it had been losing as the Cold War came to a close and most Latin America guerrillas began to ebb? There is no evidence that either Thurman or his successor, Gen. George Joulwan, SOUTHCOM's CINC starting in November 1990, ever argued for budget increases on Capitol Hill or with their superiors at the Pentagon in the name of the drug war.[7] Neither Thurman nor Joulwan used drug war rhetoric to maintain or acquire assets for SOUTHCOM or to gain or maintain a foothold in the anti-narcotics policy space. In fact, in spite of the fact that Joulwan (1999 interview) "got everything [assets] ripped off for Desert Storm" in late 1990 and 1991 "by someone that had a higher priority (the Persian Gulf War)," he hardly made any efforts to lobby Pentagon officials to retain any of his Command's already dwindling assets on account of the drug war. Nothing suggests that SOUTHCOM, as an organization, acted according to imperialistic motives to either defend its existing resources or to increase them or to secure a place in the war on drugs. It did not do so even though its resources were dwindling and its mission was in recession. On the contrary, throughout the 1980s both the Pentagon and SOUTHCOM argued against any military involvement in the drug war. Nevertheless, when Congress finally forced their hand in 1988 and 1989, they both implemented the mission, regardless of the rhetoric. That they did so begs the question: what accounts for Thurman and later Joulwan's turnaround to implementing the drug war?

The course of action that Thurman and Joulwan chose to implement the drug war in SOUTHCOM reflects two factors. First, the generals' dedication came from their personal vibrancy and verve more than an organizational desire to retain or acquire material resources or a slice of jurisdiction in the anti-narcotics policy space. There is wide agreement among the bureaucrats interviewed for this study that both of these men were highly motivated and intense personalities. In fact, Thurman had argued ardently against involving the military in the drug war.[8] Nevertheless, once "commanded" to engage the drug war, he did with a high energy level, as did Joulwan. But it is quite possible that the generals would have gladly withdrawn from the war on drugs if they had been told to do so. Their successor, Gen. Barry McCaffrey in fact took the step of downgrading the drug war within SOUTHCOM's priorities. Thus, Thurman and Joulwan's devotion to their job—e.g., implementing the drug war—can also be accounted for by their high level of energy and commitment to their badges. Second, their implementation of the drug war stemmed from the military's deeply ingrained culture of obedience rather than a commitment to increase SOUTHCOM's material assets and clout by appealing to the drug war. Once they were commanded to do it, they set out to do it as best they knew. They were accustomed to obey and this they did, even if they disagreed with Congress' desire that the military should play a role in that.

Both of these reasons also apply to the lower level military stationed in South America. Once their commanders ordered them to engage the drug war, they did so.

But the war on drugs was always eyed with suspicion by all—a suspicion attributable to the Posse Comitatus culture of the military. If they had had their druthers, they would have never engaged the drug war; and if they had been given an opportunity to say no, they would have abandoned it.

The Inverse Relationship between Numbers and Possibilities

Until the summer of 1990, Gen. Maxwell Thurman, SOUTHCOM's CINC, was charged by the Pentagon with implementing the military's drug war in South America. Although Thurman was not CINC for long because of personal illness,[9] he and his subalterns first focused on bringing SOUTHCOM's assets to bear in the war on drugs in South America not on the area of *interdiction* (detection and monitoring) but on building SOUTHCOM's anti-narcotics *intelligence* capabilities. SOUTHCOM would be, under Thurman's design, the coordinator of all intelligence operations in the drug war because that area was, according to the General, where SOUTHCOM could do better. The law, after all, made the Defense Department not only the lead agency for detection and monitoring (interdiction) but also for command, communications, control, and intelligence (C^3I) in the international drug war. As Thurman's director of operations, Gen. Bill Hartzog, explained, in 1989-1990 the primary focus was to sort out how to use SOUTHCOM's intelligence capabilities in the drug war, not so much how to interdict drug carrying craft and vessels.[10]

Unfortunately, Thurman and his officers had chosen to begin their participation in the drug war in a very crowded corner of the anti-narcotics policy space: intelligence. By the time SOUTHCOM came into the drug war, there were twenty intelligence centers dedicated to collecting, analyzing, and distributing drug trafficking intelligence.[11] Thurman, expectedly, faced stiff opposition from law enforcement agencies (LEAs). LEA personnel refused to centralize their intelligence efforts under SOUTHCOM's control, regardless of the arguments made by SOUTHCOM concerning the fact that DOD was by the 1989 law the lead agency for C^3I. Gen. Thurman's move was perceived as "offensive" to the agencies already working on anti-narcotics intelligence in Latin America. Their natural reaction was therefore to resist his efforts. Thurman even had a special building constructed to house all anti-narcotics intelligence coordination activities under SOUTHCOM. The building that Thurman had built to house a counter-drug intelligence center at Howard Air Force Base, Panama, however, was never put to use for intelligence purposes. LEA agents gave numerous arguments not to comply and none ever moved their operations into that building. Some argued that their intelligence did not serve the military's anti-drug purposes; others argued that military intelligence was not useful for enforcement purposes, perhaps with the exception of real-time detection and monitoring intelligence.[12] All in all, these and many other arguments held sway and LEAs ultimately stifled any attempts by SOUTHCOM to centralize and coordinate all drug-related intelligence activities. Unfortunately, this result was in contravention with the intentions of the law that brought the military into the drug war. Thurman's difficulties in making any inroads in the anti-narcotics intelligence area were directly related to the number of agencies already working in it and willing to protect their turf on intelligence issues. He should have realized that the stakes on the area of intelligence were not only many but high. He should have been able to predict that resistance to his efforts to centralize intelligence was going to be nearly insurmountable.

Gen. George Joulwan, Thurman's successor, arrived in South America from his previous position in Europe in late 1990. Because he was uncertain on "how to engage the lower end" (drugs) with military capabilities, Joulwan took a sixty day retreat to "analyze the threat." In this retreat Joulwan (1999 interview) produced his "strategy" to deal with the issue of drugs in South America. SOUTHCOM, he believed, could make a major contribution in the area of interdiction—precisely where his predecessor believed he could not make an important contribution. For that purpose, Joulwan designed a slogan, "One Team; One Fight." He compared the low-flying, cocaine-carrying planes to scud missiles hitting the United States with a load of 600 kilos of a chemical agent called cocaine. He visited LEA headquarters in Washington and abroad. He met with the heads of LEAs and with U.S. Ambassadors in South America to discuss the issue. He referred to the issue as a "national security threat" and put SOUTHCOM's assets, including AWACS planes and radars, to work in the detection and monitoring of drug-carrying aircraft and vessels. He developed an "air bridge" (interdiction program) to curtail the air transportation of illegal drugs. He visited foreign officials, including some Latin American presidents, and carried with him charts that he continually laid down on other people's desks to show the strategy he had designed. In effect, Joulwan militarized the drug war. He turned it into a "real war." Joulwan's enthusiasm, energy and dedication to his work were ranked very high among drug war bureaucrats.[13] In the end, Joulwan is remembered as a very successful drug warrior. He largely succeeded in involving SOUTHCOM in interdiction efforts and in getting the cooperation of LEAs for his efforts in intercepting illegal drugs en route to the United States.

From an inter-agency perspective, it is useful to compare Thurman's failure to centralize intelligence efforts in SOUTHCOM with Joulwan's successes in interdiction. Why did Thurman fail to get other agencies to cooperate with SOUTHCOM in his C^3I centralization efforts and why did Joulwan succeed in getting inter-agency support in his interdiction efforts? Joulwan was successful in part because he moved away from the crowded and competitive counter-narcotics intelligence field and chose to focus on interdiction, a less crowded area where the stakes on turf were less. His shift to a less crowded and competitive policy area is at least partly responsible for Joulwan's success among drug war bureaucrats. In that area—interdiction—SOUTHCOM's capabilities were not only complementary of LEAs' efforts, without taking anything away in assets or jurisdiction efforts, but they also enhanced LEAs' ability to claim credit in the war on drugs. SOUTHCOM's detection and monitoring capabilities added a valuable element to the work of the U.S. Customs Service and the U.S. Coast Guard. Both Customs agents and Coast Guard operatives were delighted to have SOUTHCOM use its own resources for interdiction operations, where Customs and the Coast Guard were heavily involved and generally took all the credit. And DEA had no real quarrel with SOUTHCOM's role in interdiction efforts because its agents did not believe that interdiction made any serious difference in the war on drugs anyway (Green, 2000 interview). DEA appeared to dislike interdiction as a tactic to fight illegal drugs. Also, the eagerness of LEAs to take credit for drug war operational and tactical successes did not conflict with Joulwan's plans because SOUTHCOM did not exhibit the same preoccupation with statistics.[14] SOUTHCOM was not a direct competitor to LEAs, hence no conflict was expected. LEAs were happy to free ride on SOUTHCOM's assets and take all the credit for successes.

The relationship between numbers and possibilities in bureaucratic politics is further demonstrated by the fact that, although Joulwan was quite adept at building consensus among the various LEAs operating in the SOUTHCOM theater area on the matter of interdiction and he got their full cooperation on most matters, he was not successful at centralizing all information on aircraft deployed by all agencies in his theater area. He wanted to have a single roster showing at any one point where each aircraft was in order to be "more effective" in controlling interdiction efforts, coordinating anti-drug actions, and efficientizing the use of resources. His efforts were to no avail. Each agency preferred to control its own aircraft and have its own registration, clearance, and reporting requirements separate from both SOUTHCOM and other agencies' requirements. In this specific case, Joulwan's personal skills and highly admired leadership qualities did not serve him as well. Agencies were not about to let SOUTHCOM overrun their autonomy over the use of their assets. That this is the case is a testimony to the reluctance of agencies to allow any encroachment on their autonomous control of both their assets and their activities.

Organizational Priorities: To Protect and To Defend

Inter-agency environments are almost always intense. Moreover, the level of inter-agency tension is a factor of the number of agencies that participate in a policy space. Abroad, Embassies have become skeins of bureaucrats from a sundry of agencies, almost all of whom consider the defense and advancement of their agency's interests crucial. This section examines the interaction between the Military Groups (MilGroups), a component of the military, and the State Department's own personnel at U.S. Embassies.

The MilGroups at U.S. Embassies were originally created to help the U.S. government exert influence over other governments' militaries by establishing regularized contacts, including military training and exchanges. MilGroups were generally made up of statisticians and a few operators and advisors. MilGroups personnel, though military, were paid by the State Department through the foreign assistance budget and foreign assistant sales. When the military was legislated into the drug war in late 1988 and 1989, MilGroups in South America were instructed to take on the war on drugs. In addition to their regular activities, the MilGroups now had to coordinate military support operations for anti-narcotics programs. Their workload increased considerably on tasks related to drug trafficking. The MilGroups, like every bureaucrat abroad, regardless of the agency they worked for at home, were primarily accountable to the Ambassador. State's Foreign Service officers (FSOs) and diplomats often reminded military personnel at U.S. Embassies of this "fact." But the MilGroups also had a chain of command that led up to the CINC. In effect, they worked for two masters: DOS and DOD.

By late 1989, the Andean Embassies' MilGroups's interaction with SOUTHCOM's personnel on drug war issues had increased enormously because of the expansion of the Command's anti-drug activities in South America. Over time, the MilGroups began to neglect reporting programs and operational details to Embassy personnel. They preferred to follow their "natural" command and report directly to the CINC. Although they continued to report to the Ambassador and Embassy personnel, MilGroups constituents felt that since the CINC was now engaged in the war on drugs, their primary responsibility should be to report all details to him, while giving Embassy personnel only broad programmatic and operational information. Embassy personnel disagreed.

State's FSOs and diplomats began to feel that the MilGroups' personnel were acquiring an unjustified level of autonomy from Embassy control. Dealing directly with the CINC without reporting the details of their programs and operational activities to the Embassy, first for approval and after implementation for review, was unacceptable to FSOs. DOS personnel wanted the MilGroups to cease operating with the high level of autonomy into which they had drifted and to submit all their programs and operational details to the Embassies before and after implementation. MilGroups members protested these requests as a petty bureaucratic quibble and argued that micromanagement would mean more (paper) work for the MilGroup and delays in military support operations. Some MilGroups personnel complained to the Pentagon that, while they understood they were working for the Ambassador, they were also working for the CINC and excessive control by DOS personnel was unwarranted if not outright obtrusive. Their complaints were to no avail. DOS personnel prevailed not only because DOS considers "everything that happens in [that] country its exclusive jurisdiction," and constantly reminds everyone so (Snyder, 1999 interview), but also because DOS enjoys nearly absolute statutory jurisdiction over all official U.S. activities abroad—an authority that they defend intensely. A version of the same problem occurred in Bolivia, Colombia, and Peru.[15]

Bureaucratic politics would easily have predicted this conflict. The MilGroups performed a coordinating role that overlapped with the job of the Narcotics Affairs Sections (NAS) of U.S. Embassies. NAS statutorily supervises and coordinates all anti-narcotics activities for the U.S. Embassy, including the activities of military and LEA personnel within the host country's territory. When NAS and the MilGroups were at loggerheads, NAS diplomats generally prevailed for two reasons. First, they held the jurisdictional upper hand by serving as the Ambassador's own arm in supervising all manner of counter-drug activities in the host country, not just military support. Second, they had influence over the purse strings at the Embassy because DOS controlled all anti-drug spending abroad. As the comment of a military interviewee shows, NAS had these two important advantages,

> The NAS people are sort of orchestrating. I mean, they hold [the resources]. They say, 'wait a minute, I will give him this much and withhold the rest of it. I am going to control the equipment and the parts and everything. I will give it to them little by little. If I give it to them all at once, they are going to steal it, squander it, lose it, or whatever. I have been through this before.' It is like a reward system. The name of the tactic was a 'tit-for-tat'.[16]

MilGroups at the Embassy disliked NAS's tactics; but these tactics served DOS personnel well in preserving their jurisdictional authority intact at U.S. Embassies and keeping a tight control over all U.S. operatives in any given country. The MilGroups saw these tactics as petty and wasteful but did not have the leverage to overcome DOS's preeminence in the drug war. At the same time, the proclivity of DOS personnel to want to keep a close eye on any U.S. official activities abroad is understandable. The foreign drug war, they claim, is their turf—a legislated responsibility for which they are answerable.[17] In other words, DOS was merely protecting its turf and preventing the MilGroups from setting a dangerous precedent in regard to DOS control of its turf.

What the case of the MilGroups shows is that the members of an agency seek a relative level of operational autonomy. Correspondingly, however, the "affected" agency (DOS), whom military and LEA bureaucrats have to report to is simply defending and preserving their jurisdictional authority over U.S. activities abroad. DOS personnel prevailed because they had the upper hand statutorily and because they controlled the purse strings for all spending abroad. Moreover, they were quite willing to use their influence to maintain control over any activities in what they considered their territory. The behavior of the MilGroups could not be interpreted as anything but "aggressive" by State and State's behavior could be nothing but defensive. This was clearly a functional conflict between the two and State had the ability to prevail and the willingness to use this ability to rein in the MilGroups. And that they did.

The Logic of Organizational Growth: The Case of DOMS

Bureaucratic politics in general appears to fail in explaining the behavior of the military (Pentagon and Commands) in the drug war, but it seems to explain well the behavior of the Directorate of Military Support (DOMS), the Department of Defense's agency in charge of coordinating all military support to civilian authorities during emergencies and natural disasters.[18] DOMS's behavior more closely adheres to the idea that agencies will seek to acquire new missions if these provide greater budgets and jurisdictional prerogatives, particularly during times when the mission of an agency is receding. So, what explains the *political* behavior of this agency *within* the military? Why did DOMS not prevail in its attempts to acquire the anti-drug mission at the Pentagon?

During the early to mid-1980s, the requests for and coordination of military resources for domestic drug law enforcement was handled by DOMS, a relatively small office under the then Assistant Secretary of the Army for Installations, Logistics, and Environment (ASA-IL&E).[19] DOMS was assigned to coordinate counter-drug support for civilian agencies because "it was not that big of a project" (Keravouri, 2000 interview). The requests from counter-drug LEAs for military support for their operations, mostly asset loans and personnel training, were handled by contractual arrangements between LEAs and DOMS. These contractual arrangements were called *Interagency Support Agreements* (ISAs). ISAs enabled DOD to fulfill legal requirements imposed on the Pentagon under the 1981 Amendment to the Posse Comitatus Act of 1868[20] and the 1986 Omnibus Drug Control Act.[21] DOMS received the requests for equipment and personnel support by LEAs; found the equipment and personnel from DOD stocks and services; and coordinated their temporary transfer in support of LEA operations or training. LEAs would then reimburse DOD generally only for operational costs. Every request, however, had to go through an exhaustive approval process in which the effect on the military units whose resources or personnel would be temporarily expropriated was considered very carefully. Request often brought about some turmoil in the affected units because "there are moving and training requirements" and "if you keep taking out critical communications equipment, and vehicles, and helicopters, whatever it is, it all adds up. [Unit] commanders are very resistant." This was a veritable "balancing act" (Keravouri, 2000 interview). Striking is the fact that during this period LEA agents "floated" military support requests to DOMS informally and DOMS personnel would report back to LEA agents the feasibility or infeasibility of the request. If DOMS signaled that the request was "politically" feasible inside the Pentagon, the LEA would then formalize its request. If DOMS signaled that the request was "politically" infeasible, LEAs would not proceed to formalize a request. These informal, back-channel assessments were done by simple phone calls between LEA and DOMS bureaucrats. This point illustrates how LEA bureaucrats learned to avoid conflict and political embarrassment through the creation of informal channels of communication. Such political communication is not uncommon.

When the 1988 Defense Authorization Act legislating the military involvement in the war on drugs passed, DOMS personnel quickly became enthusiastic about the new law. They saw themselves as the natural recipients of the Act's mandate. They believed their mission would simply expand to include coordination of all counter-drug military support abroad—since they had already been doing it domestically. To DOMS personnel, the mission abroad looked like an extension of the support they already provided civilian authorities during natural and other disasters and domestic drug law enforcement. Simply put, "DOMS wanted to do it" (Newberry, 1999 interview). They were ready to build an empire on the drug war. DOMS personnel began to make preparations to grow. They also began a lobbying campaign among top military officials, including the Secretary of Defense and the Joint Chiefs of Staff (JCS). The object of the campaign was to gain top brass favor in acquiring the new mission.

But DOMS enthusiasm for the mission came to be perceived as an "offensive" position at the Pentagon. Much to DOMS personnel's dismay, the Secretary of Defense and the JCS disagreed with their proposal to allow them to coordinate all military counter-drug support for LEAs at home and abroad. The Secretary of Defense, the JCS and other top level military viewed DOMS as "too small for the task." The JCS argued that DOMS should not extend its mission abroad because, by statute, the JCS is the lead actor in all decisions that involved deployment abroad—clearly a *defensive* position by the JCS. DOMS was not going to be allowed to become either a direct competitor or an arm of the JCS without a relatively major reorganization within DOD.[22] During the late 1988 and early 1989 negotiations to find DOD's anti-narcotics mission an operational lodging at the Pentagon, DOMS personnel were just guests at the table, even as they continued to chair the meetings when military support was considered for domestic counter-drug operations. As Keravouri (2000 interview) of DOMS put it, "One minute we were chairing the proceedings (domestic), while the next minute we were the guests (international)." Although DOMS lobbied aggressively to acquire the out-of-country counter-drug mission, they lost the battle. Top level military, principally the JCS, thought that coordinating sustained actions from all branches of the military and their assets did not compare with DOMS's ad hoc coordination of support for natural disasters and domestic counter drug support. "Counter drugs was becoming bigger. It involved multiple theaters, outside the United States" (Newberry 1999 interview). DOMS, apparently, could not be allowed to rival the JCS in coordinating anything abroad. And DOMS simply did not have the clout within the Pentagon to overcome JCS opposition to its ambitions. Structurally it could not, and even within the Pentagon, DOMS was a unit created to respond to low-level priorities not to be an important component of the Defense Department. DOMS was in fact a way of isolating and minimizing an unwanted burden. And, on top of that, they were strictly civilian bureaucrats inside a military culture. Making DOMS the coordinating arm of all military anti-drug operations abroad would have meant giving civilian bureaucrats control of military personnel and assets. This was simply unacceptable inside the military culture of the Pentagon.

The Chairman of the JCS had been asked to chair the meetings to find an organizational location for the new mission at the Pentagon. He and other top brass had opposed the DOMS proposal. But, while the JCS did not want DOMS to do it, it also opposed coordination of military anti-drug support directly from the JCS Office. How ironic: the JCS did not want DOMS to have it; but it did not want it either. Given this, the decision was made instead to create a separate office within the Pentagon: the Office of Drug Enforcement Policy and Support. This, of course, had the effect of creating a jurisdictional overlap with DOMS. Both offices would now coordinate military support for counter-drug operations within the United States, but DOMS would coordinate military support for domestic non-counter drug activities as well and the Office of Drug Enforcement Policy and Support would coordinate military counter-drug support both at home and abroad. Functionally, both agencies would fulfill LEAs requests for military support from the same military stock and personnel.[23] This made them direct competitors since they drew from the same assets and had a confusing overlap in the domestic drug war already, something not easily distinguishable from the international drug war. In addition, this kept the drug war mission fragmented and weak within the Pentagon.

Organizational Culture: The Military

Organizations, like individuals, possess specific traits that help determine how they respond to external stimuli. Some organizations, such as the military, possess strong cultures. Over time, the military has developed specific doctrines, norms, and standard operating procedures (SOPs) underlain by basic attitudes and assumptions that individuals integrate into their behavior as they go about performing their activities. The U.S. military, as an organization, favors its doctrines, norms, and SOPs in what it does. Its members come to believe in their military doctrines, norms and SOPs and shape their practices according to them. History is a major contributor to cultural identification and therefore organization. These practices are passed down through vigorous and effective training and socialization processes that closely resemble indoctrination, intense both psychologically and physically. The military's doctrines, norms, and SOPs are widely accepted and practiced throughout the organization.[24] Its members tend to carry their general attitudes and assumptions within wherever they go. Because the military has a strong culture, the case is ideal to test the effects of organizational culture on behavior. If organizational culture does not work in the case of a "strong culture," then its explanatory power is relatively weak. But if the military exhibits a behavior consistent with organizational culture, then its explanatory power is confirmed, albeit weakly because for the purposes of confirmation a "strong" culture should be an easy case.

What Is First Is First

There is some consensus among government bureaucrats and academics of the U.S. drug war that the military was reluctant to get involved in counter-narcotics efforts.[25] This consensus is well founded. The entrance of the military into the drug war was perhaps the most controversial drug war component to come about in the 1980s. The idea of having the military enforce laws was foreign to U.S. political thinking in general. Opponents argued that,

> . . . drug interdiction is a law enforcement mission, not a military mission; that drug enforcement is an unconventional war which the military is ill-equipped to fight; that a drug enforcement role exposes the military to corruption; that it is unwise public policy to require the U.S. military to operate against U.S. citizens; and that the use of the military may have serious political and diplomatic repercussions overseas. Moreover, some in the military are reluctant to accept an expanded role, seeing themselves as possible scapegoats for policies that have failed, or are likely to fail.[26]

Others argued that "if [the military] were to become substantively committed in what is or may be considered a police role, your military forces would become better policemen and concomitantly weaker military men" (*Military Role*, 1989, p. 25). But even as the opponents of giving the military a role in the war on drugs grew louder, the pressure on Congress to do something about illegal drugs mounted throughout the 1980s. Faced with this pressure, Congress found the military attractive to fight the so-called war on drugs. To many members of Congress, the military seemed ideal to manage a unified anti-narcotics control, command, communications, and intelligence (C^3I) system. The military also had enviable technical capabilities and experience in monitoring the skies and the oceans, both valuable for interdiction efforts. The military could also train foreign police and military forces to combat drugs. Moreover, military capabilities would be relatively inexpensive since they already existed and would not have to be created.

The first thrust to involve the military in the war on drugs came in 1981. That year, Congress passed Public Law 97-86 easing some of the restrictions of the Posse Comitatus Act (18 U.S.C. 1385) and requiring the military to provide law enforcement agencies (LEAs) with anti-narcotics support. Throughout most of the 1980s, this support consisted in providing training assistance to LEA personnel, lending military equipment or personnel for specific tactical operations, providing operational support, and sharing intelligence. Public Law 97-86 forced DOD to make some resources available for law enforcement. But there was widespread dislike for the mission among the top military ranks, principally because they believed that it distracted from the readiness of the armed forces as a whole. Fortunately for the top brass, the law did not establish precise guidelines. It simply stated that the military was to provide LEAs with support in their efforts against illegal drugs. The vague character of the law enabled the military, for the most part, to stay away from the drug war throughout the 1980s. Through DOMS, this mission was handled without any real disruptions to the "real" mission of the military. In effect, drugs were at best a subculture within the Pentagon.

By 1986 media and public pressure mounted again on elected officials to do something about the crack epidemic affecting major U.S. cities. LEA agents also began to complain that getting DOD to ante up its stock in support of drug law enforcement operations was becoming nearly impossible. Under these pressures, the Omnibus Drug Control Act of 1986 was passed. It obliged the Pentagon to prepare an inventory of its counter-drug capabilities and a plan for their use in counternarcotics operations. The idea was to inform LEAs of what military support was available to them. The 1986 Act did not have a warm reception in the halls of the Pentagon. Among the top level military, there was reluctance to "aggressively advertise" the availability of military resources for fear they might generate even more support requests from LEAs (Newberry, 1999 interview).

After 1986, several more aggressive bills attempting to deepen the involvement of the military in the war on drugs were proposed. Most were defeated. In 1988, Senator John Warner (R-VA) and Senate Armed Services Committee Chairman Sam Nunn had proposed a bill that would have given the military the authority to seal the U.S.-Mexico border and handed every soldier vast, de facto powers to arrest civilians. This bill quickly died. On May 18, 1989, Senator Pete Wilson (R-CA) proposed to create a special joint-service command to direct military drug interdiction missions. This bill also died in the committee. The bill would have made a senior Pentagon official responsible and accountable for implementing congressional mandates on the war on drugs and would have given him the authority to move and command troops as he saw fit for the purposes of the war on drugs. All of these bills faced criticism, opposition, and strong lobbying from top level military officials.[27]

Again, to be sure, the military did participate in important anti-drug operations in the early to mid-1980s. LEAs were well aware of the 1981 and 1986 laws and they intended to make extensive use of military support for their anti-narcotics activities. DEA, for example, requested SOUTHCOM's support for its paramilitary operations in Bolivia. SOUTHCOM forces supported DEA in one of the most important anti-narcotics operations in South America in the 1980s, Operation Blast Furnace. Blast Furnace was a major offensive against cocaine processing laboratories in Bolivia. The operation resembled a military offensive and lasted from July to November 1986. Another major operation was Blast Furnace's follow-up, Operation Snow Cap, a low-key LEA offensive with considerably diminished military participation. Snowcap began in 1987 and continued into 1990. By 1990, Snowcap was virtually an all-DEA operation.[28] In spite of operations such as Blast Furnace and Snow Cap, military participation in the 1980s boiled down to ad hoc, occasional support for LEA operations. The military Southern Command's (SOUTHCOM) participation was also kept to a minimal level, particularly because SOUTHCOM's Commander-in-Chief (CINC) in the 1980s, Gen. Frederick Woerner did not want the military to have anything to do with the drug war. Military participation in anti-drug efforts in the 1980s followed only the minimal requirements of the law. The focus of the military apparatus remained the Soviet bloc and, for SOUTHCOM in Latin America, the leftist insurgencies.[29]

In early 1987, the Under Secretary of Defense for Policy, Fred Charles Ikle, anticipating increased pressure from Congress to involve the military in counter-narcotics activities in a more systematic way, commissioned a study conducted by the RAND Corporation. The product of that study, *Sealing the Borders: The Effect of Increased Military Participation in Drug Interdiction*, satisfied the Under Secretary's wishes by arguing strongly against further military involvement in the war on drugs. It stated that further military involvement in drug interdiction operations would not make any difference in drug trafficking. It also made the case that if LEAs made too many requests for military resources, this could affect the military in other ways.[30] Military officials outlined a long litany of ways in which the military would be affected by further participation. General Stephen Olmstead, then Deputy Assistant Secretary for Drug Policy and Enforcement, argued that the military was capable of doing the job but warned that civilians would not like the way it would be done because the military would use machine guns and not worry about Miranda rights. Olmstead (1988) warned that,

> [The Posse Comitatus Act] is a pretty good Act. I am not hiding behind the Act, but it's a pretty good Act that separates the civilians and the military. I don't want a bunch of untrained soldiers performing law enforcement missions. . . . Let me just leave you with two very fundamental things. One of the strengths of our union is the distinction between military and civilian police powers. The second one is, I am really worried about the big war all the time. If you are going to detract from the mission readiness of the Department of Defense, you need to be very careful.

Resistance by high level military to enter the war on drugs in the 1980s was considerable, in spite of enormous congressional pressure. The Secretary of Defense until early 1989, Frank C. Carlucci, had adamantly argued against involving the military in the war on drugs; as had Gen. Woerner of SOUTHCOM and the Chairman of the JCS, William J. Crowe. The late 1988 and early 1989 military's inaction to implement the 1989 Defense Authorization Act's anti-drug provisions for the military is to a large extent explained by Carlucci's and other top level military's opposition to it and their unwillingness to move the matter forward within the Pentagon. In the end, Carlucci, Crowe, and other senior Pentagon officials decided to wait it out until the new Secretary of Defense took over (Perl, 1999 interview). The mission was just unpalatable to them.

The potential effects on military readiness had been the primary rationalization by Pentagon officials against participation in the war on drugs. This argument continued well into the 1990s. In mid-1989, the new Secretary of Defense, Richard B. Cheney, was still skeptical. He stated that "society should not expect the Department of Defense to resolve every problem that comes down the pike just because we're big and have a lot of resources."[31] Nevertheless, President George Bush had made it clear that the military had to play a role in the drug war; and Secretary Cheney began to come around.

Under heavy congressional and executive pressure, on September 18, 1989, a year after the 1989 Defense Authorization Act had passed and legislated the military into the war on drugs, Secretary Cheney threw in the towel. Resistance was becoming futile. Cheney issued a directive to Pentagon officials to start seeking ways to cooperate with the war on drugs. This directive seemed an about-face for the military. But this about-face did not symbolize a newfound willingness to take on the war on drugs. It meant instead that Congress and the President had forced their hand. By 1989, it had become increasingly difficult for the military to stay out of the drug war. The Pentagon *had* to move to take on a role in the war on drugs. Chairman Les Aspin (D-WI) of the House Armed Services Committee said: "The train is moving and cannot be stopped. The pressure on us to do something about drugs is coming from outside the Beltway so we have to do something about it."[32] Congressman Larry Hopkins (R-NY) put it bluntly to the military,

> We are serious about your active role in the war on drugs, even if it means we have to drag you screaming every step of the way.[33]

Secretary Cheney's September 1989 directive obeyed the directions of the National Defense Authorization Act of 1989 (Public Law 100-456 passed on September 29, 1988) which made the military the "lead agency for detection and monitoring of aerial and maritime transit of illegal drugs into the United States." This clause transformed the military into the lead agency for drug trafficking surveillance at sea and in the air (and later on land[34]). While the actual counter-narcotics operations were to be carried out by civilian LEA personnel, the military was to conduct the surveillance of all drug trafficking, that is, the detection and monitoring of craft and vessels carrying illegal drugs. The Act also ordered the military to "integrate command, control, communications and technical intelligence assets dedicated to drug interdiction into an effective network." Finally, it approved and funded governors' plans for expanded use of the National Guard in support of drug interdiction and law enforcement operations.[35] Under the US Code 10, Sections 371-374, DOD may provide information obtained during military activities or operations not related to the war on drugs and "to the maximum extent practicable" consider the information needs of LEAs in their operations and training. Also, the military may share intelligence with LEAs to the extent "consistent with national security."[36] This overlapping jurisdiction arrangement was precisely the kind of arrangement that all agencies dislike the most—a situation that was sure to exacerbate the dislike of the drug mission within the military.

The resistance of the top level, Washington-based military to the drug war is consistent with organizational culture. The entire organization of the Pentagon throughout the previous 45 years had focused on the Soviet Union and the communist threat. Its fundamental doctrines and plans were geared toward the conduct of a major war. From the Pentagon's perspective, the military existed to fight major wars. Within the organization, this perspective generated a culture that valued fighting militarized wars, especially major wars, above all else. The cold reception the war on drugs received in the halls of the Pentagon had already been given to other missions considered beyond the military's central mission. In 1986, for example, when the Goldwater-Nichols Defense Department Reorganization Act created the Office of the Special Operations and Low Intensity Conflict (SO/LIC), the action was not welcome at the Pentagon. The Washington military did not look favorably on the charge of looking after terrorist threats, managing counter-proliferation, peace engagement (peacemaking and peacekeeping), transnational dangers, and other "asymmetric threats" and "wild cards" (Keravouri, 2000 interview). To ask the military to serve as "global scouts" was already unacceptable when the counternarcotics mission was formalized in 1989.[37] Leading the war on drugs was not as important as leading a battalion. In the war on drugs, the enemy is elusive and certainly ignoble. Military rules of engagement did not apply. Fighting drug traffickers is more of a cat and mouse game fit for the underworld of crime but not for the high-minded tasks of the world's first rate military. In a way, the goals of the war on drugs are nothing like the goals of a traditional military, which are attained through the application of military power to destroy enemy military forces. Moreover, in the war on drugs, the military does not lead. Its mandate is to use its assets in support of other agencies, a frustrating task for an agency that is accustomed to employ unilateral, comprehensive, and unrestricted means, including in the interdiction campaigns conducted during war. The prospect of a "permanent, no-end" effort with little possibility of measurable success was not attractive.[38] Thus the organization model of the military seems to explain well the behavior of the Pentagon in regard to the drug war while bureaucratic politics, as we defined, is unable to explain why the Pentagon resisted participation in the drug war. The war on drugs was simply not central to the mission and tasks of the Pentagon; it did not speak to the organization's basic assumptions and attitudes regarding their role in U.S. national security. Therefore, even if it had implied a rainfall of resources, the drug war was spurned. That policy space was one in which the military desired no part.

The Ugly Duckling

After the military *had* to enter the drug war, particularly with the passage of the 1989 Defense Authorization Act and more so after Cheney issued the Pentagon's counter-drug directive on 19 September 1989, the military began to make preparations to implement the new mission.[39] Carlucci and Cheney's directives raised a fundamental question that was to intensify another internal fight within the halls of the Pentagon: where in the organizational chart should the new mission be located? Who should be in charge of it?

In late 1988, Secretary of Defense Carlucci had given Chairman of the Joint Chiefs of Staff, William Crowe responsibility for determining the organizational location of the mission. On October 13, 1988, a small office within the office of the Assistant Secretary of Defense for Force Management and Personnel was created. Its job was to coordinate the implementation of Title XI of FY89 National Defense Authorization Act—even as the final organizational location of the new mission was still being debated. The new office was not given sufficient funds or authority to "order" any military body to implement its determinations. For months, the office remained an insignificant bureau designed to fulfill the very minimal requirements of the law. The internal tug of war over the final organizational location of the new office went on. Through late 1988 and early 1989, JSC Chairman Crowe met several times with top level officials at the Pentagon to find the drug war an organizational location. By early 1989, Crowe decided to wait the 1989 Act's implementation out and leave it to the incoming Secretary of Defense to implement it. The debate over the organizational location of the drug war mission continued after Richard Cheney took office as Secretary of Defense on 21 March 1989. The final outcome of the debate was to create a whole new "division" called Office of the Coordinator for Drug Enforcement Policy and Support (CDEP&S). The new office was not attached to any other office at the Pentagon. Instead, it became an autonomous free-floating agency within the Pentagon. The final outcome of the debate over the organizational location of the drug mission begs the question: what explains Defense Secretary Carlucci and JCS Chairman Crowe's decision to first create a small, powerless office within the Pentagon and then to put off implementing the mission until the new administration came in? Finally, what explains the decision to create a separate division for drug law enforcement duties at the Pentagon rather than place the mission within the JCS office as the statutes regulating foreign troop deployments would suggest?

The delay in implementing the law by Carlucci and Crowe is perhaps understandable from the perspective that it was likely that the men would finish their terms within a year and were not likely to remain in their posts much after January 1989. Perhaps in consideration for the incoming administration, they deferred the implementation of the law. The whole picture, however, suggests that there were other reasons for their actions. Both Carlucci and Crowe had vigorously argued against involving the military in the war on drugs prior to the 1989 Defense Authorization Act. They did not want to take on a task that, in their view, did not belong in the military. It is possible to argue that they delayed implementation of the mission, at least in part, based on the intensity with which they had argued against it earlier. Also, their decision to create a small, powerless office within the office of an assistant secretary suggests that they did not consider the mission an important component of defense. The weak nature of the office also suggests that they were delaying full implementation of the Act rather than set in motion a full program with which they did not agree, e.g., act on organizational cultural understandings.

As stated, once the new Secretary of Defense, Richard Cheney, took office, the Pentagon created the Office of the Coordinator for Drug Enforcement Policy and Support (CDEP&S), a relatively isolated, autonomous office within the Pentagon.[40] The first coordinator of CDEP&S, Stephen M. Duncan, also wore the hat of Assistant Secretary of Defense for Force Management and Personnel. In the spring of 1989, Duncan was asked to permanently head the new office. He reported directly to the Secretary of Defense. The JCS had, in effect, rid itself entirely of any responsibility in the war on drugs even though the JCS would have been a natural place for a mission like the military drug war since that office statutorily oversaw all U.S. military deployments abroad. Although this point must be qualified by the fact that within the Pentagon it is nearly impossible to find a "civilian" office, like CDEP&S, answer to a military body, like the JCS, nevertheless, the JCS *were* directly and actively involved in accommodating the mission within the Pentagon and had an ultimate agenda regarding the place of the mission within the Pentagon. The JCS clearly showed no interest in even contemplating making the drug war any part of its endeavors. It did not do so under Adm. Crowe or later under Gen. Colin Powell. Duncan (1999 interview) reports that he was left very much on his own at CDEP&S and that the Secretary of Defense Cheney "was just happy to be informed from time to time."

Why did Secretary Cheney make the decision to create a separate, isolated office to handle the military's drug war mission? Several points stand out from the way the Pentagon handled the new mission. First, the Pentagon took a whole year to determine the "appropriate" place of the mission within the military and its organizational location at the Pentagon. Second, it was evident that the JCS did not want to handle the mission. As Robert Newberry (1999 interview) put it, "I have no doubt that the JCS saw this kind of thing as a hot potato that he might not want to handle." In addition, the mission puzzled Secretary Cheney, who was uncertain as to where to place it. Third, the unwanted mission was finally isolated from every major bureau within the Pentagon. Fourth, as late as the summer of 1989, some at the Pentagon still did not believe that the Department of Defense was in for the long haul. As Thomas W. Kelly, Director of Operations for the JCS, put it, "they [LEAs] are in the business [the drug war] forever, we are in it just as long as we are told to be in it" (*Military Role*, 1989). Fifth, though CDEP&S began the military's systematic cooperation with LEAs against illegal drugs, its budget never grew to more than one third of one percent of DOD's budget. In FY89, the total budget assigned by the Pentagon to the drug war was $300 million, not enough to make even a dent in drug trafficking. Moreover, as of June 1989, only $30.2 million of the $300 million had been transferred by the Pentagon's comptroller to military departments for counter-drug support.[41] The resources allocated to CDEP&S remained under 0.4 percent of the Pentagon's budget, even at its peak in 1992 when the CDEP&S budget reached $1.2 billion dollars. (By FY2000, CDEP&S's budget had decreased to roughly $950 million dollars.) Even as the overall drug budget continued to grow, the CDEP&S budget had not grown dramatically; over the 1990s it lost acquisition power. Finally, the bureau is not likely to become a major bureau within the Pentagon (Lin, 1997 interview).

These observations intimate that the mission remained an unwanted mission at the Pentagon. The mission, like a hot potato, was passed along until it landed in a nook of its own, isolated from the rest of the major structures of the Pentagon. Cheney's decision to create CDEP&S and "leave it alone" with "occasional updates" from the Coordinator reflects the undesirability of the mission. The process and the outcome are consistent with a strong organizational culture, which would predict that the drug war mission would not be welcome by the military. But because they could not avoid it, given that the Pentagon's political masters would not have it any other way, the mission was taken in but given a venue that would not "distract" the military from its central mission and tasks. But the mission was clearly a "secondary" if not a "tertiary" mission, an ugly duckling.

The Ugly Duckling, Part II

This section argues that among the forward deployed forces, the response to the new mission was not much different, although it did vary from command to command. This variation, however, does not originate in variance of motivation, but in the differences in the fundamental circumstances in which each command operated. Briefly stated, this is how each of the relevant commands responded to the drug war mission. The Southern Command (SOUTHCOM) made the decision to handle the mission as part of its day-to-day responsibilities. Three commands, the Pacific Command (PACOM), the Atlantic Command (LANTCOM), and the Forces Command (FORSCOM) decided to create a separate office to handle their counter-drug responsibilities. Finally, the North American Aerospace Defense Command (NORAD) created an organizational niche for the mission within its existing structure. PACOM created the Joint Interagency Task Force West (JIATF-West, later known as JIATF-5) housed in Alameda, CA. LANTCOM created the Joint Interagency Task Force East (JIATF-East, later known as JIATF-4) headquartered in Key West, FL. FORSCOM created a Joint Interagency Task Force (JIATF-6) headquartered in El Paso, TX. NORAD created the NORAD Tactical Intelligence Cell (NORTIC), headquartered in Cheyenne Mountain Air Force Base, CO.

It is noteworthy that PACOM, LANTCOM, and FORSCOM's CINCs decided not to handle counter-drug operations directly but created instead Joint Interagency Task Forces (JIATFs) as their primary agencies for counter-drug operations. LANTCOM's JIATF-East monitored the Atlantic Ocean and the Caribbean along the coasts of South America, Central America and Mexico. The purpose of the new JIATF-East was to provide early detection of drug traffickers and early notification to LEAs regarding the location and direction of the smuggling vessels. Once detected, an illegal drug-carrying vessel would be monitored until it could be "handed off" to an LEA—Coast Guard, U.S. Customs or the U.S. Customs-Coast Guard joint C^3I East Center located in the Southeast United States. Through its interagency Joint Operations Control Center, LANTCOM's JIATF-East had some notable successes. JIATF-East, however, was created, assigned permanent personnel and assets, and funded but it remained largely isolated from the day-to-day operations of the Command. Though it is hard to determine what motivated LANTCOM's CINC to do this, the outcome points to a decision designed to fulfill the requirements of Defense Secretary Cheney's directive with the minimal disruption to the core activities of the command. As Newberry (1999 interview) put it,

> LANTCOM got to take care of the Atlantic Ocean and to fight WWIII on the ocean. . . . So, they kind of went, "hey, I can't devote my whole time to this. I will create a joint task force. Let them focus their effort on [that]."

PACOM's CINC established JIATF-West to handle the drug war mission for the command. The CINC's area of responsibility included almost the entire Pacific Ocean, except the ocean area off the coasts of South and Central America where its jurisdiction "chopped" to LANTCOM. Initially, JIATF-West was assigned two to four ships supported by P-3 maritime patrol flights. The random patrols they conducted in the vast ocean soon proved disappointing and wasteful. JIATF-West was then reorganized as an intelligence center with detecting and monitoring responsibilities. But JIATF-West, like JIATF-East, was assigned its personnel and assets and separated from the command's day-to-day planning and activities. The realization that the drug war in the Pacific theater, if it was to be effective, required greater resources fell on deaf ears both at the Command's headquarters and at the Pentagon. JIATF-West remained a small, isolated office vastly undersupplied and underfunded for the enormous task they were given. It appears that PACOM's admirals too found the new mission potentially distracting from their principal mission, to prepare "to fight WWIII" (Newberry, 1999 interview). It is also significant that both PACOM and LANTCOM's top level military handed the main JIATF posts in their counter-drug operations to Coast Guard Admirals although, they argued, the Admirals would report to DOD and not to the Department of Transportation. This was another sign that they viewed the drug mission as "distracting" from their personnel and resources.

FORSCOM created JIATF-6 which served as its planning and coordination headquarters for counter-drug support. The tasks that FORSCOM conducted were primarily improvement of the roads along the Southwest border to ease the movement of LEA personnel and reconnaissance patrols to cover the Southwest border. They also manned listening and observation posts and placed remote sensors. The activities FORSCOM personnel conducted along the Southwest border, however, resembled practice and training exercises. The picture is one of soldiers in fatigue with painted faces dragging their bodies along the border caught between the sand and heat of the desert. While all these enterprises were useful for the purposes of the drug war, the military's counter-drug operations along the Southwest border were really training grounds for "real time" Army and Marine troops. Duncan (1999 interview) of CDEP&S recognized this very point,

> The first time that one goes down it's kind of exciting. And, there's an attempt to make the training as good as it can be. If you're going to go there, do a lot of night work, night reconnaissance patrolling, and a lot of small unit kind of stuff, it can be good training and it can be . . . troops like good training. If it's good, realistic, hard training, [the soldiers] will go to the mountains of New Mexico and have a ball. Life is good. That's part of why they joined the army. An eighteen, nineteen year old kid out there climbing big mountains at night and all that. . . . So, once you get there on the ground, you keep it exciting. They like being there. They come back and they tell great stories about it; what was going on in the Southwest; the drug smugglers they interdicted, etc.

The office itself, located in El Paso, Texas, remained small and underfunded. Its contribution to the drug war is hard to measure. It is likely that it had no substantial effect on drug smuggling through the U.S.-Mexico border. Then, as now, about 70 percent of all the cocaine that enters the U.S. comes in through the U.S.-Mexico border.[42] But whatever the result, JIATF-6 became not FORSCOM's major contribution to the drug war but a good excuse to train soldiers under "real conditions." For FORSCOM, as for LANTCOM and PACOM, the drug war was really a secondary mission that was either to be isolated or used to support primary missions.

The North American Aerospace Defense Command (NORAD) is a binational United States and Canadian organization charged with the missions of aerospace warning and control for North America. Aerospace warning includes the monitoring of man-made objects in space, and the detection, validation, and warning of attack against North America, whether by aircraft, missiles, or space vehicles, utilizing mutual support arrangements with other commands. Aerospace control includes providing surveillance and control of the airspace of Canada and the United States.[43] In the eyes of Congress, this capacity was ideal for fighting the air drug war. NORAD was therefore given the primary responsibility for detection and monitoring of all aircraft suspected of transporting illegal drugs into the United States. To do that, NORAD created the NORAD Tactical Intelligence Center (NORTIC) in 1990. NORTIC produced a comprehensive air picture of drug trafficking from all sorts of air tracking sources already in place. NORTIC personnel would sort out and separate information relevant to drug trafficking from information already collected by NORAD's assets and then make it available to DOD and LEAs organizations for their purposes. NORAD managed to avoid going deeply into the drug war by simply capturing information in main stream and handing it over to LEAs as "drug trafficking" intelligence—often doubtful in its utility for that purpose because it was neither "real time" information nor did it provide information that LEAs did not know already, e.g., information on smuggling routes.

Gen. Maxwell Thurman, SOUTHCOM's CINC from 1989 to 1991, also received Secretary Cheney's 18 September 1989 directive. He was to find a permanent, prominent operational location for the drug war within SOUTHCOM. Thurman, his Director of Operations, and other SOUTHCOM leaders began the process of decision making to find the drug war its place within SOUTHCOM's force structure. Up to then, SOUTHCOM had provided informal, ad-hoc support for LEA operations throughout the 1980s, but now they were being asked to integrate the mission into their command structure and activities. Thurman and other SOUTHCOM leaders created the Office of the Deputy Director for Drugs, under the J3 Operations, which came to be known as J3-DDD. DDD would handle all counter-drug operations. Within a few years, the office of the DDD grew substantially. It took an autonomous life and became the driving factor in SOUTHCOM's counter-drug activities. DDD was led by an aggressive former Ranger battalion commander, Col. Keith Nightengale. The office was staffed with officers with special operations backgrounds. The overall tone in the office was militaristic and aggressive.

PACOM and LANTCOM's responses are identical. They both created JIATFs that effectively isolated the anti-drug mission. Both missions, however, were underfunded and understaffed. This response is not unlike the Pentagon's. An unwanted mission that cannot be avoided is conveniently positioned in a niche where it can neither become central to the organization nor distract it from its main mission and tasks. In addition, the underfunding and understaffing signal the low priority of the drug mission within these two commands. FORSCOM's response is also similar; it created a JIATF to handle the drug war mission because it had to. However, the activities of the JIATF largely resembled the training activities of the Army and the Marine Corps. In effect, the drug war mission was reconceived in order to allow the Command to use its resources and its day-to-day activities to serve the training needs of the organization. This response is quite consistent with a military organizational culture. In the case of NORAD, creating an office, NORTIC, which would fish for drug war-related bits of data through a stream of information produced for other purposes than the drug war is the equivalent of a minimal effort to fulfill the congressionally mandated role in the drug war. The task was simply not central to

NORAD. The mission had to be adapted in such as way that it would not disrupt the central concerns of the organization. Moreover, NORAD's existing equipment was entirely inadequate for the detection and monitoring of small, low-flying aircraft, the type most used by drug smugglers. NORAD made little or no effort to adjust its hardware and activities to perform the new mission's tasks. In the minds of NORAD's officers detecting small, low-flying aircraft was not different from detecting a Soviet MiG and they made no attempt at adjusting to the drug war—even though they could not really detect the small, low-flying, drug-carrying aircraft at all.

Only SOUTHCOM made the effort to integrate the drug war mission fully into its operational and tactical activities. But, does that mean that SOUTHCOM embraced the mission in spite of its military character? I argue that SOUTHCOM did not behave differently, but that its different circumstances compelled them to integrate the anti-drug mission differently. The explanation that SOUTHCOM leaders gave at the time for not creating a separate office to handle counter-drug activities, and which the evidence confirms, is that SOUTHCOM was generally a resource-starved command. Newberry (1999) argued that "Odds are he [Gen. Thurman] did not have a bunch of people to draw from to make a JTF." This might indicate that they might have done just that, if they had had the resources and personnel to do so. Lack of resources was further exacerbated by the fact that the debate to find an organizational location for the drug mission within SOUTHCOM's force structure was being made simultaneously with the implementation of another September 1989 order by the National Security Council, through the JCS: to begin military surveillance of Gen. Manuel Noriega in Panama. In effect, Gen. Thurman had to begin planning the military's actions in Panama. Taking personnel out of the Command's sensitive activities to organize and man a separate counter-drug office in the Fall of 1989 would affect the ongoing preparations to depose Gen. Noriega. Thus, it appears that SOUTHCOM did not have the resources to handle both tasks at the same time. Thurman explained at the time that "of the 497 permanently assigned USSOUTHCOM staff personnel, 55 are dedicated to counter-narcotics related activities as part of their overall duty responsibilities." No personnel were assigned full-time permanently to counter-narcotics activities (*International Aspects*, 1990, p. 183). It is likely, however, that Thurman would have preferred to isolate the mission within SOUTHCOM but was unable to do so because of the important activities being conducted for Gen. Noriega's overthrow.[44]

In sum, the responses of the various U.S. Commands appear consistent with our view of the organizational culture of the military. None of the Commands appears to have embraced the mission so as to transform it into a central mission within their organizational and force structure. Instead, they isolated it where it would not interfere with the Command's priorities (PACOM and LANTCOM) and kept it undernourished; they used its resources to give their low-level soldiers "real time" training (FORSCOM); created a small office to pick the anti-drug relevant information from an existing stream without making major adjustments to the hardware and operations of the organization (NORAD); or simply were forced to adopt it because the circumstances did not enable the Command to compartmentalize the mission away (SOUTHCOM). In the end, the mission remained the "ugly duckling" among the activities more attractive to the military.

To a Hammer, Everything Looks Like a Nail: Culture and Preferred Solutions

The Chairman of the JCS issued his counter-drug planning guidance to SOUTHCOM on 19 September 1989, a day after Secretary Cheney issued the military's overall counter-drug directive. SOUTHCOM's CINC, Gen. Thurman was instructed to find ways to accommodate the new directive. Thurman then began to comply and geared for the drug war. Thurman's dedication to the drug war, however, was affected by two important factors. First, Operation Just Cause, the operation against Gen. Noriega in Panama, was being planned and implemented toward the end of 1989. The counter-drug mission quickly came to be considered a distraction from Thurman's work on Just Cause. The most serious efforts to implement the military's drug war within SOUTHCOM had to be put off until the invasion of Panama was over. Second, in 1990 Thurman was diagnosed with leukemia and was absent from SOUTHCOM from July to November 1990. This further delayed the transition although some preliminary steps were taken to identify the areas where SOUTHCOM might make a difference in the drug war.[45] These two factors make it difficult to judge the behavior of SOUTHCOM under Thurman. But in November 1990, Gen. George Joulwan became SOUTHCOM's CINC. Joulwan began the transformation of SOUTHCOM into an operational headquarters for the drug war. Joulwan's enthusiasm for the mission was unmatched. He made the war on drugs a "top priority." He outlined a plan to employ military assets and personnel in support of a comprehensive regional counter-drug effort that he himself conceived. Joulwan was a hands-on CINC; he conducted his own public relations campaigns; and he continually called meetings to which he invited the Ambassadors, important elements of the country team and other officials. He regularly traveled to Washington, DC, to pitch his case both at the Pentagon and other agencies. His personal skills earned him the support and respect of most of the people he interacted with. Joulwan led the way and came up with a comprehensive plan that included an interagency slogan (One Team, One Fight), a strategy slogan (Hit the Beehive, Not the Bees) and numerous charts where he showed how drug trafficking organizations would be defeated (Joulwan, 1999 interview). Gen. Joulwan believed that the military had valuable assets for interdiction and intelligence that could help formulate a comprehensive approach to combat drug trafficking.[46] But the drug war was nothing like what Joulwan had done in the past. For the military, it was a new problem, a law enforcement problem, with which they had little or no prior experience.

To cope with this new type of problem, Joulwan took a sixty-day retreat to figure out and put together a "comprehensive theater strategy" to respond to the drug threat. To configure that strategy, Joulwan used many of the precepts outlined in a well-known military doctrine: Low Intensity Conflict (LIC).[47] LIC, later known as OOTW (Operations Other Than War), has a long history in U.S. government policy. It was more or less known in the 1960s as "stability operations." A child of the policy of containment, LIC's fundamental focus was to identify insurgency movements throughout the Third World and provide support for combating these groups. Making a reference to these "operations," President Kennedy spoke of,

> This new type of war, new in its intensity, ancient in its origins—war by guerrillas, subversives, insurgents, assassins: war by ambush instead of by combat; by infiltration, instead of aggression, seeking victory by eroding and exhausting the enemy instead of engaging him. It requires in those situations where we must counter it a whole new kind of strategy, a whole different kind of force, and therefore, a new and wholly different kind of military training.[48]

Up to the 1950s the military had used standard, large-army tactics to combat guerrilla movements. By the early 1960s, President Kennedy promoted the newly conceived "stability operations" and demanded that the armed forces include this new counter-insurgency training in the curriculum of all military schools. President Kennedy's "Flexible Response" doctrine was partly based on this new type of guerrilla warfare.[49] Propelled by the desire to be effective in dealing with guerrilla tactics, the U.S. military developed specific operational concepts to deal with such non-conventional threats as insurgency movements. The operational concepts by which the military guides its actions are contained in the U.S. Army doctrinal publications. These publications, known as FMs (Field Manuals) are the capstones that embody the Army's culture. The FM series provide the detailed guidance by which Army personnel do what they do. The Army, which dominates SOUTHCOM, takes its direction and guides its activities from the doctrine presented in the FM 100-5 (*Operations*). As Richard Duncan Downie (1998, p. 52), a well-known Army historian writes,

> Implementing doctrinal publications is denoted by an FM number other than 100 (e.g., FM 31-21, *Guerrilla Warfare and Special Forces Operations*). This information, contained in these manuals is directed toward specific elements or subelements of the Army, such as divisions, brigades, battalions, and lower echelons. Implementing doctrinal manuals describe the "how-to" details that permit each of these types of units to perform the particular set of functional missions that it is assigned by capstone doctrine. These manuals delineate and clarify specific tactical information derived from the more generalized concepts contained in the capstone

> doctrine. Implementing doctrinal manuals also provide the necessary details for the organization, equipment, education, and training of specific kinds of units.

The end of the Vietnam War in the 1970s brought with it a strong opposition to counter-insurgency operations in the U.S. Army which, coupled with a new emphasis on the European conventional and nuclear theaters, moved away from such non-conventional doctrines as "stability operations" or counter-insurgency. The 1970s editions of FM 100-5 deemphasized these operations. It was not until 1986 that FM 100-5, *Operations*, included again references to counter-insurgency operations. But by then the term *Low Intensity Conflict* began to be used. Low intensity conflict denoted an *environment* but no longer an *activity*, non-conventional military operations rather than specific activities such as anti-guerrilla warfare. By the late 1980s, LIC included five different environments, including anti-narcotics. The FM 100-20 of those years dealt directly with that term. By 1990, the Army published its FM 100-20 retitled *Military Operations for Low Intensity Conflict* (LIC). This version included a substantial discussion concerning what the Army now refers to as OOTW.

SOUTHCOM had collaborated with law enforcement agencies in the 1980s, particularly in Bolivia, through the conduct of operations such as Blast Furnace and Snow Cap, but these operations involved only the provision of support to specific tactical operations and logistical aid for LEAs. Although these operations did have a military flavor, they did not require the use of any overarching principles or guidelines for military action. They were small and sporadic to require a doctrine for their application. But in late 1990, when Joulwan became CINC, SOUTHCOM adopted and adapted the 1990 edition of FM 100-20 which embodied the LIC doctrine to guide its anti-drug operations. In effect, Joulwan applied LIC doctrine precepts systematically to conduct a drug war.[50]

The "anti-drug" strategies that arose from the application of the principles of the FM 100-20 (and its derivative FMs) clashed with reality. The first clash had to do with the conceptualization of the nature of the enemy, a misguided conceptualization based primarily on Cold War images of the enemy. Drug traffickers were a business that did not operate anything like leftist insurgencies. LIC tactics proved inadequate to thwart the modus operandi of drug traffickers. The second is the mobilization operations of the Army. The military, for example, moved in obvious ways. They sent scouts to prepare the terrain and set up their tents. As Al Matano (1999) explains,

> The traffickers knew what was coming because when the U.S. military does anything, nothing is covert. They send advance parties . . . the maintenance. . . . The U.S. military does things overtly. They did it in support of DEA. . . . Big show. The traffickers went on vacation weeks before [the operations]. They dismantled their operations.

Just based on these two items, LIC doctrine proved inadequate for fighting drugs without important adjustments to the nature of the enemy.[51] It took SOUTHCOM's operatives several years to learn the difference between the drug war and leftist insurgencies and readjust for it. LIC doctrinal concepts could not be simply applied to the drug war. Clearly, the military was using old solutions to new problems. If the drug war was a real war, surely war manuals would suffice. That was obviously not the case.

A second important illustration also shows how an organization employs old and familiar tools to solve new problems. In September 1990, with Gen. Thurman absent due to illness, SOUTHCOM was authorized by the Army Chief of Staff to use the U.S. Army Decision Systems Management Agency to design, acquire, integrate, and implement a Command Management System to support SOUTHCOM's counter-drug efforts.[52] According to one account, the intention was to create a communications network resembling the television game show "Hollywood Squares." The system would greatly enhance communications and enable an interagency initiative to function smoothly. The result of these efforts turned out to be not a "Hollywood Squares" kind of strategy—an "Andean Squares" equivalent—but the creation of SOUTHCOM's Counter-Drug War Games section. According to Holden-Rhodes (1997, p. 75),

> Under the aegis of the J5, the first game—a development exercise—was conducted in 1991. In spite of advice and warning to the contrary that the games must be viewed as the SOUTHCOM team aligned against a business—La Empresa Coordinadora—the game was basically a Cold War "Red vs. Blue" exercise.

As the game exercises proceeded, it started to become clear that there was a gap between the acknowledged premise that drug trafficking was a business and the military-like responses that underlay SOUTHCOM's team's response to the threat. SOUTHCOM was treating La Empresa Coordinadora as if it were a Soviet Army, not a drug business. As Holden-Rhodes (1997, p. 74) notes again,

> The Red Team [the drug traffickers] stymied SOUTHCOM and country team players [the Blue Team] on every move. Red Team successes, structured on current narcotraficante business operations, appeared to mystify the Washington interagency players. In several cases, this led to verbal fist-fights and the promise of physical mayhem.

Clearly, initially SOUTHCOM's anti-drug efforts, though genuine and enthusiastic, were circumscribed by the "way the military does things." SOUTHCOM's operatives drew on existing military doctrines, concepts, and experiences to conceive a response to what was really a new problem. Although the picture may be mixed, there is sufficient evidence here to show that agencies will often resort to preestablished practices, doctrines, and basic assumptions and attitudes to face changes in their environments, more specifically, to deal with policy problems that they have never seen before. In effect, to a hammer, everything will look like a nail.

Culture Blinds: Why Agencies Often Cannot Anticipate Consequences

Organizational culture would predict that members of organizations take on attitudes and basic assumptions about the world that make them regard as important only consequences or phenomena that they were socialized to regard as part of their job, but will have little or no regard for those that they have not been taught to consider significant. Because the military had never dealt with the drug war, it should have never been expected to recognize potential problems with or consequences of "the way it does things" once it engaged the drug war. Thus while other agencies saw the military modus operandi as having potentially disastrous consequences on U.S. relations with the governments of drug-producing nations, the military was unable to take such diplomatic perils into considerations because, simply put, soldiers are not diplomats. The following analysis demonstrates how this prediction worked out in the military anti-drug war in South America.

DOD is by far the largest bureaucracy in the United States. In the drug war, the military was sometimes referred to as "the 800-pound gorilla." The military displays its largess in its operations. The war on drugs is no exception. As an interviewee states,

> We [the military] . . . we do things big and we end up getting nothing out of it or falling apart, and we kind of accept that sometimes. We just quickly see that we have more money than other people and we take losses with our gains. We say, 'well, if we want a gain, we gotta try it. If we lose, we'll try and stop short; but we don't go half-way or otherwise you have a half-ass problem'.[53]

This characteristic is sometimes troublesome for the Department of State personnel stationed in drug-producing countries with which there is wide anti-drug cooperation. The military's overt and massive modus operandi can cause diplomatic concerns among FSOs and diplomats because the operations of the military often become too visible. As Matano (1999 interview) explained, "it can look like an invasion." Indeed, the military is not known for taking seriously any concerns with the sovereignty of other countries or with upsetting other publics or other governments. The State Department is. Diplomats worry about what the operations of the military, particularly massive operations, tend to do to the perceptions of the U.S. by other governments and publics. To confirm this, David Westrate (2000 interview) of DEA also said that,

> In the early days, [during] Operation Blast Furnace . . . [the military] brought with them their C5As, with C5s, which are huge airplanes. And, when they went, it looked like, I think there were a hundred and twenty-five military people or more. I mean, they went in with a chaplain, with cooks, with a complete medical back up. . . . It astounded me. [When confronted], they said, we can't go, our thinking, our way of doing business does not allow us to commit troops to something like this without the basic elements of our military structure. . . . And, it didn't get much done because . . . a village idiot could figure it out. It was time to get out . . .

The relative insensitivity of the military for issues of sovereignty caused some difficulties between the U.S. government and the governments of drug-producing countries where the military is most active. The diplomatic fallout is often the problem of DOS. DOD was not accustomed to taking such impacts into consideration. It could not be sensitive to what it was not taught to be sensitive to, to what it has not been trained to perceive as important. The maintenance of good relations with other publics and governments is not the concern of the military and they are not likely to think about that when they conduct their work.

Another example mentioned in some conversations with drug war bureaucrats and which demonstrates how culture can make us blind to certain realities was that the military is not trained in law enforcement techniques. The military is not equipped to handle evidence with the savoir-faire of a law enforcement officer. Gen. Hartzog (2000 interview) recognized that when he said that "We didn't know police skills. We still don't know police skills for that kind of threat." Westrate of DEA also explained that the 24,000 soldiers that invaded Panama in December 1989 mangled up the useful law enforcement evidence against Manuel Noriega in Panama. Many of the records could not be used in court against Noriega because they were seized and removed by the military. The evidence was then declared potentially tainted. What the military could have provided to prosecute Noriega was lost. Westrate (2000 interview) explained that,

> When the 82nd Airborne went into Panama to take Noriega out of there, they were basically serving an arrest warrant for a narcotics charge. . . . But, the military went in and they scooped every record from the Panamanian Defense Forces. They put all this stuff in a warehouse and we were stuck with a huge conglomeration of stuff. Everything from his personal photos to the maintenance records of his jeeps to. . . . Well, when we went down there as investigators to look at it, nobody knew who seized it, who transported it. . . . And so, as evidence in a criminal trial it would have been very difficult to use any of it. The way to get around those things [was] not to let the military get too close to investigative things. They are not to do any seizing.

Clearly, however, military actions in Panama were an invasion and military operatives should not have been expected to behave like cops. The military did what they do in such operations with little or no regard for the law enforcement intricacies behind the U.S. government action. Soldiers, simply put, are not cops.

A third example of how culture blinds us to certain phenomena is that "the members of our armed forces are not used to playing support of anything" (Duncan 1999 interview). Military personnel prefer to lead. Carl H. Builder (1989, p. 1) put it best,

> Unlike most combat operations, which the military prefers to design and conduct according to its own concepts and doctrines, current peacetime military operations in support of drug interdiction must be designed and conducted in close coordination with civilian agencies, imposing significant limitations on both the scope and means of the military operations.

Thus, the fundamental problem with the foot soldiers, as Hartzog explained, is not that they do not like or like the drug war but that they feel frustrated by their inability to see the end game of a [drug war] operation. According to Hartzog (2000 interview),

> My lieutenants, lieutenant colonels, colonels were frustrated by putting all this training into [the foreign military or police forces] and then having to sit down and watch them go away in an operation and never know whether the training is any good or not.

The foot soldier wants to plan the action, conduct the operation, and then claim victory over the enemy. Stopping short of the entire process is quite frustrating to military personnel. Their frustration often turns into dislike for the mission itself.

These examples illustrate the fact that many agencies operate without regard for important consequences that they do not consider so because they are not trained for it, but which, to the trained eye of another bureaucrat, a diplomat or a cop, for example, may be crucial for the preservation of good relations with a foreign government or a building of a good prosecutorial case in court. It is precisely in these cases where it is possible to appreciate the difference that organizational culture makes in the behavior of agencies.

Rainfall Missions: The More Things Change the More They Stay the Same

Although the military resisted its incorporation in the drug war, Congress and the Executive were determined to make use of the military's capabilities to "stem the drug flow" into the country. While the resistance to accept a mission that is not concordant with the organization's way of doing things is understandable from the perspective of an organizational culture, it is critical to ask how an agency responds when it can no longer defer its adoption.

When Secretary of Defense Cheney sent out DOD's directive in September 18, 1989, the Air Force was compelled to enter the drug war. At that time the Air Force was undergoing a budget review because of the announced $80 billion dollar defense budget cut coming up over the following five years after 1989. At the same time, Congress kept increasing the drug war budget every year and, along with it, DOD's appropriations for counter-narcotics operations, which reached a peak of $1.2 billion in FY1992. The Air Force then made the decision to enter the war on drugs and actively dipped into the new funds for "counter-narcotics operations." What the Air Force did was consistent with its organizational culture in at least one regard: the money was put to use for propping up existing activities within the Air Force, with little real adjustment for fighting a drug war. One example of this is the Over-The-Horizon Backscatter (OTH-B) Radar Program.

The OTH-B Radar program was a highly popular program within the Air Force (AF). OTH-B was developed to support the North American Aerospace Defense Command's (NORAD) continental air defense mission. The mission consisted of tactical warning and assessment (detecting, tracking, and assessing the threat targets) and tactical airspace control. The OTH-B system included four separate systems containing two or more radars each. There were an East Coast Radar System (Eastern System) with three operational sectors; a West Coast Radar System (Western System) with three operational sectors; an Alaskan Radar System with two operational sectors; and a Central Radar System with four operational sectors. The four systems covered the entire United States.

In FY1991, AF requested $242.8 million for OTH-B procurement and construction. Most of these $242.8 million were to procure and install the Central Radar System. That same year the Pentagon began experiencing the sharp budgetary reductions previously announced by President Bush. The OTH-B was one of the programs earmarked for elimination, particularly because of the collapse of the Soviet Union and the reduced threat of incoming long-range missiles. But AF officials were very enthusiastic about the program and did not want to see it eliminated. After some serious search for ways to rescue the program, the Deputy Secretary of Defense came up with a plan to rescue the program. He directed that the first sector of the Central Radar System be positioned toward the Southwest instead of the East. Positioned that way, it was argued, the Central Radar System could be used for counter-narcotics purposes, such as detection and monitoring of aircraft carrying illegal drugs. The entire $242.8 million budget for the Radar System was then moved out of the AF budget that year to the counter-narcotics budget at CDEP&S, the small anti-drug agency inside the Pentagon. In effect, the Central Radar System was to be financed with counter-drug money, where it would constitute a little less than a third of DOD's FY1991 counter-drug budget.

Several relevant points stand out in this decision. First, OTH-B was not a radar system that could detect and track small, low-flying aviation aircraft, which is the kind of aircraft that narcotraffickers coming from Latin America use. The AF responded to this by arguing that the Central Radar System could be coupled with a second radar system more apt for monitoring and tracking small aircraft. The large radar system would detect that something was in the sky. The second system would locate it, identify it, track and monitor it, and target it for interdiction.[54] This would leave the Central Radar System intact. Second, when Pentagon officials were confronted with the objection that there were no missile or bomber threats coming from the South, particularly coming from Latin America, AF officials responded that the Soviets (and later the Russians) were capable of launching an attack on the United States from any direction. A critical GAO report concluded that the AF desired to save this program and was willing to go to greater lengths to do so. It noted that "several DOD representatives stated that despite these actions, the primary purpose of the Central Radar System was still to support NORAD's air defense mission" (GAO, 1991). Pentagon officials, including Secretary Cheney and the JCS justified the OTH-B's contribution to the counter-drug mission as an extension of the airspace control element of NORAD's air defense system.

A second example of how the Air Force and the Navy used counter-drug resources to pursue familiar and useful activities emerges from their participation in interdiction efforts. AF and Navy officials, like their counterparts in the other services, were ordered to help the Pentagon's anti-drug mission. The AF was presumably in a good position to help the Pentagon because an important part of the overall tasks of the organization was to conduct air surveillance—an activity useful in anti-drug efforts. The Navy was in the ideal position to aid LEAs in the detection and monitoring of drug-smuggling vessels. Neither the AF nor the Navy assigns assets permanently to any task. Instead, their assets are managed by a system of operating costs where the units are "flying hours" and "steaming days." The collection of all flying hours and steaming days is referred to as the "operating tempo" (OPTEMPO) of the service. Between 1989 and 1993, the Department of Defense spent $3.3 billion on detection and monitoring. Two-thirds of the money went to programs and procurements and close to a third of the money into operating AF aircraft and Navy vessels in support of the drug war. The AF and the Navy's dipping into the anti-drug budget to fund their OPTEMPO begs the question of whether their activities were in effect supporting the war on drugs or whether their participation in it was an opportunity to fund OPTEMPO operations that would otherwise be cut because of the overall defense budget cuts.

After all, OPTEMPO funds taken from the Pentagon's counter-drug budget by the AF and Navy had increased by 300 percent from about $212 million in 1989 to $844 million in 1993. Both the AF and the Navy had been steadily increasing the number of flying hours and steaming days that they billed to the counter-narcotics budget. But, were the AF and Navy being effective in stemming the flow of illegal drugs to the United States?

Table 3.1 Air Force OPTEMPO operations billed to the Pentagon drug war budget in millions of dollars.

Year	1989	1990	1991	1992	1993	Total
Programs, etc.	$139.7	$364.1	$551.0	$686.3	$550.5	$2,291.6
OPTEMPO	$71.8	$119.5	$215.5	$275.7	$293.1	$975.6
Total	$211.5	$483.6	$766.5	$962	$843.6	$3,267.2

According to a GAO report, when the OPTEMPO billed to the drug budget is assessed against interdiction and supply reduction results, the services' flying hours and steaming days did not provide a reasonable return on investment. Since 1989, the flow of cocaine actually increased, most shipments were still not interdicted, and the supply on the streets did not decrease at all. The same GAO report accused AF and Navy officials of using expensive equipment for doing something (surveillance) that could be done less expensively with other equipment. State-of-the-art surveillance, which the AF and the Navy were doing, is inherently expensive and this was especially the case because the services were using high technology systems originally designed to detect and control highly sophisticated weapons systems in combat situations to track smuggling aircraft and vessels—which could be a small propeller driven plane or a small wooden boat.

All this led some members of other federal agencies involved in drug trafficking to suspect that the AF and the Navy were simply transferring costs from the operations of high technology assets into the drug budget and using these operations to train and practice maneuvers that they needed to practice while labeling these activities counter-drug operations and drawing from DOD's counter-drug budget. Because it is hard to show how state-of-the-art submarines and surface combatant vessels can help monitor and track small, slow drug-trafficking aircraft or wooden vessels or commercial and private small planes, the evidence seems to suggest that the AF and the Navy justified the continuation of routine activities slated for cuts after 1989 with the drug war. This is further reinforced by the fact that the military crews conducting surveillance at sea or air received little training related to counter-drug surveillance and their flying hours and steaming days resembled more the traditional missions and training of the military. Moreover, the AF and the Navy billed the drug budget for the flying hours and steaming days of ships that even happened to have been incidentally in the area, regardless of whether these ships guaranteed a plausible electronic coverage for the detection and monitoring of smuggling aircraft or vessels. There were large gaps in the electronic coverage that the AF or Navy would not cover.

Table 3.2 Navy OPTEMPO operations billed to the Pentagon drug war budget in millions of dollars.

Year	1989	1990	1991	1992	1993
Flying Hours	18,436	48,026	78,168	70,733	94,623
Steaming Days	2,081	3,830	5,051	4,091	4,968
OPTEMPO costs	$71.8	$119.5	$215.5	$275.7	$293.11

Finally, the AF and the Navy retained assets scheduled for deactivation and rededicated them to the counter-drug mission. For example, the Navy retained an E-2C squadron and rededicated it to the drug mission. It also gave a larger counter-drug role to its P-3 aircraft and retained three T-AGOS ships that could no longer be justified by the submarine threat they were intended to counter. Six hydrofoils were also rescued from deactivation. NORAD partially justified its inventory of fighter aircraft on the basis of "ever increasing challenges from drug smugglers." But, while these ships and aircraft were modified especially for counter-drug operations, many of them were modified by adding equipment of a "roll-on, roll-off" type that can be transferred among aircraft or of a temporary nature such that the equipment can be removed if the vessels or aircraft were needed for another mission.[55]

An analysis of the AF and Navy's participation in the drug interdiction suggests that when organizations accept, or are imposed, additional discordant missions that they did not want in the first place, they will use those resources in such a way so as to reinforce what the organization is already doing. Clearly, the AF and the Navy had a stake in trying to find funding for their programs and OPTEMPO since they were facing budgetary cuts. But, what if the AF and the Navy had not been facing budgetary cuts? Would they have dipped into counter-drug funds for the programs and activities slated for budget cuts? It is hard to speculate on what they would have done. We can guess that they would probably have rejected the mission altogether or at a minimum, shirk. What organizational culture predicts, however, came true. The AF and the Navy dipped into the counter-drug budget to do what they were doing anyway, to reinforce and support their preferred missions, and to free funds from OPTEMPO or other programs for other more desirables activities that go directly to what the organization values the most.

To Survive and Prosper: The U.S. National Guard

The National Guard (NG) falls under the jurisdiction of the governor of each state or territory. Although in the 1980s some governors had requested sporadic NG support for law enforcement activities against illegal drugs, NG entered the federal and international drug war along with DOD through the National Defense Authorization Act of 1989. In that year, all state and territorial components of the NG began to implement counter-drug programs to support LEA efforts against illegal drugs.[56] The NG created a national office to handle drug law enforcement support; the State guards created special divisions for counter-drug programs; and NG leaders opened the NG Counter-Narcotics Institute in San Luis Obispo, CA. NG leaders began to speak enthusiastically about NG's counter drug activities, even though many of them "had spent the 1980s trying to avoid getting into it [the drug war]."[57] The *Annual Review of the National Chief* of the National Guard had no mention of the drug war in 1989 or before. The 1990 *Review* contains a small paragraph on the subject. But by 1993 the *Review* dedicates well over four pages to NG counter-drug activities. In March 1990, the *National Guard* magazine published a special issue dedicated to detailing and praising the contributions of the National Guard to the drug war. In sum, by late 1989, NG leaders across the country actively sought to participate in the drug war. They also began to show an unprecedented zeal for their newly acquired mission. What explains NG's about-face in the drug war? Moreover, what explains the sudden enthusiasm for the new mission? The eagerness of NG leaders to enter the drug war is puzzling because law enforcement is not a fundamental part of the NG mission. Moreover, NG leaders view themselves as military—an institution that had openly resisted participation in the drug war.

There is a view among some of the interviewees that the NG sought the mission because they had always been complaining that they never had enough resources and that the drug war gave them an opportunity to acquire additional resources. New resources means the ability to recruit or retain more personnel—in an era of declining numbers—and the ability to have jobs for the reserve forces to do. In addition to this, the drug war offers the opportunity to train more of its personnel.

In general, it was the prospect of keeping jobs at a time of downsizing that motivated the NG to embrace the new mission. As Leonard Wolfson (1999 interview) put it,

> This is not as derogatory as it sounds, because it's real life. We fund the National Guard, the fifty state plans plus the four territories, each year, as a composite of something like 160 to 200 million dollars [for the drug war]. You divide that by fifty-four. It's not a huge amount. . . . Do they do useful things? Yes. Are they doing something strategic that's going to resolve the drug problem? No. Do they contribute? Yes. But, what is their basic motivation? Jobs. . . . [The added funds they get for the war on drugs] mean several hundreds of jobs for National Guardsmen. Good jobs. You know, doing meaningful things. You give them one billion dollars; they'd take it.

The conditions faced by the NG during those years were indeed severe cuts in its budget and personnel. From FY89 to FY93, NG personnel were cut from 456,960 to 422,725, with steady reductions every year. The *Reserve Component Programs* publications issued by the Reserve Forces Policy Board of the Department of Defense from FY90 to FY93 expressed serious concerns about these reductions in the NG. At about the same time, NG leaders began to use the rhetoric of the war on drugs to argue for increased funding for the NG. They justified these requests both to the Pentagon and before Congress by playing a numbers game. Every year the *Annual Review of the National Chief* displayed prominently and laudingly the contributions of the NG to the drug war in quantifiable terms. The *Review* tables of 1992 and 1993 are illustrative.

In addition, NG exhibited a curious penchant for "taking credit." In a hearing Lt. Gen. John B. Conway, the NG's national leader, argued that, in contrast to the *Annual Review* charts,

> The results of drug enforcement operations during which the National Guard provided support for local, state, and federal law enforcement agencies during FY89 were: Cash was confiscated in the amount of $1,735,745. Cultivated marijuana plants eradicated/destroyed totaled 4,076,662. Drugs seized were: processed marijuana pounds - 49,917; cocaine pounds - 10,887; heroin pounds - 39.5. Other property seized during support operations were: 95 ammunition. The arrest of 859 individuals was a result of operations the National Guard supported. The street value of the drugs plus the cash confiscated reflects a net value of approximately $12 billion.[58]

Getting credit for its contribution to the drug war was a major preoccupation within the NG. Credit was important because it constituted the best argument for getting additional funds or stemming the loss of existing funds.[59]

Table 3.3 An illustration of the National Guard performance report and review.

Seizures	1992 Figures	1993 Figures
Cash	$61,784,709	$170,360,318
Marijuana plants eradicated	83,433,586	206,035,207
Processed marijuana	445,248 lbs.	891,693 lbs.
Cocaine	165,758 lbs.	180,351 lbs.
Heroine	1,047 lbs.	3,320 lbs.
Opium	631 lbs.	2,668 lbs.
Vehicles	5,153	6,433
Weapons	5,099	12,205
Arrests (contributed)	22,097	69,173

And initial examination of NG's about-face in the drug war appears well explained by bureaucratic politics. NG was faced with severe budgetary cuts and the drug mission provided the opportunity to keep the flow of funds going. Counter-drug funds would make up for at least some of the resource losses. Yet, while it appears that more (or at least not less) budget and jobs and credit motivated the NG to enter the war on drugs, it is difficult to argue that the activities of NG were changing fundamentally. All along, NG operatives were simply doing what they had been doing before. As Lt. Gen. John B. Conway put it, in regard to the National Guard interdiction and counter-drug activities, "National Guard personnel were assigned duties that conformed, as nearly as possible, to their individual military occupational specialty" (Department of Defense, 1990, p. 595). This shows a preoccupation with doing something about the drug war but without making major adjustments in the activities of the organization from what they normally did. To support this point is the fact that the FY1989 *Report of the Reserve Forces Police Board* stated that the war on drugs permitted guardsmen to train in a "real-time" mission and to use the NG's capabilities daily. It recommended that each person be given a task that reinforces his or her personal occupational specialty in the Guard. Thus NG began to send its engineers to build roads and bridges that would presumably contribute to the drug war. Its Deployable Medical System personnel rotated duties in South America in operations labeled "counter-drug activities," even when these had little to do with drug combatting. F-16s were being flown to chase small, low flying drug-carrying planes with little results. Handheld Global Positioning Systems (GPS) were acquired in the name of the drug war without specifying how these would be used. Light armored vehicles and combat planes were mobilized for the drug war with a hard-to-measure impact on drug trafficking. Every year, the NG argued for more money to acquire assets and to train in the name of the drug war, but only to keep doing what they had already been doing before the drug war.

The Overseas Deployment Program, which already existed prior to the NG's involvement in the war on drugs abroad, was coupled with drug-war fighting capabilities. The program was ideal because the guardsmen took tours of 2 to 6 weeks training abroad. The SOF (special operations forces) program was also used to help combat drugs although the program was touted more as a program in support of the Goldwater-Nichols Department of Defense Reorganization Act of 1986. Even VCRs and cell phones were acquired in the name of the drug war.

Thus, even if NG's behavior of aggressive acquisition of the "new mission" can be explained by bureaucratic politics, the reality is that they did not change their activities and tasks substantially, but they continued to do what the organization had always done—something consistent with organizational culture predictions. In sum, the case of the National Guard, like the Air Force and Navy in the previous section, shows how an organization will not necessarily become imperialistic for the sake of building turf. It appears instead that agencies will adopt unwanted missions only to prop up and support what they are already doing. To adopt a mission completely dissonant with the existing mission would require the organization to make long and painful adjustments. To say yes to a mission, without such adjustments, particularly when the new mission comes accompanied of resources, is simply to enhance the current mission without any real costs to the agency.

Conclusion

In this chapter, it became clear that the evidence for making the case that organizational culture heavily influences the behavior of the military is compelling. Indeed, the military resisted the drug war largely based on the fact that it was inconsistent with the core mission of the military. Moreover, when the military finally took on the drug war, they did so with an apparent enthusiasm that reflected more their culture of obedience than a real desire to fight the drug war. Finally, once Congress and the President persuaded the reluctant drug war warrior to come on board, the military did the minimum and, as soon as there was an opportunity, they downgraded and starved the mission. And when they did something about the drug war, they did so in ways that seemed to serve their existing mission and operations, rather than make real adjustments to a war of a different nature. Thus, an examination of the behavior of the military and its various component parts in the drug war reveals that the behavior of the military is more likely to be explained by its organizational culture than any other explanation. That the military resisted the drug war; that it gave no prominent role to the counter-drug mission on its organizational chart; that it downgraded and starved the mission; that it employed familiar concepts to conceive its counter-narcotics role; and even that it used drug-war funds to sustain programs and activities that it favored at a time of large budget cuts are all actions well explained by the military's organizational culture.

But in regard to bureaucratic politics, it is clear that the military defended its autonomy as much as any other agency. Some military even argued that the military did not want to have the responsibility for a failed war, if it failed, because they should not be held accountable for law enforcement activities. These belonged somewhere else, many said. Moreover, the relationship between the military and its political masters reveals a more interesting fact, that is, when the principals of an agency (Congress and the Executive) ultimately persuaded the agent (the military) to come on board and fight the drug war, the organization never really did so on their terms but on its own terms. Through various mechanisms that included threats, incentives, and rhetoric, the military finally accepted to fight the drug war, but they never really embraced the mission and got rid of it as soon as they could.

Notes

1. See Ron Chepesiuk. *Hard Target: The United States War Against International Drug Trafficking* (Jefferson, NC: McFarland & Company, Inc. Publishers, 1999).

2. See also Donald J. Mabry, "The U.S. Military and the War on Drugs," in Bruce Bagley and William O. Walker III, eds., *Drug Trafficking in the Americas* (New Brunswick, NJ: Transaction, 1994).

3. See Lorna S. Jaffe, *The Development of the Base Force: 1989-1992*, Joint History Office, Office of the Chairman of the Joint Chiefs of Staff, July 1993. Document found in http://www.dtic.mil:80/jcs/.

4. Newberry, 1999 interview.

5. Total Federal drug control budget (in millions)

FY 1989 actual	$ 6,663.7
FY 1990 actual	$ 9,758.9
FY 1991 actual	$10,957.6
FY 1992 actual	$11,910.1

FY 1993 actual $12,171.1

Although, to be sure, it would be a long shot to bet on the war on drugs to recover the many billions of dollars that the Pentagon was supposed to lose under these budget cuts. Nevertheless, the rhetoric should be enough to show our case, regardless of the dollar numbers involved.

6. Interview with Dave McGinnis, April 11, 2000. Mr. McGinnis argued that the phrase "slippery slope" became the buzz word at the Pentagon among those who argued against military involvement in the war on drugs. The phrase appealed to the power of a political tradition embodied in the Posse Comitatus Act of 1868, which forbade the military from participating in law enforcement activities.

7. Review of Gen. Maxwell Thurman's records at Carlisle Barracks, PA; and interview with General George Joulwan, September 23, 1999.

8. While it is hard to guess whether Joulwan would have argued against the drug war if he had had the opportunity to do so, the fact is that he probably never had the opportunity to express an opinion on the matter before he became SOUTHCOM's CINC.

9. Within a year of his appointment as SOUTHCOM's CINC, Gen. Thurman was diagnosed with leukemia and left SOUTHCOM.

10. Interview with Bill Hartzog, February 15, 2000. This view is confirmed by the statement of the Director of Operations, JCS, Thomas W. Kelly, who said on June 9, 1989, that "SOUTHCOM is primarily at this time involved in intelligence operations." See *Federal Drug Interdiction: Role of the Department of Defense*, Hearing before the Permanent Subcommittee on Investigations of the Committee on Governmental Affairs of the United States Senate (Washington, DC: GPO, June 9, 1989); p. 35.

11. Drug Control: Inadequate Guidance Results in Duplicate Intelligence Production Efforts, GAO Report, April 1992.

12. Self-servingly so because this kind of intelligence did help LEAs get to smuggling craft and vessels first and then claim credit quickly without long-term commitments to work with SOUTHCOM.

13. All US Ambassadors (Bolivia's Richard Bowers; Colombia's Morris Busby; and Peru's Anthony Quainton) and all heads of LEAs interviewed for this study agreed that Joulwan was a highly energetic and committed individual.

A clarification is pertinent here. Joulwan's enthusiasm for his job in the drug war was largely based on his personality and the high value that the military places on duty and obedience. There is little evidence that Joulwan used drug war rhetoric to argue for greater resources or greater jurisdictional prerogatives for SOUTHCOM in the drug war. He simply used the assets that came and went under his control as effectively as was possible. It is possible to argue that if Congress had decided that SOUTCOM had no role in the drug war, Joulwan would have simply let go the mission as easily as it came.

14. Some interviewees argued that the military did not pursue the taking of credit because they had an image of themselves as being "above that kind of pettiness." This argument is, of course, more compatible with organizational culture than bureaucratic politics.

15. Interviews with Ambassadors Morris Busby (Colombia), March 21, 2000; Richard Bowers (Bolivia), March 24, 2000; and Anthony Quainton (Peru), April 26, 2000.

16. Newberry, 1999 interview.

17. This proclivity of "diplomats" is further explored in Chapter 5.

18. DOD Directive 3025.1 of the Secretary of Defense, issued in 1968, instructed that

the Secretary of the Army be the Executive Agent to task DOD components to plan for and commit DOD support in response to requests from civil authorities. The Director of Military Support serves as the Secretary of the Army's action agent for planning and executing DOD's support mission to civilian authorities within the United States. The directive intended to organize the channeling of military support to civil authorities facing civil riots in 1968. Later, the organization stayed in place and began providing support for missions that ranged from natural disasters to forest fires to Olympic Games support.

19. www.dtic.mil/doms.

20. This amendment has caused some important controversy among academics. See "The Posse Comitatus Act: A Principle in Need of Renewal," *Washington University Law Quarterly*, Vol. 75, No. 2 (Summer 1997). See full text at http://www.wulaw.wustl.edu/WULQ/75-2/752-10.html.

21. International Narcotics Control Act of 1986. Title II of Public Law 99-570 [Anti-Drug Abuse Act of 1986], 100 Stat. 3207-60, approved October 27, 1986.

22. It is unclear whether the JCS saw a threat to its power in DOMS's ambitions to expand to coordinate all military support for LEAs abroad. It is also possible to speculate whether the JCS may have been worried that DOMS was excessively attuned to the needs of LEAs and would not be able to "fence off" LEA demands when these impinged on DOD's priorities. What is clear is that the JCS adamantly opposed this idea.

23. Few at DOMS realized that even if they had been charged with the military's international drug war, they would have had to contend with the budgetary and jurisdictional claims of the State Department in the international drug war. That bridge, of course, was never crossed, at least not by DOMS.

24. For a more detailed analysis of the "personalities" of each of the military services see Chapter 2, "Five Faces of the Service Personality," and Chapter 3, "The Service Identities and Behavior," in Carl H. Builder, *The Masks of War: American Military Styles in Strategy and Analysis* (Baltimore: The Johns Hopkins University Press, 1989).

25. Of about forty-five bureaucrats interviewed for this study, not one disagreed with this general premise.

26. *Narcotics*, 1988.

27. Besides the heavy lobbying from the military against these bills, there was some concern in Congress regarding the importance of the Posse Comitatus Act in the history of the United States democracy. Many Congress members were not willing to go any further beyond the 1981 amendment to the Posse Comitatus Act to grant the military greater law enforcement responsibilities.

28. See Donald J. Mabry, "The U.S. Military and the War on Drugs," and Eduardo Gamarra, "U.S.-Bolivia Counternarcotics Efforts During the Paz-Zamora Administration: 1989-1992," in *Drug Trafficking in the Americas*, Bruce M. Bagley and William O. Walker III, eds. (Boulder, CO: Lynne Rienner Publishers, 1994); pp. 43-60 and 217-256.

29. SOUTHCOM's CINC in the mid 1980s, General Woerner, continually warned against distracting SOUTHCOM personnel from the vital task of fighting guerrillas in Central America. He argued vehemently against any involvement of the military in the war on drugs until the day he left his post.

30. Peter Reuter, Gordon Crawford, Jonathan Cave, with Patrick Murphy, Donald Putnam Henry, William Lisowski, and Eleanor Wainstein, *Sealing the Borders: The Effects of Increased Military Participation in Drug Interdiction* (Santa Monica, CA: RAND Corpora-

tion, January 1988). In an interview, Dr. William Olson has pointed out that since the study was published important questions regarding its validity have emerged. Studies by the Institute for Defense Analyses have questioned RAND's study. See http://www.ida.org/IDAnew/Research/Force/nssi.html#natsec.

31. *Air Force Times*, October 2, 1989.

32. *The Washington Post,* May 13, 1989; A1.

33. Cited in David Isenberg, "Military Options in the War on Drugs," *USA Today*, July 7, 1990.

34. Public Law 101-510, FY1990 Defense Authorization Act of 5 November 1990.

35. National Defense Authorization Act of 1989.

36. The Act gave the military a two-pronged role. The military was put in charge of all surveillance (detection and monitoring) and of coordinating all intelligence efforts among the various law enforcement agencies. See Title 10, U.S. Code, "Armed Forces legislation," in *International Narcotics Control and United States Foreign Policy: A Compilation of Laws, Treaties, Executive Documents, and Related Materials*, Report prepared for the Committee on Foreign Affairs of the U.S. House of Representatives by the Congressional Research Service, Library of Congress, December 1994; pp. 213-218.

37. For the type of study that the Pentagon uses to justify its resistance to operations other than war (OOTW) see Jennifer Morrison Taw, David Persselin, and Maren Leed, *Meeting Peace Operations' Requirements While Maintaining MTW Readiness* (Santa Monica, CA: RAND, 1998). In this study, the authors argue that OOTW, such as peace keeping or drug enforcement, have a negative effect on military force structure, readiness, training, and equipment, acquisition, supply, and maintenance. MTW stands for "major theater war."

38. The military prefers to lead, is unaccustomed to intervene anywhere in a supporting role, and it prefers missions that have a beginning, a definite end and at least an inkling of measurable success. For these features of military doctrine see Carl H. Builder, *Measuring the Leverage: Assessing Military Contributions to Drug Interdiction* (Santa Monica, CA: RAND, 1993).

39. While this decision making process was going on, DOD top level military, in order to fulfill the minimum requirements of the 1988 law, created an office to handle drug enforcement matters. That office was headed by a Deputy Assistant Secretary of Defense for Drug Policy and Enforcement, Stephen Olmstead, who had previously opposed any military role in the drug war. Again, to placate Congress, the office was given a budget, $300 million, which was not enough to make a difference in drug trafficking law enforcement. In justifying the delay in DOD's implementation of the law, Gen. Olmstead argued that involving the military in the drug war required that DOD move "deliberately and prudently. . . While any delay whatsoever in meeting the threat posed by the importation of illegal drugs into this country is too long, the significance of our new responsibilities and the importance of carrying them out correctly dictated a thoughtful approach." *Federal Drug Interdiction: The Role of the Department of Defense*, Hearing before the Permanent Sub-Committee on Investigations of the Committee on Governmental Affairs of the United States Senate, 101st Congress, First Session, June 9, 1989. Was this foot-dragging or shirking?

40. The Office of the Coordinator for Drug Enforcement Policy and Support reported directly to the Secretary of Defense. It is technically not located within any of the major bureaus of the Pentagon. According to the organizational chart, "the role of the Coordinator as the principal staff assistant and advisor to the Secretary of Defense for drug control policy,

requirements, priorities, systems, resources, and programs. This includes developing policies, conducting analysis, providing advice, making recommendations, and issuing guidance on DOD drug control plans and programs; developing systems and standards for the administration and management of these plans and programs; promulgating plans, programs, actions, and tasks pertaining to the DOD drug control program; reviewing, evaluating, coordinating, and monitoring drug control plans and programs to ensure adherence to approved policies and standards; promoting coordination, cooperation, and mutual understanding within the Department of Defense, Congress, and between the DOD and other Federal Agencies, State and local governments, and the civilian community." See the following web site, http://ardor.nara.gov/secdef/osd2200.html.

41. Memorandum from the Office of the Assistant Secretary of Defense for Force Management and Personnel, June 1989, signed by Dale H. Clark, Director for Requirements, Plans, and Programs.

42. The figure of 70 percent, an estimate, has remained steady throughout the 1990s. It has been reported repeatedly in the White House's *National Drug Control Strategy Report* and in the Department of State's annual drug trafficking reports year after year.

43. www.spacecom.af.mil/norad/noradfs.htm

44. Recall also that Gen. Thurman had in the past argued against military involvement in the drug war.

45. Gen. Thurman's Director of Operations, Gen. Bill Hartzog, explained in an interview (February 15, 2000) that SOUTHCOM's military personnel worked closely with LEAs to break down every single activity required in the drug war and identify those in which military personnel could help. The catalogue of activities listed 1200 different activities. Of these, several hundred types of activities were identified as activities in which military personnel could participate.

46. For some agencies, Joulwan's enthusiasm was actually a concern. Department of State diplomats and FSOs, for example, feared that his enthusiasm would get the better of him on the policy end and that this would cause some problems with foreign governments, problems which State would have to clear later.

47. To be sure, LIC concepts had been put to use by the military since 1986 in the drug war, but it was Joulwan who used LIC doctrine to put together a comprehensive, systematic strategy for SOUTHCOM's drug war. In any event, that the military used LIC concepts against the drug war even before Gen. Joulwan went to South America only reinforces the point of this section, organizations will try to deal with new problems using old, well-known solutions.

48. Hilsman, 1967, p. 413.

49. For a thorough explanation of the development of the counter-insurgency doctrine during the Kennedy Administration and the resistance of the military top-brass to adopt and integrate such doctrine see Richard Duncan Downie, *Learning From Conflict: The U.S. Military in Vietnam, El Salvador, and the Drug War* (Westport, CT: Praeger, 1998); 47-52.

50. See Downie, *Learning from Conflict*.

51. Here, it is important to introduce a caveat to the use of the Army FM manuals for LIC in the drug war. Clearly, SOUTHCOM is a multi-service command. It is not exclusively an Army-based command. Nevertheless, the Army dominates SOUTHCOM and the principles and manuals used for SOUTHCOM's LIC-based anti-narcotics campaigns, though touted to be multi-service principles, were largely based on the Army's LIC doctrine as pub-

lished in the Army's FMs.

52. This had been Thurman's idea, though he was not there to implement it.

53. Newberry, 1999 interview.

54. The necessity of keeping this expensive, high-tech program going is further in doubt if one considers that the Pentagon was already using multiple other assets for detection and monitoring of drug trafficking aircraft, including land and sea based aerostats, the Caribbean Radar Basin Network, fixed and mobile ground-based radars, several AWACS, and Navy aircraft ships with powerful surveillance capabilities.

55. After 1993, the Air Force and the Navy began a process of disengagement from the war on drugs. A note in the *Washington Post* stated that there is a "near disappearance of U.S. radars and planes from the Andean." An Air force official cited in the article argued that "we [the military] get asked to do everything and when this one (Air Force supports in South America) came through the door and we had to do it with our own money, there was a feeling of 'Hey, why shouldn't the Navy or somebody else take care of it?' . . . At this point the entire fleet of AWACS is committed to missions where Americans are in harm's way or where there is a high threat of conflict, and so if any planes go to Manta (Ecuador) on a regular basis, someone is going to have to decide whether it is Iraq or Korea or someplace else that has to give them up." See *The Washington Post*, March 13, 2000; A.

56. After 1989, practically every National Guard in every state and territory has a counter-drug program that looks much like this mission statement of the Texas National Guard, "The Texas National Guard Counter-drug Program is a joint task force, made up of Army and Air National Guard Personnel. Counter-drug support began in Texas over ten years ago, providing aviation/aerial observation support to the Department of Public Safety by use of Texas National Guard personnel in state active duty and annual training status. The program provides quiet, honest, and professional support to approved enforcement and community agencies statewide. The Texas National Guard takes great pride in being involved in the fight against drugs as members of the nation's armed forces, state military forces, and as volunteers in community DDR programs throughout the state."

57. Conversation with Col. Robert Perkins, May 10, 2000.

58. Department of Defense, 1990, p. 595.

59. State NG leaders also learned to play the credit game. Texas is illustrative. In their web page the Texas National Guard takes credit for the following numbers—without any reference to what they mean exactly,

Law Enforcement Seizures with Texas National Guard Support
Fiscal Year 1986: $73 million
Fiscal Year 1994: $904 million
Fiscal Year 1996: $1.2 billion.

Chapter 4
Diplomats

The U.S. war on drugs is waged on many fronts, both at home and abroad. Over the last three decades of the 20th century, U.S. anti-narcotics efforts expanded from the streets of U.S. cities into the jungles of Colombia, the mountains of Peru and Mexico, and the waters of the Caribbean and the Atlantic and Pacific Oceans. As the drug war became an international endeavor, U.S. diplomats and Foreign Service officers (FSOs) were forced to incorporate it into their goals and strategies and their daily activities. Diplomats not only had to learn to balance the American "national interest," as they had traditionally viewed it, with the increasingly internationalized drug war mission but they were also forced to learn to balance their organizational interests with the organizational interests of other agencies involved in the international drug war, particularly those that sought to expand their operations abroad. In countries such as Bolivia, Colombia, Mexico, and Peru, the practices of the diplomatic corps became intertwined with the dynamics of the drug war.

This chapter examines the behavior of diplomats and FSOs in the drug war. How did the U.S. diplomatic corps, both at the Department of State and at U.S. Embassies, respond to the war on drugs as it moved into the realm where diplomatic culture ruled? What factors determined the behavior of U.S. diplomatic agencies in the drug war? Can bureaucratic politics help explain diplomatic behavior in the anti-narcotics policy space? How did organizational culture shape the way the State Department behaved in adapting to the drug war mission? What is evidence of DOS culture (e.g., diplomatic culture)?

Bureaucratic Politics: The Diplomatic Corps

The Department of State's (DOS) Bureau of International Narcotics Matters (INM) was created only in 1978.[1] The decision to create a bureau within DOS that dealt exclusively with international anti-narcotics policy was a congressional decision that signaled a general shift in governmental focus toward greater attention to the supply side of the issue. If drugs were to be combated successfully, the effort had to include diplomatic pressure on foreign governments and internationally based plans and programs to aid efforts in fighting illegal drugs. Under this logic, the drug war became an international endeavor. Hundreds of U.S. diplomats and FSOs were thereby forced to take on the drug war mission as part of their day-to-day activities. Many within State did not view the mission favorably. They believed that it would only complicate their work both at home and abroad. Nevertheless, FSOs and diplomats took the mission and made it their own. And it is this attitude toward the drug war that raises the question of the motivations that State had to adapt to the mission. In addition, it is also pertinent to ask what were the most important factors that determined how the Department of State and U.S. Embassies, as organizations, dealt with the drug war.

Diplomacy and the War on Drugs: A Historical Caveat

The political behavior of DOS in the drug war must be understood in the historical context of the gradual erosion of its supremacy in foreign policy causing a devolution of its culture. Since at least the Kennedy administration, there had emerged a consensus in Washington that much foreign policy making power had shifted from DOS to the President's team of foreign policy advisors inside the White House.[2] While the supremacy of DOS in foreign policy making was first challenged by the creation of the National Security Council (NSC) in 1947, it was not until the Kennedy administration that NSC began to acquire the foreign policy prominence that it has today. As the power of the National Security Advisor grew over time, particularly in the 1960s, DOS was often obliged to allow NSC to take the lead in U.S. foreign policy making.[3] But, while, and because, there is little diplomats and FSOs can do to change the tendency of the president and other prominent figures to turn to White House staff rather than DOS bureaucrats, the shift of foreign policy power from DOS to NSC was a traumatic experience for DOS and the diplomatic corps (Gelb, 1980). The increased prominence of NSC and the President's advisors on foreign policy making has had the effect of making DOS concerned over the erosion of its supremacy in foreign policy and overprotective of its foreign policy prerogatives.[4]

Parallel to State's gradual loss of its foreign policy making monopoly, U.S.

embassies and missions abroad have also seen an erosion of their influence as well. As Barry Rubin put it, "U.S. embassies abroad are routinely passed over as Washington or special envoys conduct negotiations, gather information, and maintain contact."[5] Indeed, presidents sometimes distrust DOS and view it as a sluggish institution incapable of responding with the flexibility and swiftness that international crises often require. The consequence of this is that not only DOS but also its Embassies abroad have developed a natural defensiveness to the inclinations of the sitting President to bypass DOS and U.S. Embassies and missions in conducting foreign policy.

It is in this important historical context that DOS was summoned by Congress and the Executive to participate in the drug war, specifically its international aspects. Starting in the late 1970s and early 1980s, diplomats had to begin to develop, implement, and coordinate U.S. anti-narcotics policy and programs abroad. In those years, most diplomats viewed the drug war as a hindrance to the "real" labor of diplomacy, that is, its cultural policy space. It was considered an unsavory subject that had little to do with the traditional work of diplomacy. Drugs were, in effect, a dirty task, an unwanted mission. Nevertheless, had the DOS refused to enter the war on drugs, its already battered primacy in the construction of foreign policy would have been further eroded. Multiple agencies, from the military to Treasury and law enforcement agencies would have been free to deal with foreign governments and gain a foothold in *foreign* drug policy making, encroaching inevitably into State's jurisdictional territory. Thus DOS had to respond to the changing nature of the anti-narcotics issue and become a "drug warrior," simply for the protection of its interests.[6]

The activities State diplomats and FSOs performed in the drug war came to include drug eradication programs, negotiations over U.S. anti-narcotics aid, management and transfer of U.S. anti-narcotics aid to foreign governments, coordination of the actions and programs of other U.S. anti-drug agencies operating abroad, and pressuring foreign governments to cooperate with U.S. anti-drug policies. The activities of diplomats and FSOs regarding the war on drugs acquired an interactive character not only toward foreign governments but increasingly toward organizational interests of other U.S. agencies that sought to wage their drug war abroad. The number of voices at the international anti-narcotics table was increasing and likely to increase further in the future. With each year passing, more and more individuals from numerous U.S. agencies were sitting at the conference room tables of U.S. Embassies particularly across South America pushing their own role in the war to stop illegal drugs from reaching the United States. State often struggled to maintain control of their activities in those nations. The dilemma for DOS was clear. State had to either become an actor in the war or lose an important say on a growing issue of U.S. foreign policy.

Given the historical erosion of State's monopoly in foreign policy making, it is possible to make the case that the Department of State's participation in the drug war was largely motivated by a desire to protect its jurisdictional power over *foreign* policy. Foreign policy, even if it involved a drug war abroad, was important for State because of its claims to jurisdiction over *any* issue the U.S. government dealt with abroad. Thus the historical evolution of U.S. diplomacy over the past forty years, specifically the erosion of DOS's foreign policy making supremacy, influenced the overall behavior of the diplomatic corps in the drug war. Much of the eventual entrance of State into the drug war was motivated by the normal desire of an agency to protect its "turf." Nevertheless, it is a difficult task to discern exactly how much of DOS's political organizational behavior activated by its own self-conscious awareness of its culture was a response to the erosion of its bureaucratic power in foreign policy (defensive behavior) and how much is because of the instinctive cultural tendency of all organizations to want to protect and enhance their bureaucratic power (offensive behavior). The result, however, is much the same. But, while it is hard to sort out the influence of each of these two motivations over the behavior of State, this study contends that much of State's political behavior was intrinsic to it as an organization *defending* its jurisdictional power over foreign policy, including foreign drug policy, rather than wanting the mission as a way to expand the bureaucratic power of the organization. The historical fact that DOS's supremacy in foreign policy was contested by other governmental agencies is likely to have had an exacerbating effect on the instinctual organizational tendency of State to protect its "turf" when it came to the drug war. Thus, this historical variable, unique to DOS, is likely to be a contributing variable to its response. But DOS exhibited much of the same political behavior as other bureaucratic organizations as it will be shown ahead.

Diplomacy and Turf at Home

From very early on, the drug war represented a challenge for DOS. It took several years for State bureaucrats to figure out what the role of diplomacy would be in the drug war. By the time President Reagan came into office, however, State's diplomats and FSOs had determined that they had no part in the domestic drug war, but that State's role was not only crucial but unique in the *foreign* drug war (Gifford, 1999 interview). It was in this facet of the drug war that DOS decided to focus. This focus put State on a collision course with other agencies working on their own drug wars in South America. The first salvo shots in that regard, however, were fired at home, with President Reagan's own attention to the drug war.

From the early years of the Reagan administration, there was a desire to develop and coordinate anti-drug policy in an integrated, coherent manner. To do this, Congress created the National Drug Policy Board (NDPB), chaired by Attorney General Edward Meese III and comprised of the heads of some 15 U.S. government agencies. The purpose of the NDPB was to direct and coordinate all federal efforts against illegal drugs. The NDPB gave DOS's INM the chair of the International Standing Committee (ISC), which dealt with drug policy in the Andean countries. DOS, however, never really accepted the role that NDPB played in theory in the international drug war. Soon after the NDPB asked State to chair the ISC, State bureaucrats used Section 400 of the Foreign Assistant Act as a justification to assert their jurisdiction over the drug war abroad. The ISC, in other words, could not be chaired by anyone else but State because it pertained directly to the *foreign* drug war. The reality was that State never recognized NDPB's jurisdictional claims over the foreign drug war because DOS personnel believed that anything bearing the word international was a matter that fell well within the purview of State. To drive this point home, DOS personnel employed various tactics to make it clear that the NDPB had no legitimate claims over the foreign drug war. State, for example, failed to provide NDPB with the information required to do more than compile the plans and ideas submitted by the various government agencies involved in the Board. The result was a fragmented and disjointed drug war ("Issues Surrounding Increased Use," 1988, p. 15). But withholding the information the NDPB required to create a truly comprehensive, well-coordinated plan for the drug war was not the only ploy the State Department used to make it clear to other agencies that it alone represented the U.S. government in the drug war abroad. Failing to send representatives to meetings or sending low-ranking personnel to the joint meetings was another way to convey State's displeasure with the NDPB's tendency to mix the domestic and the foreign drug wars. DOS insisted that the foreign drug war was their work, not the NDPB's. To be fair, however, DOS never made any claims to the domestic drug war either; it remained utterly uninterested in it, but it asserted aggressively its control over the foreign drug war.

Over the next few years, DOS would become the prominent actor within the NDPB in all aspects of the foreign drug war, all in the name of its claim to anything international. By the late 1980s, INM was writing and coordinating most of the NDPB's inter-organizational strategic and implementation plans. The strategy was clear. Since State could not make the NDPB disappear, they would certainly ensure that anything it did at the international level was well under full control of the Department. Unfortunately for State, when the NDPB ceased to exist, State's INM immediately lost the hard-fought-for control over NDPB's coordination powers of the drug war abroad. Not surprisingly, State's rejection of the NDPB's claims to the foreign drug war was transferred over to its successor organization, the Office of National Drug Control Policy (ONDCP) or the Office of the "Drug Czar." The NDPB's successor, the ONDCP, created in 1988, meant that DOS was sent back to square one. It had to start rebuilding its clout within the new institution. DOS responded with many of the same ploys it had used with the NDPB to show ONDCP that it was still the premier agency in control of the foreign drug war. In 1989, when the ONDCP finally got started, State often left its liaison seats unfilled at the

ONDCP and even the El Paso Intelligence Center (EPIC).[7] The ploys were, of course, a sheer power game to demonstrate their influence on the subject. ONDCP was handled in the same way as the NDPB had been.

Diplomacy and Turf Abroad

The domestic interaction between State and NDPB (and later its successor, the ONDCP) is interesting enough already, but as the war on drugs moved abroad, State moved aggressively to control fully all U.S. agents working the drug war in South America. State personnel established their own narcotics units within the "country teams" (CT). The "country teams" were composed of personnel from all the other agencies participating in the drug war. To assure its control over these "country teams, State appointed a narcotics coordinator, usually the Deputy Chief of Mission (DCM), and sometimes another diplomat or FSO appointed officially as the head of the Narcotics Affairs Units (NAU) of the embassy.[8] These narcotics teams within CTs included representatives from various U.S. agencies, including the military and numerous law enforcement and intelligence agencies.[9] The narcotics teams were responsible for developing counter-narcotics plans, assigning responsibilities, and coordinating all the operations of U.S. agencies waging the drug war abroad. Narcotics CT personnel also reported on progress made in foreign countries and supplied valuable input for the creation of new programs and plans at home. In many ways, country teams became the first line warriors of all U.S. anti-narcotics efforts abroad.[10] Though headed by the DCM or a DOS-designated person, narcotics CTs were under the authority of the Ambassador.

At first glance, the drug war lines of authority from DOS's INM to the Ambassador to the narcotics CTs appear both sensible and clear. But the multi-organizational arrangements within U.S. Embassies' CTs and then within drug war teams are, in reality, ideal for the proliferation of inter-agency struggles. There were simply too many agencies, with too many interests, represented at the narcotics CT table. For the student of the drug war it quickly became evident that membership in the narcotics CT did not guarantee that participants' interests coincide. As Sherman Henson put it, while "inside the beltway [Washington, DC] there is only one individual who is in legitimate line of command over everybody. In the U.S. Embassy meeting room [abroad], where you have a representative from each agency, the lines of command are less clear." Although most country team members acknowledge that "at a post abroad, the Ambassador was the ultimate authority, if you ask the Administrator of the DEA whether the Ambassador can tell the [DEA] country attaché what to do, the Administrator will indignantly tell you that there are all sorts of reasons why he can't or should not." The problem, Henson further explained, is that the Ambassador can tell you to pack your bags, get on a plane, and get out of the country within 24 hours.[11] And sometimes Ambassadors used that prerogative or at least threatened to do so.

Indeed, DOS was quickly overwhelmed because throughout the 1980s multiple U.S. government agencies moved to operate abroad and set up various offices in other countries in order to conduct the drug war. The many moves by various agencies implied direct challenges to the authority of DOS in making and implementing foreign drug policy. DOS had to be prepared to act aggressively to defend its jurisdiction over the foreign drug war. To allow any degree of autonomy to any one agency would mean for State opening Pandora's Box. DOS had to find ways to rein in the many agencies seeking actively to operate abroad—or risk having its foreign policy making power further eroded until DOS became one more agency operating abroad. The question was now, how to keep a firm hold of the numerous activities that other agencies would be conducting in foreign land? What were the channels of action open to State to control the foreign drug war?

There are available formal and informal channels of action in order to bring about an actor's preferences. State happened to have resorted to two important *formal* channels of action in order to protect its turf. State personnel became determined not to allow these to be wrestled away and, in fact, used these formal channels of action quite effectively to keep a short leash on the personnel and activities of other agencies operating abroad. One of these sources of control goes back to the Kennedy administration. President Kennedy, in various National Security Action memoranda (NSAM), ordered that the foreign aid budget be separated from all budget items (NSAM-1) and issued orders that all foreign aid plans be reorganized (NSAM-6). Then, in a directive to DOS, President Kennedy ordered that all U.S. governmental activities be centralized under the control of the Ambassador in each country. This directive, mentioned even today in every letter of ambassadorial designation, was often cited by DOS personnel to the members of other anti-drug agencies operating abroad as giving DOS all jurisdictions over any *official* U.S. action abroad. No matter whom an agent worked for at home, DOS personnel often reminded other agencies' personnel abroad, that they worked for the Ambassador first, then for their agency. As John Hensley (1999 interview) of U.S. Customs, put it,

> You work for the Ambassador. You work for your own agency only secondarily. When you are at the Embassy, it's made clear to you, the Ambassador is in charge. . . . You are part of [his] team. So, if the Ambassador really doesn't want you doing anything, you are not going to do it.

Similarly, every FSO interviewed agreed that it was a priority to let members of other government agencies stationed abroad know that whatever is done abroad must be first approved by DOS before its implementation. In all planning, programming, and implementation, the Ambassador is the ultimate arbiter. FSOs, of course, took care to explain to other agencies' personnel why State must vet all their activities abroad. The official justification does not look like bureaucratic politics. In fact, it appears, like in every other case, quite reasonable. DOS personnel generally argue that maintaining a close tab on the activities of other agencies abroad is crucial for good relations with other countries because it centralizes all actions enabling a coherent U.S. policy. A coherent policy was portrayed as beneficial to the job of State and the resulting good status of relations with the host government, it was argued, benefited the overall undertakings of U.S. foreign policy. Everything, FSOs argued, was the ultimate responsibility of the Ambassador. If something went wrong and serious recriminations ensued by a foreign government, it was the Ambassador and his team who had to repair the damage. And to many FSOs, much of the damage is done by "rogue" LEA agents and military personnel operating outside the approval, consent and supervision of the Ambassador in turn. As Mel Levitsky put it, "the Ambassador and DOS have ultimate jurisdiction over any actions or operations they might want to carry out in foreign land." Then he went on to add that Ambassadors and FSOs are particularly concerned with "rogue operations" by other agencies and, therefore, they had to keep a watchful eye on everyone (Levitsky, 1999 interview). Such were the arguments under which most Ambassadors and DCMs protected their authority and strongly exercised their right to know and vet all the details of every LEA or military-led anti-narcotics operation before it was carried out.[12] These stands look less coherent, however, when viewed under a different light. If the Ambassador was not interested and preferred a hands-off approach to the drug war, for example, the rest of DOS personnel at the Embassy took on the role of scrutinizing very closely any action by other bureaucracies picking up the ambassadors slack in defending the interests of State before other agencies. This fact alone suggests that maintaining control and preventing any other agency from encroaching on State's jurisdiction was considerably more important than success or failure in the drug war.

The second source of formal power to which DOS bureaucrats resorted to keep close control of the drug war abroad is the 1988 Anti-Drug Abuse Act which gave the Secretary of State responsibility for coordinating all assistance provided by the United States in support of counter-narcotics efforts. State diplomats and FSOs are fond of citing to other agencies' anti-drug personnel operating abroad whenever the latter protest imposed limits on their activities. That law reads as follows,

> Consistent with subtitle A of Title I of the Anti-Drug Abuse Act of 1988, the Secretary of State shall be responsible for coordinating all assistance provided by the United States Government to support international efforts to combat illicit narcotics production and trafficking.[13]

This law is important because it enabled DOS to eliminate an important source of influence and leverage that other agencies may conceivably have in the foreign drug war, namely, the items in their own budgets dedicated to anti-drug operations abroad. Since 1988, those funds had to be concentrated in the Embassy and disbursed by State as its personnel saw fit. That was the equivalent of giving DOS the power of the purse in the drug war abroad, a fact that made many a drug war bureaucracy extremely resentful of State. Moreover, all foreign aid—and nearly all drug traffic related aid to foreign countries is considered foreign aid—must, by law, be channeled through DOS. The result of this was that it became impossible for any other U.S. agency, outside DOS, to spend a single dollar in the drug war that was not first approved by State and went through the Ambassador and DOS personnel at U.S. Embassies. This gave DOS enormous power and control over the activities of other agencies. State had become, as an interviewee put it, the landlord that rents and pays for all U.S. activities abroad, although it may later bill the sums spent to the agency that conducted the operation,

> We look at DOS as the landlord. They bill us for everything. When you are part of the Country Team, you're a renter of Embassy space. You pay a premium for everything, [including] your housing. And they are the landlord. They tell you where to live. They tell you how big your office can be. You can protest it, but it's like dealing with a landlord. . . .[14]

The 1988 Anti-Drug Abuse Act provision on foreign aid is an important document for DOS and constantly waved by DOS personnel before other agencies' bureaucrats as a reminder that all operations abroad are under the direct jurisdiction and control of State. The fact that all anti-drug foreign assistance for law enforcement operations abroad is paid for through INM makes it impossible for other agencies personnel to initiate any action without Embassy personnel knowing about it (Snyder, 1999 interview).

This particular examples shows why formal channels of influence and the willingness to use them is crucial for bureaucratic politics. State became very effective at using such channels of action to bring about its preferences and to protect its autonomy from encroachment by other agencies. Although other agencies appeal to informal channels of action, the reality is that State does not have a particularly strong set of allies and patrons in the U.S. domestic political scene and must consequently seek to maximize its leverage based on the statutes that give it a say in official U.S. actions abroad. Other agencies have not been able to reduce the statutory leverage that State enjoys.

Informal Channels of Influence and Control

Exacerbating State's need to keep firm control of all anti-drug activities by other U.S. agencies is the fact that over time the number of agencies operating abroad has grown to more than thirty, with quite a few of these involved in the foreign drug war. But even as the number of agencies operating abroad grew substantially, State's resources deteriorated over time to the point that Ambassadors lack the resources "necessary to coordinate and oversee the resources and personnel deployed to their missions by a myriad of agencies."[15] Indeed, at many Embassies, non-DOS personnel outnumber State personnel. This is certainly true in the major drug-producing countries of Latin America. This situation forced State to become a very efficient agency in the exercise of its authority to defend its turf in the drug war.

One example of State's efficient bureaucratic control abroad is the use of two specific ploys that DOS Embassy personnel impose on other agencies: clearance and reporting. And while State does have the statutory authority to clear every U.S. action abroad and to demand periodical reports on it, FSOs and ambassadors appeared to employ this clearance and reporting requirement more as an instrument to guard their turf at Embassies and missions from encroachments by other agencies than as planning and evaluation mechanisms for success in the international drug war. The extent to which State's personnel go to keep a close eye on the activities of other agencies is stated in a cable,

> . . . many hours are spent in cables, phone calls, etc., trying to insure that everyone stays within their limits.[16]

Although this statement is made in the form of a complaint by an FSO stationed abroad, it is not sheer coincidence that these strict clearance and reporting requirements were demanded. In effect, the high level of control that Embassy personnel impose on other agencies work has been the source of frustrations and complaints by other drug war agencies. The fleet-footed, independent-minded DEA agents are one example. Accustomed to having great flexibility on the field, it took DEA agents a long time to learn to comply with DOS's clearance and reporting requirements. Part of the reasoning behind Administrator Bonner's attempt to build a DEA interdiction capability of its own was DEA's frustration with its dependence on other agencies (and their assets) to accomplish its drug enforcement mission. DEA agents considered that DOS had excessive discretionary power over DEA's operations abroad. Its field agents did not appreciate having to clear and then report their every move to DOS personnel at U.S. Embassies.[17]

In addition, DOS appears continually preoccupied with protecting its image in Washington. The disagreements between Embassy personnel and LEA officers, such as those that emerged in the Embassy in La Paz, Bolivia, between the 29 DEA permanent agents and the 31 NAS's employees over what should be done and when, had a debilitating effect on the execution of the operational aspects of drug policy.[18] These disagreements tend to undermine the well functioning of CT efforts. This in turn has the potential of making the Ambassador appear incompetent and DOS's drug war abroad a failure—an image State can ill afford in Washington. So, when disagreements emerge, DOS generally preferred to find a solution before word got to Washington regarding turf battles at Embassies. Although sometimes solutions were a compromise, these compromises tended to favor State's assertion of its jurisdictional power over the foreign drug war. Regardless of the solution, disputes often gave rise to many long meetings at Embassy rooms and often the disputes reached Washington anyway (Bowers, 2000 interview).

Oddly, in the drug war, State did not appear focused on exercising these control ploys in order to expand its budgetary share on Capitol Hill, a logical inference in bureaucratic politics. In spite of the ballooning anti-drug budget, State hardly profited materially. There simply did not appear to be a great interest in "more and more money."[19] Instead, although there were increases in INM's anti-narcotics budget, State's control ploys appeared designed to contain and maybe even reverse the gradual erosion of its autonomy on foreign policy matters, including the international drug war. In view of this, we can plausibly conclude that it is entirely possible that government agencies value autonomy even more than they value resources.

State and Capitol Hill

From analyzing DOS's overall behavior in the drug war, it is possible to conclude as fact that State is highly concerned with its image in Washington—though normal to any government agency—it could also be interpreted as being a matter of preserving its autonomy and protecting the Department from congressional meddling and criticism. Agencies profoundly dislike congressional oversight, even if they know and understand it as a reality of American political life. In the case of State, it is somewhat evident that this concern had more to do with fending off congressional discipline than with being effective or efficacious in the drug war. From a bureaucratic politics perspective, the behavior of State in the drug war has been mostly on the defensive not just for historical reasons but also because of the emergence of multiple contenders for the making of foreign drug policy. DOS's "defensiveness" in the drug policy field only increased as the drug war abroad grew.

Congressional dynamics also exacerbated DOS's rather cagey reactions in the drug war as well. Through the George H.W. Bush administration, the drug war had a high profile in Congress. Members of Congress were under enormous pressure to show "results" to their constituencies. In the international drug war, State's success in controlling all activities also meant that State could not simply be inconspicuous about its role in the drug war. If it controlled the purse and all anti-drug activities abroad, success or failure could also be attributed to State. DOS bureaucrats were quite aware of this. DOS personnel were often "hauled up to Congress" to participate in congressional hearings regarding progress in the drug war in South America. In a 1992 hearing, for example, Mel Levitsky and Bernard Aronson's had to make major efforts to defend DOS and INM from the onslaught of Senator John F. Kerry and others over the performance of State in the drug war and the overall results of U.S. efforts abroad.[20] In that hearing, Senator Kerry cited a GAO report that maintained that there was little evidence that drug war aid, an area managed by INM, was used effectively and as intended. Thus, an important task of drug war State bureaucrats vis-à-vis Congress became defending the DOS against harsh criticism from Congress as the drug war appeared as losing enterprise. Mr. Aronson and Mr. Levitsky, for example, had to defend State's record stating that the GAO report Senator Kerry cited referred only to one country, Colombia, but that in Peru and Bolivia the aid programs were being very successful. Aronson went on to say that the criteria used by the GAO report could be the culprit in why the numbers did not look good. The negative, he suggested, was being emphasized and a lot of positive was being omitted.

Inter-agency dynamics also put State in a tough spot to defend. All bureaucrats are sometimes forced to question other agencies' reports and evaluation criteria and to exalt their own record, independently of the facts on the ground. State bureaucrats often attributed failures to other agencies in what could be viewed as clearly a defensive position designed to repair the image of State and stave off further criticism that could jeopardize State's control over the drug war abroad if Congress were to declare it incompetent and reorganize drug war lines cutting into State's jurisdictional power. This would be the ultimate threat to State and it had to be avoided at all costs. Although it was often chastised by Congress for individual failures in the drug war, there was never a very serious threat from Capitol Hill to shave off State's jurisdiction over the international aspects of the war on drugs.

Examining the relationship between Capitol Hill and State, it is obvious that the politics of bureaucracy are not entirely directed at other agencies. Studying government agencies hardly makes sense if their relationship to Congress is not taken into account. Although the Executive branch is also important, Congress is the crucial life-line of bureaucracy. Much of the politics of a bureaucracy is both elicited by and directed toward legislative bodies. Because of the nature of the legislature-bureaucracy relationship, it is impossible to organize a bureaucracy without unintended perverse incentives and disincentives. The funding and oversight powers of Congress in particular provide bureaucracies with incentives that both create and preserve organizational behaviors designed to help them cope with congressional pressures and demands. Even for organizations such as DOS, with its lack of a permanent and solid constituency inside the United States, it is difficult to escape the oft-unhealthy dynamics of congressional processes.[21] "The American constitutional framework provides especially with respect to the bureaucracy a set of opportunities, incentives and lacunae that invites assertiveness and struggle" (Aberbach, 1990, pp. 7-8). Thus the irrationalities of which governmental organizations are often accused may sometimes be natural and calculated responses by organizations to congressional dynamics—as could be the tendency to hide or manipulate information so as to present rosier scenarios.

Regarding the proverbial "power of the purse," a major difficulty that DOS faces is that there is often a gap, and sometimes a serious lag[22] between the funds *authorized* by Congress and the funds *appropriated* by Congress. The anti-narcotics Andean Initiative of the Bush Administration is an example. The $2.2 billion dollars authorized to be spent over five years in the major anti-drug offensive in South America were never fully appropriated. The gap created difficulties for drug war diplomats. First, it became very hard for DOS personnel to make accurate assessments of the effectiveness of the Initiative's programs because many programs were cut short. The planned effect of the Initiative's programs was never realized because the programs were not "given a chance to work." There were also problems with the lag between authorization and appropriation of funds for the Initiative. For example, in a cable from the U.S. Embassy in Bogotá, Colombia, DOS employees complain that,

> Oddly enough, we get caught in the planning/budget cycle trap. We attempt to estimate realistic source requirements for FY1993, units, equipment, and programs whose effectiveness have not yet been tested because FY1990 program resources are still in the pipeline . . . a year and a half into the process . . . monies [for the U.S. mission in La Paz, Bolivia] . . . ultimately did not become available for six months hence. [23]

Congress, nevertheless, demanded "results" and chastised the lack of effectiveness of the Initiative. It often became a practice among bureaucrats to find ways to preempt chastisement, embarrassment and avoid threats to the agency from members of Congress. To satisfy Congress' constant demands for reports on the effectiveness of anti-narcotics programs, DOS often repeated the same numbers in report after report and generally presented rosy scenarios regarding progress in anti-narcotics programs.[24] Inevitably, the process provided diplomats with incentives to manipulate DOS reports to emphasize the positive and deemphasize the negative. This in turn was the source of numerous congressional accusations that diplomats' view of the world was a very rosy view—yet it may not be because they see the world that way but because they prefer to save themselves generous doses of congressional badgering, a position that constitutes defending the autonomy of the organization from its political masters.[25] Another important consequence of the lag and the gap between authorization and appropriation is that the process might provide an incentive for governmental organizations to request more money than might otherwise be needed. What may sometimes be seen as organizational imperialism may be a calculated response to congressional behavior.

In addition to what congressional dysfunctional budgetary behavior adds to the strain drug war agencies already face, the congressional power of oversight also contributes to the development and nourishment of bureaucratic pathologies. Because of the intense interest of Congress in the drug war, DOS was increasingly under pressure to produce numerous reports on the effectiveness of anti-narcotics programs.[26] As Mel Levitsky put it, "if you look at the law that has been passed, signed by the President, passed by Congress, it requires us to report so much..." DOS was required to produce numerous reports on the progress in the drug war. As of 1992, INM alone was required to produce 39 reports annually.[27] This level of congressional micro-management of the drug war led DOS to "cook the books." DOS reported the same data over and over because often not much had changed on the ground from one report to the next. A quick survey of various reports over the years reveals that they often look alike year after year, with only marginal changes and updates from one to another. This kind of congressional micro-management also obliges government agencies to report "optimistic" figures for fear of being criticized by Congress for lack of progress. The 1992 annual certification report of the State Department's INM, for example, states that,

> In 1991, for the second year in a row, the USG-led anti-drug effort registered important gains. The most salient progress occurred in the Western Hemisphere, where governments stepped up their coordinated campaign against the cocaine cartels. By year's end, several important indicators showed that the effort was paying off: coca cultivation was down, US-bound cocaine seizures reached an all-time high, and traffickers came under great pressure.[28]

At the same time, Andean Ridge country reports and other independent assessments suggested otherwise. In some estimates, coca production was up and seizure figures, while "higher," were unclear since there was no base line against which to compare them. Moreover, the touted foreign cooperation was judged by some to be purely perfunctory. Sometimes the gap between DOS's figures and others' figures regarding progress in the drug war was wider than at other times, but there was always a variance. And it may be no one's fault. It is very hard to tell what the exact numbers are because the base line regarding the production and trafficking of illegal drugs is at best an educated guess.

Congressional budgetary and oversight dynamics, together with inter-agency competition, created an overall unhealthy environment in the international drug war. In that environment, anti-drug agencies—as evidenced by the Department of State and U.S. Embassies in South America—were forced to react, producing bureaucratic pathologies because the ultimate goal ceases to be to win the drug war but to play the bureaucratic political game in such a way that the agency is able to stave off any damage to its image and thereby to its jurisdiction or material resources. In effect, the war on drugs was relegated to a secondary plane. Organizational goals became the priority.

Organizational Culture: The Diplomatic Corps

Clearly, the behavior of the State Department was heavily influenced by bureaucratic politics. However, like "cops" and "soldiers," diplomats are also entirely susceptible to the influence of the behaviors that flow from the organization's culture. State has a defined culture, a diplomatic culture, which guides the behavior of its employees and often determines the overall reaction of the organization to external stimuli. If this is so, we should be able to discern a diplomatic culture that guides the diplomatic corps' way of thinking about policy problems and solutions in the drug war as well as the mechanism by which the culture of State influences the final actions of its members.

The Bureau that Nobody Wanted

The Assistant Secretary for International Narcotics and Law Enforcement Affairs (INL), known in the 1980s as the Bureau of International Narcotics Matters (INM), reports to the Under Secretary for Global Affairs. The bureau develops, coordinates, implements, and supervises DOS's international narcotics control activities. It is also responsible for developing, coordinating, and implementing U.S. policy and programs directed at U.S. government objectives abroad on criminal justice issues. INL also supervises the activities of the Office of Resource Management responsible for financial planning, budget execution, personnel management, administration, and acquisition management in the war on drugs. INL works closely with both U.S. Embassies abroad and foreign governments in the implementation of anti-narcotics policy and programs.[29] The agency is dedicated to addressing concerns regarding the illegal drug supply coming from abroad and the desire to increase diplomatic pressure on foreign governments to aid the United States in its war against drugs.[30]

From very early on, however, it became clear that the diplomatic corps disliked the issue of illegal drugs. They had come into it not because they thought it an important national interest but because they had to do so in order to prevent the further erosion of DOS's jurisdictional power over foreign policy. The issue of narcotics was not seen as directly pertinent to diplomacy, but was regarded as an irritant and a distraction to the central work of DOS. INM was, from the beginning, an "unwanted bureau." Up until Mel Levitsky became head of INM, diplomats and FSOs steered clear of assignments at INM. INM ranked low in the hierarchy of desirable posts within State. This lack of acceptance of INM within DOS is well explained by the organizational culture of the State Department. DOS is charged with establishing and maintaining relations with foreign governments. Drugs is generally a diplomatic irritant and therefore not a contributor to the major mission of the State Department. Hardly anybody within State was convinced that the drug war was something that State should wage. State was not in the business of conducting wars; it was in the business of making peace. The drug war could only be a distraction to the important business of maintaining smooth inter-governmental relations. Within State as within the military before, the mission was rejected, which confirms the idea that organizations will at a minimum neglect and at a maximum reject missions that are not perceived as being compatible with the fundamental culture of the organization. The marginal place that INM occupied within State confirms that secondary missions within an organization will not reach a central place. Like at the Pentagon, the drug war mission was compartmentalized and accommodated within DOS in ways that would not distract the organization from the tasks that are considered central to it.[31] This case also shows that agencies seek out their preferred problems and solutions rather than seek to grow randomly and imperiously. It was very likely that Congress would have granted greater resources to State for the drug war, if it had requested them. Many of the resources for the drug war were even granted by Congress without a request from State. DOS took what it was given, without pressing for further resources. State's lack of assertiveness in pursuing greater budgets for the drug war appears to indicate something that had already become evident. Government agencies may say yes to growth, but only if that growth follows the lines of the organization's culture. An organizational culture analysis of the State Department confirms what was already discovered in the other two cases, that there is such a thing as unwanted resources—when these impose an unwanted mission on the organization.

DOS and Its Central Mission: First Things First

DOS considered its primary responsibility the maintenance of good relations with foreign governments. Narcotics could not be allowed to monopolize or cloud relations with foreign governments. While Congress tried to cajole State to take a hard line against countries considered "not cooperating" with the drug war, DOS ran a rear-guard effort to soften any sanctions mandated by Congress against other governments. It is not a coincidence that starting in 1986, Congress mandated the application of an infamous "certification" process which involved "certifying" those governments cooperating with the U.S. in the drug war and "decertifying" those that were deemed uncooperative. In a way, the certification process was a way of forcing State to involve harder diplomacy in dealing with governments of illegal drug producing nations. State, expectedly, resisted the process. A survey of the annual reports of the decertification process shows that the overwhelming majority of the decertified countries were nations with whom the United States had no diplomatic relations anyway. Many of these nations recommended for decertification by DOS were nations that were not really considered drug-producing nations or transit zones for illegal drugs by any stretch of the imagination. Iran, for example, in spite of a near-zero tolerance for drug production and traffic, has been decertified continuously.[32] Colombia, Mexico and other Latin American countries were not really decertified, except on rare occasions and the penalties were mostly waved anyway. It was clear that State did not want to "rock the boat" and preferred to punish easy targets that produced no real consequences on its own diplomatic mission.

In this regard, INM's role in the decertification process was complicated by the multilayered nature of the dealings of State with other governments. INM, for example, had to deal not only with other government agencies for which the issue of illegal narcotics is not a central issue but also with some bureaus within State that had a different agenda, often removed from the drug war. The Bureau of Latin American Affairs is one example. It served as a constant advocate and apologist for various Latin American countries whose performance in the narcotics issue has been less than that required by Congress and which INM would have had to decertify if it followed the rules. Thus, the process was mired not only in the inter-agency struggles between departments but also in the inter-bureau struggles within State itself. Overall though, the issue of drugs was seen as counter to the central mission of State as an organization. Under this reasoning, drugs could not be allowed to interfere with other important issues in U.S. foreign relations—such as maintaining good relations with Latin America. INM's position was quite weakened by this understanding and there was little its bureaucrats could do but negotiate their annual certification stand with other bureaucrats and often declare as certified countries that would have been easily decertified.

The Forest and the Trees: Bureaucracies and Parochialism

State is by definition an agency that deals with multiple issues in many regions of the world. DOS continually makes the argument that State and its Embassies cannot be allowed to be captured by a single issue. Instead, they claim, State has to worry about economics, democracy, development, technology and weapons, human rights, terrorism and maintaining U.S. presence and interests abroad. In the "big picture," narcotics are but one aspect among many (Baker, 1999 interview). In a hearing, for example, State personnel argued that,

> While the Department of State as an institution and agency of the U.S. government was to control the anti-drug activities of each Country Team, it also had other interests in each country, including promoting democracy, open and competitive economies and human rights issues among others.[33]

In a similar vein, Bernard Aronson of State argued that,

> . . . we must recognize that in Latin America, the war against drugs is also a fight to defend democracy and to preserve the natural environment. . . . An alternative economic development [plan] is an essential part of the counter-narcotics strategy. . . . Progress in such crucial issues such as human rights is only possible through sustained engagement.[34]

Thus, DOS argues, the organization is in there for the long haul, to take care of many more issues than just the war on drugs, while other agencies are there to "take care of one problem" and then they will be gone.[35] By the late 1980s, when the Andean Strategy was being designed, State, through INM, insisted that the drug war should include five elements: crop control, developmental assistance, enforcement of drug laws, training for LEAs, and public education campaigns against drugs and drug use (Menzel, 1996, p. 29). In addition, CT activities should include micro-credits for economic development, immunization programs for children, crop substitution efforts, food programs, drug awareness programs, and even scholarships to familiarize people with democratic processes. And all of these as part of an anti-drug program designed by INM![36] The approach, State argued, should be a comprehensive approach of deep and continual engagement of the whole society of the target countries.[37] As former Secretary of State Baker (1999 interview) said,

> DEA are the hardest liners, of course, on the question of narcotics . . . they would like a free hand to just go in any of these countries and cowboy the operation in whatever way they like. But that is not how the real world works. You've got to consider all of these other national interests. We have a national interest in the war on drugs, but we also have a national interest in good relationships with other countries around the world.

This argument was not welcome in other government agencies, particularly those that dealt with single issues, such as DEA. DEA argued that crop eradication had no effect on the overall drug problem. They showed little faith in interdiction and other aspects of the drug war (Burke, 2000 interview). Thus while DOS was convinced that they had the "whole picture" and that other agencies were too parochial in their understanding of the context of the drug problem, other agencies viewed State as uninterested in the drug problem. In the field, these interpretations of the problem provoked conflicts between State and other agencies. The argument that State had the "big picture," while other agencies had the "narrow picture," often led diplomatic agents to restrain, modify, or even cancel an anti-drug operation on account of other non narcotics-related considerations. This led many LEA anti-drug bureaucrats to doubt State's commitment to the drug war and often provoked virulent reactions among non-State drug war bureaucrats who complained bitterly that State had no appreciation for the damage that drugs were doing to the nation. The clashing conceptions of the issue as "broad and complex" or as "narrow and simple" (the standard views) were probably neither right nor wrong. They were instead two visions diametrically opposed to each other. Such visions of the issue were the logical product of the function that each agency was designed to perform. State's mission is inevitably broad and multifaceted whereas DEA's mission is narrowly focused. Drugs are the sole issue that preoccupies DEA. It is quite understandable that when State postponed or even canceled an anti-drug operation on account of other considerations, DEA, whose central focus was that alone, did react with outrage; it was its entire agenda that was being put on hold. State diplomats, however, would not sacrifice their focus on the maintenance of good relations with other governments for a single anti-drug operation. The operation had to await a more propitious moment when State would see the way ahead to avoid stressing the international relationship heavily.

Going Native: State Department Clientelism and the Drug War

Diplomats are often accused of being unpatriotic. This charge emerges from the tendency of many FSOs (and some diplomatic appointees) to develop a sense of advocacy on behalf of the host country in which they are assigned to serve. This sense of advocacy amounts to a sort of "clientelism," which is what in turn raises questions regarding the patriotism of diplomats.[38] Some presidents have complained about this. President Lyndon B. Johnson perceptively discerned this tendency. As Rubin put it, President Johnson told "a startled Indian ambassador as he left a White House meeting in 1968" to tell the Prime Minister of India, Indira Ghandi, not to worry because "She's got two ambassadors workin' for her…you here and [U.S. Ambassador Chester] Bowles over there [in New Delhi]."[39] At another level, this "clientelism" has often driven a wedge between FSOs and the more transient diplomatic political appointees who sometimes claim that FSOs are all too willing to sacrifice U.S. goals and interests in order to preserve a congenial relationship with the host country. In *Secrets of State*, Rubin (1985, p. 128) refers to this issue in the following way,

> . . . defenders of political appointees believe FSOs are too eager to maintain cordial relations with the country in which they serve, becoming more concerned with the nation's requirements than with U.S. interests.

The explanation to the development of clientelism at DOS can be found in the social function that State was created to perform and which gives rise to the fundamental conception that cordial country-to-country relations are the goal. But, how do diplomats make the leap between their explicit mission and the attitudes and basic assumptions about what they really do? It is crucial to clarify this before proceeding to examine whether clientelism has any effect on State's organizational behavior in the drug war. The formal, explicit mission of State reads:

> . . . the Department of State is the lead U.S. foreign affairs agency, and the Secretary of State is the President's principal foreign policy advisor. The Department advances U.S. objectives and interests in shaping a freer, more secure, and more prosperous world through its primary role in developing and implementing the President's foreign policy.[40]

This mission implies that State bureaucrats both at home and abroad must seek ways to represent and advance U.S. interests in foreign lands. Viewed this way, the mission appears to be fairly clear and simple. However, besides the difficulty of discerning *what* those interests are—and they do change over time, there is the difficulty of discerning *how* U.S. interests are best represented and advanced overseas. For a very long time, State bureaucrats believed that those interests were best represented and advanced *by building and maintaining good relations* with foreign governments. One corollary to this is that relations, when broken, must be repaired as quickly as it is possible. Another corollary is that one must avoid anything that may adversely affect relations with foreign governments. Thus the central focus of State bureaucrats has been the building and maintenance of functional relations with foreign governments, sometimes even when these governments operate against current U.S. interests or fail to cooperate with U.S. policy goals.[41] The way diplomats have come to conceive their central mission and the consequent activities that they perform or cease to perform from day to day have often been the source of serious misunderstandings—cultural clashes—between State and other governmental agencies operating abroad.

The differences among the cultures of DOS and other government agencies, principally anti-drug LEAs, stand out by comparing the priorities of each group. LEAs ask whether U.S. interests—e.g., stemming the flow of illegal drugs—should be sacrificed for the sake of maintaining cordial relations with foreign governments. State diplomats turn this question on its head and ask whether specific U.S. interests—e.g., stemming the flow of illegal drugs— should be pursued blindly at the expense of cordial relations with a host government. These questions reveal the fundamental difference between how each views its role. State bureaucrats consider cordial relations an asset for U.S. interests, even in fighting illegal drugs, while other U.S. government operatives view State's protective seal as an obstacle to policy success. In the drug war, disagreements seem to be heightened and reveal what the culturally determined priorities of each agency are and how these often collide with one another.

To be fair, State does criticize host countries sometimes, but it is clear that often State bureaucrats do become advocates for the country they are assigned to.

Diplomats tend to soften the faults of other governments and even self-flog in defense of the host country. The following statement taken from a cable from Bogotá, Colombia, is one example,

> How many times have we as individuals, agencies, mission teams, or as a government as a whole criticized an HC [host country] for not implementing a new law or regulation or for not taking swift action to establish a CN [counter-narcotics] agency, or deploy personnel to a more target-rich environment? A smug USG [U.S. government], more often than not, interprets such actions as foot dragging probably attributed to corruptive influence. [But] We take a year or more to implement a simple project and no one says anything.[42]

State's tendency to protect cordial relations has caused it to paint rosy scenarios where reality is a lot darker. On July 30, 1991, Acting Secretary of State Larry Eagleburger signed a determination stating that Peruvian security forces were not engaged in a consistent pattern of gross violations of internationally recognized human rights, that the human rights situation in Peru was improving, and that the military answered to civilian control. Interestingly, a rebuttal to this statement could be found in State's own Country Reports on Human Rights Practices for 1990. It said that Peru's security forces were responsible for widespread and egregious human rights violations. Moreover, at a March 1991 congressional hearing, State's Bernard Aronson described Peru's security forces record of abuses as "long-standing and systematic."[43] But the reports came from different parts of the organization. This tendency of diplomats to soften the shortcomings and deficiencies of foreign governments or to advocate their interests in Washington has created an underlying conflict among government agencies in drug war because, as he said,

> The information that would provide the grist for [the foreign drug war] decisions was to be provided by the State Department, an agency whose views are driven by an entirely different set of guidelines [from law enforcement]. Simply put, optimistic figures of cocaine trafficking activities painted each year by the Department of State belie the truth.[44]

But there are exceptions to these generalities. Such exceptions are those driven by the personality of the individuals involved. Some political appointees, for example, can, and often do, place what they view as U.S. interests above cordial relations with the host country. The brazenness of some political appointees, however, often drives a wedge between them and State regular bureaucrats. Robert Gelbard, Ambassador to Bolivia, for example, is well known for having angered a lot of people in Bolivia because he pushed the Government of Bolivia very hard on issues of drug trafficking. Gelbard's attitude not only upset many Bolivians but also caused panic among FSOs. State Department personnel were horrified by the way in which Ambassador Gelbard treated the Bolivian Government. Eventually, some FSOs argued,

Gelbard gained so much ill-will in Bolivia that he had to leave because interaction with the Bolivian government became very difficult.[45] FSOs saw Gelbard's attitude as an obstacle to progress in all matters, including the war on drugs, even as Gelbard saw his attitude as the right attitude for doing something about what he considered the central interest of the U.S. in Bolivia. Not surprisingly, Ambassador Gelbard was popular among LEA agents stationed in Bolivia. He was a hero and a patriot to them.[46] He was, however, profoundly unpopular among State bureaucrats both at home and abroad.

In another case, DEA agents in Colombia in the early 1990s began to develop a deep contempt for what they perceived as an excessive "tolerance" of State for the drug trafficking problem around the Colombian cartels and the Colombian Government. By 1994, Joe Toft, the head of DEA-Colombia became upset and quit his job. He then called a conference and leaked out confidential information that the U.S. Embassy in Colombia had kept undisclosed and that pointed to Colombia's President Ernesto Samper's involvement in drug trafficking. DOS's cautiousness in handling this delicate information made DEA agents accuse State of ignoring it. To Toft, it was unacceptable that State valued continued contact with the Colombian Government under such circumstances, however minimal these contacts were. To State personnel, continued and even relatively cordial contact was necessary in order to extract Colombian cooperation on a number of issues and even other aspects of the drug war itself. President Samper's alleged involvement with drug traffickers should not be allowed to get in the way of the many programs that State was running in Colombia. Joe Toft's conference, nevertheless, cooled relations between the U.S. and Colombia and caused a great deal of turmoil among State personnel in Colombia and at home. And perhaps State bureaucrats were right. While Toft went on with his life, State bureaucrats were left with a broken relationship that they had to repair. Joe Toft's explosive declarations are illustrative of the discrepancies in the way DOS and other organizations prefer to handle the issue of drugs. It also shows that FSOs are often frustrated because they cannot always control what other organizations do when agencies feel frustration that stems from the FSOs and diplomats' belief that cordial relations are an asset for U.S. interests, even when they do not seem to be.

DOS v. DEA: Patience and Tentativeness v. Stamina and Decisiveness

An analysis of the interaction between DOS and other drug war agencies shows that the diplomatic mind is often incompatible with the Weltanschauung of other Washington bureaucracies. This observation goes right to the heart of the fundamental culturally motivated differences between State and other drug war agencies. The diplomatic mind of State bureaucrats values specific instruments and practices that have served State well for a long time but which contrast with the "virtues" valued among cops and soldiers. One such value, for example, is ambiguity. Diplomatic life is full of uncertainties. Circumstances in the foreign policy landscape can be unchanging over a very long period of time or they can be changing abruptly and continuously from one day to the next. To cope with uncertainty, diplomats have learned to live with and even value ambiguity. Ambiguity is what enables diplomats to offer face-saving solutions to diplomatic problems or to press harder for specific concessions, depending on the circumstances. For a diplomat, what exactly is meant by what is said often implies ongoing clarification. "We hope," "possibly," and "if things work out right" are an integral part of an FSO's language. As Monteagle Stearns (1996, p. 36) put it,

> Avoiding unpleasant surprises is always an important purpose of diplomacy, but it is usually accomplished through close and careful observation of foreign conditions.

Diplomatic willingness to accept ambiguity collides with the proclivities of cops and soldiers to view persons, events, and actions in stark contrasts—black and white, good or evil and often with a strong ideological bent. DEA agents prefer to use categories that classify individuals as "criminals," "informants," "innocents;" the military uses categories such as "enemy," "target," and "ally." Diplomats feel quintessentially uncomfortable with this language. They prefer to see those same individuals, events, and actions as complex mixes of various categories that may include good and evil, black and white, where the bad may be considered an ally and the good may not necessarily be a friend. A country's dictator may be despicable from the perspective of an organization that sees human rights violations as sheer evil or from the perspective of an agency that fights illegal drugs, but that same dictator is often the person with whom State has to deal in order to protect and advance U.S. interests in that country. The tentativeness and patience of DOS bureaucrats are difficult to understand for others. They are often perceived as a lack of commitment to the drug war. Conversely, the energy and enthusiasm of LEA agents makes diplomats hold cops and soldiers suspect. Diplomats use words like "rogues" and "cowboys" to refer to DEA agents and they worry about how to "keep them in the box" (McLean, 2000 interview). Diplomats' comfort with ambiguity has important consequences for the inter-organizational environment of the drug war. Three areas stand out in this regard: measuring results, the use of rhetoric, and moral judgments. Let us turn our attention briefly to each of these aspects.

Diplomatic comfort with ambiguity collides with LEA and military penchant for concrete, measurable results. While it is clear that this penchant is often the product of bureaucratic politics, there is an important cultural component to it. The centrality of statistics in the war on drugs not only reflects the desire to fare well in the eyes of the organization's political masters, but it also the necessity of cops and soldiers to show "results" in order to feel good about the work and the contributions and progress of their organization. This need to show results evident among cops and soldiers contrasts sharply with the longer-term, more patient rhythm of diplomats who do not always expect to reap the "fruits" of their activities immediately or in tangible ways. In fact, most of the yield of diplomatic work is intangible in the short term and appreciated in the long term.

Rhetoric or language is another area where organizational cultures collide. The language of DEA agents always appears to have a sense of urgency. Threats are almost always looming large on the horizon. LEA rhetoric is more like the language used by politicians. DEA agents use terms such as "drugs and thugs," "the siege of American cities," and "public scourge." Diplomatic speak does not favor this language. This kind of discourse makes diplomats think that DEA agents are "rogues," and "cowboys" (Matano, 1999 interview). In contrast, rhetoric at State is always full of ambiguities. The mildness of diplomatic language, however, is often viewed by other drug war bureaucrats as a lack of commitment by State to ending illegal drugs. State bureaucrats know and understand the need for ambiguous and understated language. It has been useful in diplomacy for centuries. Interestingly, there is seldom a misunderstanding among diplomats as to what they mean. The difficulties in communication arise in dealing with dozens of bureaucrats from other agencies that rarely understand the need for or tolerate diplomatic discourse.

A third area where the differences between law enforcement and military personnel and diplomats emerge is the fact that the former two irradiate a great deal of passion and energy about their work. The socialization of cops and soldiers, and the risks that they may be harmed or killed in the line of duty or have to harm or kill others, involves a great deal of emotional involvement in their work. Cops and soldiers carry with them a passionate commitment to their identity as part of their agency's culture. Among diplomats, on the other hand, "the code of diplomacy stresses emotional detachment and pragmatism, expediency over morality" (Rubin, 1985, p. 233). At a subjective level, issues of good and evil are a point of contention among bureaucrats from various agencies. Whereas LEA agents visualize a moral evil, diplomats are less likely to see the matter in the absolute sense that LEA agents do. The differences in the way different agencies measure their results, the type of discourse they use regarding moral judgments have caused serious organizational culture clashes between DOS and other drug war bureaucrats.

Professionalism and the Culture of the State Department

State Department bureaucrats prefer political rather than military or law enforcement means to resolve problems and disputes. Career staff is skeptical of applying hasty moral or value judgments to international relations. FSOs are detached and cautious about what they do and what they say. Political appointees at State are to a large extent "outsiders" and are much more enthusiastic and ambitious about what can be accomplished; they are candid in their public statements and do not bother with the niceties and delicacies of diplomacy. When one compares the two groups, the career staff and the political appointee, the culture of State is generally contained in the attitudes and assumptions of career FSOs and not in the attitudes and assumptions of political appointees. Initially, many appointees believe that the cautious attitudes of the career staff sabotage their plans; many do learn, however, that the actions of the career staff seldom have anything to do with anyone at a personal level. It is State's "way of doing things." When outsiders compensate for this behavior, life generally becomes easier for everyone. Ambassador Gelbard case shows that often there is a clear distinction FSOs and appointees and the ways they conceive the work of State. The drug war has clearly demonstrated that State, like Customs, manages to operate with two subcultures, but not by keeping the two cultures separate like Customs, but by an institutional understanding of the nature of political appointees and the eventual mutual accommodation of one Weltanschauung to another. Most career staff understand that political appointees are temporary workers and they try to soften the impact that the spontaneity or enthusiasm of political appointees may have on U.S. relations with another government. State's case, in contrast with Custom's, shows that there is yet another way in which two subcultures can cohabit within an organization without provoking its demise or hindering its performance—by means of accommodation, propped up by the fact that one of the subcultures is largely transient and the other largely permanent.

Doomed to Upbeat Reporting

The section on bureaucratic politics of this chapter contains an entry titled "Defending the State Department." That section makes the argument that much of the work of State bureaucrats is to defend the organization from congressional attacks during oversight. For diplomats, however, upbeat reporting has not only a political motivation but also an organizational cultural one. While defending State through a strategy of upbeat reporting is sometimes a political strategy, in the case of State the political motivation for upbeat reporting is difficult to distinguish from what appears to be a *cultural* proclivity of diplomats for presenting rosy scenarios on the conditions and progress of U.S. interests abroad deriving from DOS mission priorities and the tendency to develop clientele relationships with foreign governments.

The involvement of State in the drug war includes plenty of examples of upbeat reporting that originates in the culture of State. As already pointed out, DOS can even be found to contradict itself. In a 1991 hearing cited above, Peru received a very positive evaluation. At the same time, DOS's Country Report on Human Rights Practices for 1990 said that Peru's

> . . . [s]ecurity forces personnel were responsible for widespread and egregious human rights violations. . . . There were widespread reports of summary executions, arbitrary detentions, and torture and rape by the military, as well as frequent reports of such abuses by the police.[47]

DOS has been accused of "cooking the books" in order to project a foreign government's positive image in Washington. In 1990, in order to improve Bolivia's record of coca elimination, the Narcotics Affairs Unit of the U.S. Embassy in La Paz, Bolivia, made a proposal that committed the Bolivian government to eradicate 1,300 hundred hectares of coca plants between January 1 and July 23. In July, if the commitment were met, the Bolivian government would receive $5.4 million for further eradication. By July, it was clear that Bolivia was not going to be able to meet that commitment. On July 21, Aníbal Aguilar Gómez, the Under Secretary for Alternative Development, met with DIRECO (Dirección de Reconversión de la Coca) officers in the Chapare region near the village of Villa Tunari. At this meeting, it was revealed that the elimination plan for the first half of 1990 had fallen 156 hectares short of the goal. In order to protect the aid for the next period, Aguilar came up with the idea that the maps should be altered in order to hide the missing 156 hectares. The Under Secretary's representatives made the case based on the importance of future U.S. aid for the overall drug efforts in Bolivia (Malamud-Goti, 1992, pp. 65-67).

Word of the ploy reached NAU officials in Cochabamba. The head of DIRECO, Mr. Zamendo, was warned not to go ahead with the ploy or a report of the maneuver would be filed at the U.S. Embassy in La Paz. Zamendo went ahead and altered the maps and, to the surprise of Cochabamba officials, the U.S. Embassy in La Paz approved DIRECO's account of eradication efforts and sent the report to Washington without even acknowledging the ploy. As a result, the aid to the Bolivian government was granted; the pertinent officials were given "due" credit; and the reputation of the program and U.S. officials in La Paz actually improved. Diplomats were willing to overlook the cooking of the books in order to protect the Bolivian Government from chastisement from Washington and to save the funds to be used in the eradication program for the second half of 1990—an at least quasi-organizational cultural motivation in our interpretation.

Thus the interest of DOS in upbeat reporting is not only political but it appears to be entangled with State's clientelist culture of "protecting" the interests of foreign governments in Washington. Upbeat reporting appears to be an area where it is difficult to disentangle bureaucratic political motivations from organizational cultural motivations. It appears that to explain State's penchant for upbeat reporting, one must appeal to a combination of both bureaucratic politics and organizational culture.

Conclusion

Diplomats came into the drug war not because they considered the drug war within their competence but because not doing so would have signified allowing other U.S. government agencies a degree of control over foreign policy—at a minimum foreign drug policy—an area which DOS considers its exclusive turf. State moved to defend its turf, a move confirmed by the actions from very early on. DOS sought to make it clear to both the NDPB and later the ONDCP that in the drug war abroad, State had all authority. Similarly, within the country teams, diplomats employed a number of tactics to keep tight control of all programs and operations. What these observations reveal is that even when agencies are relatively passive when it comes to empire building, they will become defensive and even competitive when their autonomy is encroached upon. This point offers more evidence to refine our original belief that organizations care considerably about preserving their autonomy in their area of competence, more so than about building an empire. In other words, defensive positions appear more common than offensive positions.

Interestingly, unlike LEAs, which were eager to claim credit in a highly competitive environment, DOS did not show the same zeal about the "stats." DOS's political behavior was different. Its concern with the numbers was not directed at competing with other agencies nor was it directed to empire building. State's concerns with numbers appear directly connected to congressional dynamics. State was concerned with presenting "good" statistics in order to save itself criticism from Congress more than to claim credit. DOS presented rosy scenarios and used the same information in report after report to save itself meddling by Congress rather than to claim credit for any achievements. Congressional dynamics exacerbated this problem because Congress micro-managed the drug war to some extent.

State, like the military, was initially reluctant to take on the drug war. But, unlike the Pentagon, which had to be cajoled and even coerced to do its part, DOS came on board to protect its interests—its jurisdiction over U.S. foreign policy. The case of State shows, to some extent, the limits of organizational culture. An organization will act to adopt an unwanted mission if not doing so might affect its jurisdictional power. An organization will do so even if the new mission is not considered central to the organization. Adopting the drug war mission for State meant preventing unraveling at the edges of the agency, with potentially nefarious consequences for State's autonomy in the future. But organizational culture is not useless in our analysis. The mission never became central to State's activities. In fact, the idea that organizations will isolate, or even neglect, an unwanted mission held more or less well. The drug war mission within State was lowered on the list of priorities of the Department. Moreover, the drug war mission was reconceived as a small part of a much larger diplomatic agenda. Soon the drug war included even education and economic development facets. In fact, to State, the absolutizing view that other agencies had of the drug war (e.g., DEA) was mistaking the trees for the forest.

Within DOS, DEA was continually accused of parochialism.

In a similar vein, State had a tendency to sacrifice the drug war for the sake of safeguarding their primary work: to build, maintain, and repair relationships with foreign governments. The core mission of State was not the drug war, but good relations. If the drug war was in the way of good relations, the drug war had to take a back seat. This also confirms our speculation that unwanted missions will likely be ignored when they get in the way of the organization's core tasks. Thus, as already stated, upbeat reporting was in the political interest of State inasmuch as congressional dynamics required State to perform to the satisfaction of the legislative branch but upbeat reporting seemed also motivated by the cultural dicta of State. If good relations are the goal of State, most of the actions of foreign governments will tend to be justified at some level because doing otherwise would appear, in the end, a failure in the performance of State.

Notes

1. On Oct 1, 1978, Congress, in the Foreign Relations Authorization Act for Fiscal Year 1979 (P.L. 95-426; 92 Stat. 969), authorized the position of Assistant Secretary of State for International Narcotics Matters, to be responsible for the overall coordination of the role of the Department of State in the international aspects of narcotics problems...The new Assistant Secretary, who headed the Bureau for International Narcotics Matters, replaced a Senior Advisor to the Secretary of State on Narcotics, who had served with a rank equivalent to an Assistant Secretary of State since 1971. The Department of State first supported the Department of the Treasury's Bureau of Narcotics in 1909. The title of this position was changed from International Narcotics Matters to International Narcotics and Law Enforcement Affairs, Feb 10, 1995.
Extract taken from
http://www.state.gov/www/about_state/history/officers/asinl.html.

2. See John Franklin Campbell, *The Foreign Policy Fudge Factory* (New York: Basic Books, 1971); I. M. Destler, "Making Foreign Policy: Comment," *American Political Science Review*, No. 66 (1972), 786-90; and Graham T. Allison and Peter Szanton, *Remaking Foreign Policy* (New York: Basic Books, 1976).

3. How much and when State was obliged to allow NSC to lead in foreign policy making depended largely on the preferences of the president to turn to his White House advisors rather than the State Department and on the personality of the individuals heading DOS and the NSC.

4. See *The History of The National Security Council: 1947-1997*. The text can be found at the following website: http://www.whitehouse.gov/nsc/history.html.

5. Barry Rubin, *Secrets of State: The State Department and the Struggle Over U.S. Foreign Policy* (New York: Oxford University Press, 1985); 129. See also Peter W. Rodman, "The NSC System: Why It's Here to Stay," *Foreign Service Journal* (February 1992); 24-26; and Jerel A. Rosati, *The Politics of United States Foreign Policy* (Fort Worth: Harcourt Brace College Publishers, 1993).

6. For an interesting account of the beginnings of INM at the State Department and why : was a "bureau that nobody wanted," see James J. Gormley, "Reflections of a State Depart-ıent Drug War Warrior," *Foreign Service Journal* (June 1992).

7. Interview with Al Matano, October 5, 1999. Curiously enough, DOS's liaison to :PIC was composed of people that came from Diplomatic Security (DS). These men were ardly trained to be drug agents or anything remotely related to intelligence. Diplomatic secu-ity hardly looks anything like anti-narcotics law enforcement activities. Consequently, DS li-isons often felt quite lonely in their outpost at EPIC in El Paso, Texas. This isolation was ex-cerbated by the fact that there was almost no coincidence between what DS personnel were rained to do and what other agencies' personnel at EPIC were doing. In this regard, the case f State is similar to the case made about the way the military chose to respond to the drug var: it used its readily available security detail to do a job that DS was completely unprepared nd untrained to do.

8. Narcotics Affairs Unit (NAU) was the official name until Mel Levitsky changed the ame of the subsection. It then came to be known as Narcotics Affairs Section (NAS), with all he prestige of the various other sections within the embassy. In this study, from this point on, : will be referred to as NAS.

9. For a recount of the difficulties of establishing the Peru counter-narcotics country eam and smoothing out its mission, see GAO Report, "The Drug War: U.S. Programs in Peru 'ace Serious Obstacles" (Washington, DC: General Accounting Office, 1990).

10. See Gary Williams, "State Department Narc," *Foreign Service Journal* (August 990); 22-26.

11. Interview with Sherman Henson, October 12, 1999.

12. There are variations on the level of control depending on the personality of the Am-assador. Anthony C. E. Quainton, U.S. Ambassador to Peru, is reputed to have kept a very ight control on his Embassy team, whereas Charles Richard Bowers, Ambassador to Bolivia, s said to have been more relaxed about it. When the Ambassador is lax about keeping a tight ontrol, however, the DCM and other State personnel will generally make up for the slack. 'or a quick, journalistic comparison of these two Ambassadors' styles see *The Commercial ppeal* of Memphis, TN, June 28, 1992.

13. See International Narcotics Control and United States Foreign Policy: A Compila-ion of Laws, Treaties, Executive Documents, and Related Materials, Report Prepared for the enate Caucus on International Narcotics Control and the Committee on International Rela-ions of the House of Representatives by the Congressional Research Service of the Library of 'ongress (Washington, DC: GPO, 1997); 36.

14. Hensley, 1999.

15. *State Department Reform*, Report by an Independent Task Force of the Council on oreign Relations and the Center for Strategic and International Studies (Washington, DC: 000); 7. Text available at the following website:
ttp://www.cfr.org/p/pubs/StateDepart_TaskForce.html.

16. U.S. Embassy, Bogotá, Colombia, 25 April 1991, Cable.

17. This style of diplomacy—complete control of all U.S. operations abroad through the erson of the ambassador and his collaborators—that State insists in maintaining has been re-erred to as "classic diplomacy." A study produced by The Henry L. Stimson Center argued ıat classic diplomacy is no longer adequate to represent U.S. interests successfully abroad nd "must be modified to reflect new realities," including a new institutional expression of

diplomatic representation that allows for "interagency coordination" among "the many agencies and bureaucracies . . . conducting operations overseas." See *Equipped for the Future: Managing Foreign Affairs in the 21st Century* (Washington, DC: The Henry L. Stimson Center, 1998); 3-4.

18. Many interviewees pointed out some of the conflicts between DEA and DOS personnel. Principal among these conflicts were issues having to do with aircraft support for DEA operations, approval of specific DEA operations that DOS considered likely to be irritants in U.S. relations with the host nation, and very strict reporting requirements by DOS over DEA personnel who insisted in reminding DEA agents that their programs and operations began at the embassy and ended at the embassy. See Jaime Malamud-Goti, *Smoke and Mirrors: The Paradox of the Drug War* (Boulder: Westview Press, 1992); 91-107.

19. In fact, even as State was being asked to do more in the drug war and other world issues, the international affairs budget was cut by nearly fifty percent between 1985 and 1995. See Remarks by Peter F. Krogh, "America's Diplomacy, Foreign Affairs Reporting and Diplomatic Capital," *ISD Report*, Vol. I, No. 3 (April 1995). Nevertheless, even as State's budget deteriorated in real terms, State's counter-narcotics budget actually grew steadily between 1989 and 1992.

20. *Andean Drug Initiative*, Hearing before the Subcommittee on Terrorism, Narcotics, and International Operations of the Committee on Foreign Relations of the United States Senate, 101st Congress, Second Session, February 20, 1992 (Washington, DC: GPO, 1992).

21. Presumably, the absence of a domestic constituency exacerbates the political scenario of a bureaucracy. As Aberbach puts it, American bureaucrats are likely to "pursue the interests of clienteles who can help protect their programs, and to act as advocates for interests inadequately represented through the ostensible channels of political representation. Constituencies can pressure Congress to cut some slack to certain agencies. See Joel D. Aberbach, Robert D. Putnam, and Bert A. Rockman, *Bureaucrats and Politicians in Western Democracies* (Cambridge, MA: Harvard University Press, 1981); 99.

22. I make a distinction between these two. Lag is a period of time between the authorization and the appropriation actions of Congress. A gap is the difference between the amount authorized for spending and the amount actually appropriated by Congress.

23. U.S. Embassy, Bogotá, Colombia, 25 April 1991 Cable.

24. It is possible that State Department statistics may have improved after the passage of the Government Performance Review Act, which dealt in part with the issue of government reporting.

25. Senator John F. Kerry, for example, in chastising Bernard Aronson and Melvyn Levitsky of DOS in the 1992 congressional hearing on the Andean Initiative said that he was not sure that Secretary Jim Baker's statement that "the Andean strategy has been a success in reducing the supply of cocaine to the United States" could be substantiated "[n]o matter how positive a spin we put on the facts." See "Andean Drug Initiative," *Hearing before the Subcommittee on Terrorism, Narcotics, and International Operations of the Committee on Foreign Relations of the United States Senate*, 102nd Congress, 2nd Session (February 20, 1992); 2.

26. This is exacerbated by the fact that Congress must produce its own "results" to the constituencies to which it is accountable.

27. In 1992, the INM was producing an annual International Narcotics Control Strategy Report (INCSR); a mid-year INCSR; an annual Program Operating Plan (POP); quarterly

'OPs; an annual wrap-up POP; an annual procurement estimate; an End-Use Monitoring EUM) Phase I Report; and EUM Phase II Report; an annual training requirement report; a ive-year budget projection report; four quarterly financial pipe line reports; twelve monthly ounter-narcotics activities (CN) reports; and twelve monthly CN aviation activities reports. Although the POPs are not congressionally mandated, they are produced, for a total of 39 re-orts. And this does not include the many hearings and the follow-up answers to questions hat sometimes numbered hundreds.

28. *International Narcotics*, 1992.

29. See Foreign Affairs Manual (FAM) 1 FAM 530 and 531.1 Assistant Secretary for nternational Narcotics and Law Enforcement Affairs (INL); 1-11.

30. Because this study is interested in the years 1988 to 1993, years in which INL was till known as INM, the acronym INM will be used from here onward.

31. Nevertheless, there is an important difference between the case of the military and he case of the State Department. While the mission was neglected and downgraded in the nilitary, the same has not occurred within State. The mission has actually grown and, though ot exactly a desirable one, State has taken it as part of its activities, at least with specific ountries, where drugs are an important concern for the United States. The difference, how-ver slight, is explained, I argue, by the fact that State was motivated by some bureaucratic olitics (defense of its jurisdictional power) to enter the drug war, that is, to fend off en-roachments on its foreign policy primary from other agencies. To neglect the drug mission, r even the INM, would have meant ceding power to competing and encroaching agencies. he military was not motivated by such reasons. It had nothing to lose. The mission, therefore, vas thoroughly neglected and downgraded. State simply swallowed the pill but for ulterior easons.

32. This is clearly evident from a quick review of the annual International Narcotics 'ontrol Strategy Report produced by the State Department in accordance with §489 of the oreign Assistance Act of 1961, as amended (the "FAA," 22 U.S.C. §2291).

33. *Report 101-991*, 1990.

34. *Andean Drug Initiative*, 1992, pp. 19-21.

35. Indeed, in my interviews with DOS personnel, it became puzzling to me that many f them thought that the narcotics problem was a somewhat temporary problem, one that vould eventually be resolved.

36. See *Drug Policy in the Andean Nations*, Hearings before the Senate Committee on e Judiciary, 101st Congress, 1st and 2nd Sessions, November 6, 1989, and January 18 and 1arch 22, 1990 (Washington, DC: GPO, 1989, 1990).

37. For a discussion of the difficulties that ensue from what is called a "single issue for-ign policy" and why State is correct in pursuing the study of "all sides of an issue" see Se-all H. Menzel, *Fire in the Andes: U.S. Foreign Policy and Cocaine Politics in Bolivia and eru* (Lanham: University Press of America, 1996); 106-113.

38. See David Newsom, "Are Diplomats Unpatriotic?" in *Foreign Service Journal* March 1989); and George Baker, "Clientelism in Economic Reporting," in *Foreign Service ournal* (June 1989); pp. 42-44.

39. As cited by Barry Rubin in *Secrets of State* from Roger Morris, "Clientelism in the oreign Service," *Foreign Service Journal* (February 1974); p. 24.

40. See http://www.state.gov.

41. For an insight into the consternation that a diplomatic community often goes

through when relations are affected negatively or broken see David D. Newsom, ed., *Diplomacy under a Foreign Flag: When Nations Break Relations* (Washington, DC: Institute for the Study of Diplomacy, 1990).

42. U.S. Embassy, Bogotá, Colombia, 25 April 1991 Cable.

43. See Tina Rosenberg, "Unholy Alliance: Latin American Militaries and the War on Drugs," *Foreign Service Journal* (November 1991); p. 24.

44. Holden-Rhodes 1997, p. 25.

45. See Eduardo A. Gamarra, "U.S. Bolivia Counter-narcotics Efforts During the Paz Zamora Administration: 1989-1992," in Bruce M. Bagley and William O. Walker III, *Drug Trafficking in the Americas* (Boulder, CO: Lynne Rienner Publishers, 1994); pp. 221-226.

46. Author recollection from an interview with Chris Arcos, October 14, 1999.

47. Rosenberg, 1991, p. 24.

Chapter 5
Conclusion

This book has taken a hard look at the drug war through two important lenses in the study of bureaucrats and their pathologies: bureaucratic politics and organizational culture. Both lenses proved extremely useful in discerning the problems that U.S. drug policy faces once legislation has moved from Congress to the hands of bureaucrats everywhere. The main conclusion of this work cannot be underestimated. Policy success or failure cannot be analyzed solely on the merits of the content of the legislation, funding or environmental conditions of its implementation. Policy failure and success must be looked at also in light of the material and ideological interests of the government agencies in charge of implementing the policy. Both bureaucratic politics and organizational culture are theories that can help us understand why bureaucracies do what they do. The case of the drug war is a prime example of how the interests of a particular policy can take a back seat to the interests of the organizations in charge of it.

Recapitulating Our Concepts

The fundamental premises of bureaucratic politics were the following: governmental organizations desire to maximize their material resources and their level of autonomy. Governmental organizations would like both of these goods *ad infinitum*. Because this is impossible, organizations must engage in *politics* in order to maximize one or the other or both. Therefore, the most important points where politics can be observed at work are scenarios where either resources or autonomy are at stake. Consequently, bureaucratic politics assumes that the fundamental conflict between governmental actors is either allocational or functional, depending on whether the situation (threat or opportunity) pertains to resources (allocational) or autonomy (functional). Competitive behavior for additional resources was also posited as political behavior. Accordingly, in any given situation, government agencies must assess the fundamental threats to their material resources or organizational autonomy and the key opportunities to enhance them. The stands that a governmental organization adopts when faced with a threat or an opportunity, and which constitute organizational political behavior, is classified as "defensive" or "offensive," depending on whether the situation is a threat or an opportunity to enhance the resources and autonomy of the agency. Finally, the course of action that a governmental organization adopts is shaped and colored by three factors: 1) the agencies involved; 2) the relative influence of the agencies involved; and 3) the channels of action, both formal and informal, available to an agency. In considering these elements, this study looked at two important government environments: the environment between an agency and its political masters and the environment between an agency and its fellow dwellers in a given policy space. Although other studies of bureaucratic politics focus also on interests groups, regulated interests, the public, and media, and other actors, this work assumes that the political masters of an agency and the other agencies that inhabit the same policy space should be enough to show when a government agency's behavior is motivated by politics.

But government agencies are not only motivated by politics; they are also motivated by their fundamental organizational culture. Organizational culture premises that the culture of an organization emerges from the very nature of the social function for which the organization was created. The genealogy of an organizational culture shows that it is the result of the practical experiences of an organization as its members attempt to carry out that social function. It was proposed that the emergence of a government agency's culture follows this path: 1) it starts with the legislative fiat creating the organization; 2) from which the explicit organizational mission is derived; 3) and broken into specific organizational tasks; 4) from which the functional norms and practices of the organization emerge; 5) helping members create the appropriate basic attitudes and assumptions that they carry with them as they go about performing their duties. Regardless of factual content, conceiving culture as subjective and attitudinal enables us to determine how the culture of a government agency emerges. Culture serves two important purposes for any organization: 1) internal integration and 2) external adaptation. This book was concerned primarily with the external adaptation function that culture performs. In other words, culture is what makes organizations behave similarly before external stimuli rather than what makes them behave differently. Thus we maintain that organizational behavior, when external stimuli show up at the doormat of an organization, is to a large extent determined by the organization's culture.

Through our analysis of the drug war it became evident that bureaucrats are motivated by both politics and culture. Neither analytical paradigm can best explain the overall behavior of a U.S. government agency. It is fair, therefore, to conclude that both politics and culture are important elements in understanding how U.S. government agencies operate and often the two lenses, juxtaposed, give a clearer view of why government agencies do what they do. In general both paradigms faired well collectively in explaining why the drug war has been such a difficult and painful process for all agencies involved. The importance of understanding the lessons of the drug war for understanding the future outcome of the multi-agency war on terrorism is crucial and this book clearly goes a long way in doing just that.

Lessons Learned: Bureaucratic Politics

Bureaucracies and Bureaucratic Growth

Fundamentally, bureaucratic politics is about organizational growth. It assumes that governmental organizations desire to increase both their budgets and their autonomy to the maximum extent possible. At the end of this study, we can conclude that there is enough evidence to support this general belief. Agencies do appear to desire both greater resources and greater budgets. The path to those ends is not nearly as simple as it appears, however. Contrary to the claims of crude bureaucratic politics theories, evidence shows strong support for the assumption that agencies do not seek to expand randomly and imperiously just for the sake of it. Bureaucratic growth in this instance was not linear at all. The government agencies engaged in the drug war exercised a much more cautious and piecemeal approach in the pursuit of greater resources. In effect, our study reveals that there are limits, even self-imposed limits, to bureaucratic growth that surface within the dynamics of multi-organization governmental environments. Let us consider some important qualifications to the premise that agencies pursue greater resources indiscriminately.

The Logic of Opportunity: Resources

In general, the evidence examined in this book does appear to substantiate the point that government agencies desire and seek greater resources. An examination of the annual budget requests of the agencies analyzed for this study reveals that agencies do request greater resources every year, whether they get them or not. U.S. Customs, the National Guard, DEA, and many other agencies continually made the case on Capitol Hill for steady increases in resources in order to "win the war on drugs." During the period under investigation, every agency chosen for study received greater resources from Congress for its efforts in the drug war—though this was an exceptional circumstance thanks to the willingness of Congress and the executive to indulge these requests given the popularity of the drug war. The numbers reveal that the anti-narcotics policy space grew substantially and has continued to grow nearly every year since then and that this growth obeys the concern of politicians about drugs.[1] Agencies took advantage of every opportunity to compete for the additional resources, though some attempts were tempered because with more resources came greater accountability, which implied less autonomy. It is at this juncture where the picture gets more complex.

Government agencies did not appear to spend inordinate amounts of time trying to maximize the agency's budget. While they requested larger budgets, they did so incrementally, year after year, and always with an eye for a potential reduction in autonomy. In a potential trade-off between material resources and autonomy, autonomy would be preferred over greater budgets. For real growth spurts in resources or autonomy, government agencies preferred to wait for "windows of opportunity." These windows of opportunity for quick growth were opened by new legislation, public attention to the issue of drugs, the perception of an illegal drug crisis, and a number of other reasons. Between 1989 and 1993, such a window of opportunity was wide open given the fact that the drug war was high in the priorities of politicians. Politicians dedicated considerably more resources to the effort every year during that period. Thus, during the G.H.W. Bush Administration, everybody stood to gain from the rapidly increasing drug war budgets and nearly every agency in the drug war took advantage of this opportunity to grow as quickly as they could but nowhere nearly as recklessly as some might have thought. It was not uncommon to hear bureaucrats talk about the responsibilities that come with additional resources, which might explain why some agencies appear not to have welcomed the added resources. They saw in them the threat of great accountability, which is presumed by most bureaucrats to mean a lesser degree of autonomy for the agency. A key lesson of our study in this regard is that agencies pick their "expansionary battles" carefully. Windows of opportunity appear crucial to an agency if it is to push for greater budgets, without having to spend enormous amounts of its own political capital in making an idea happen.[2] But greater budgets are never pursued if they result in a lessened level of organizational autonomy.

The Logic of Opportunity: Jurisdiction

A similar observation can be made in regard to turf. Government agencies appear to take advantage of "windows of opportunity" to gain greater autonomy—that is, to bring forth selected problems and solutions to bear on a problem. The agencies in our study generally avoided pushing hard for changes in a policy space—even though there was room to be ambitious. Instead, drug war agencies pursued a "logic of opportunity" for their jurisdictional growth. Among LEAs, for example, the shrewd use of windows of opportunity for turf expansion was quite evident. U.S. Customs proved particularly adept at using such windows of opportunity, which confirms our premise that influence and willingness to use that influence also matter. Custom's leaders were not only able but willing to take advantage of all sorts of opportunities to enhance the standing of the agency in and outside the anti-narcotics policy space. Customs, for example, took advantage of the provisions of the 1989 Defense Authorization Act to claim nearly absolute jurisdiction over air interdiction, practically expelling the Coast Guard from all air interdiction efforts. Customs also took advantage of SOUTHCOM's resource scarcity during the Gulf War to plug itself into important surveillance and monitoring operations assigned to the military—a move that enabled Customs to be first at the crime scene and claim credit for successes in the drug war and make itself appear as the "indispensable" agency with the ultimate say in anti-drug operations. In addition, Customs struck opportunely to gain ground on the field of domestic investigations of anti-narcotics matters, forcing DEA to share its jurisdiction over investigations operations—a deviation from the bureaucratic politics hypothesis whereby Customs should have been reluctant to go into a field in which it would necessarily share jurisdiction with another organization. They saw this move, however, as recovering a piece of the pie they had lost to DEA earlier. Similarly, the Coast Guard took advantage of the 1989 Defense Authorization Act to establish an important bridge with the Navy, a move which raised its profile and the morale of its personnel and gave it greater clout in marine interdiction—a clout that was not interfered with by the Navy, given that the Navy actually disliked the mission. But working in Navy ships, alongside Navy personnel, is quite the morale booster for a Coast Guard member. The move could only mean enhancement of the Coast Guard's image both inside and outside the policy space, proving that prestige can often move agencies as well. With prestige comes, of course, more autonomy. All these cases suggest that government agencies are concerned with a measurable stability and will take gradual risks rather than seek abrupt disruptions in the distribution of jurisdictional power. Agencies prefer to venture into areas where they actually increase their decision making power and not where it might actually be reduced. The Navy/Coast Guard case also suggests that sometimes agencies will seek arrangements that will allow them to profit from cooperation, although this clearly works best when they can share jurisdictional power without interfering with each other's main mission. The Navy did the sailing, placating its political masters and the Coast Guard did the law enforcement part, enhancing its image.

A "Window of Opportunity" Theory

After having established that for numerous reasons agencies prefer a piecemeal, cautious approach to bureaucratic growth, an examination of the organizational behavior of drug war bureaucracies reveals that there are other crucial factors in understanding agency behavior. An agency's behavior is influenced by the various windows of opportunities for growth in resources or autonomy that show up along the way. Agency leaders nearly always keep an eye open for such opportunities. Whether an agency makes effective use of such opportunities depends not only on the relative influence of the agency in the overall bureaucratic landscape but also on the willingness of the agency's leaders to use that influence. Both of these elements, a measure of influence and the willingness to use it, constitute a sine qua non condition to achieve an agency's organizational goals and both help determine a given course of action chosen by an agency's top bureaucrats. Willingness alone to use influence is not enough. Agency behavior is also dependent on the leadership skills of the agency's officials. While some may want to make use of an opportunity to expand, their skills may be quite limited and they may not be able to do so. Carol Hallett of U.S. Customs is a good example of a skillful agency chief. She is well remembered for her personal political abilities to take advantage of such opportunities. DEA officials, on the other hand, were not well known for their political skills. The result was that where Customs succeeded the DEA often failed. This is even more puzzling if we consider that the DEA should be expected to have considerable clout in the anti-narcotics policy space and to profit from the willingness of its leaders to make aggressive moves in an area that was very much their own. Yet they never enjoyed Custom's success in part because DEA's leaders lacked the political skills needed to maneuver through the bureaucratic thicket of the policy space. Many of them tended to be former military or law enforcement officials, not the savvy political appointees that usually get to head Customs. Of course, in a political game, organizational success is also a factor of the impact that a particular move by an agency may have about the interests of other actors in the policy space. Although an agency's action may prompt a response from other actors in its environment, the move's impact on other agencies matters considerably because it triggers a political chain reaction that the "revisionist" agency must confront. Here is where the relative influence of an agency matters most. DOMS, for example, faced a formidable opponent, the Office of Joint Chiefs of Staff, in its desires for expansion in spite of the fact that it saw the international drug war at the Pentagon as a good opportunity to grow and sought to take advantage of it. DOMS's behavior was perceived as offensive or "revisionist." It clearly wanted the mission and "fought" for it in order to capitalize on the growth opportunity of the anti-narcotics policy space but it did not succeed because its relative influence vis-à-vis the JCS was too low—its formal powers within the structure of the Pentagon were simply too small. Bureaucratic alliances could not work for DOMS either. DOMS had hardly any "powerful" allies to which it could appeal to support its cause—in effect it lacked formal and even informal channels to push for its organizational agenda. Thus, the case of DOMS confirms that the relative influence of an agency in its environment clearly matters. These observations clearly point to the fact that bureaucratic growth is more closely like a muddle-through process rather than a systematic and consistent way to explain agency behavior.

The manner in which an agency pursues its organizational agenda also depends on the type of opportunity its officials perceive they have. Whereas DOMS tried a straightforward approach, by lobbying and persuading, DEA in the Guatemalan interdiction case seems to have tried a classic end-run. DEA's push for growth in the interdiction sphere failed for numerous reasons, not the least of which was the fact that it was encroaching on the turf of very powerful agencies, e.g., Customs. DEA's attempts confirm the point that rival agencies, when faced with a threat, will respond defensively to the revisionist agency. The higher the stakes, the bigger the reaction. Indeed, DEA provoked a formidable inter-organizational alliance to prevent it from achieving its growth goals. The affected agencies viewed the Bonner plan as a threat not only to their resources but to their own stakes in air interdiction. Their reaction was as extensive as it was intensive and their combined relative influence was enormous. Bureaucratic reaction to the Bonner plan suggests that agencies view threats of potential losses with considerable alarm whereas opportunities for potential gains are assessed with less enthusiasm, much more cautiously than might be expected. Every agency fiercely fought attempts to encroach upon its turf. The inter-organizational alliance provoked against Bonner's plan is but one example—albeit a somewhat extreme one. However, Customs and SOUTHCOM also fiercely fought Bonner's proposal to turn over the west coast of South America to LANTCOM's jurisdiction. The DEA itself sought vehemently to ensure its future survival before the repeated attempts of the FBI to absorb it. Similarly, the State Department was resolute in the defense of its supremacy over the "foreign" drug war, going to great lengths—even petty behavior—to ensure that others understood its preeminence in all matters of foreign policy, including the international drug war. Lastly, when SOUTHCOM, under Gen. Thurman, attempted to centralize all intelligence efforts of anti-drug agencies in Latin America, he too provoked a strong inter-bureaucratic coalition against his efforts. All together, these cases suggest that in the organizational behavior of government agencies defensive behavior is both more common and more intense than offensive behavior. Adopting offensive stands is simply too risky a strategy for bureaucratic growth. It tends to draw too much attention to an agency and strong opposition to its organizational preferences.

The issue of inter-bureaucratic alliances has received little attention, but our cases show that they do happen and it is therefore an area that requires more exploration. It is obvious that in cases where an agency is perceived as aggressive or imperialistic at the expense of other agencies, such behavior attracts the attention of other bureaus as well as an agency's overseers. Too much attention can put the agency's freedom of action or autonomy at risk, if it were to be castigated for its offensiveness. Indeed, besides provoking inter-bureaucratic alliances, some agencies' organizational goals did catch the attention of its political masters or departmental heads who often rebuked the offending agency. For these reasons, awaiting windows of opportunity to grow and walking gingerly around the way to pursue such growth appeared to be much more attractive to government agencies than to make aggressive moves because, when faced with threats to their resources or autonomy.

Bureaucratic Imperial Growth v. Organizational Nesting

In this study, it also became clear that government agencies prefer to find nests or niches in which they can assert their jurisdiction. The government agencies considered in this study did not really seek to expand into every functional area of the drug war. Some agencies pursued expansion in the area of investigations; others stuck to interdiction; yet others kept a hold on eradication, and so forth. Seldom did an agency seek to move aggressively into an area already occupied by another agency or even several other agencies. Only U.S. Customs appears to have behaved more imperialistically—a fact partly explained by the historically aggressive posture that Customs tends to take in nearly every area of its competence and partly by the nature of its leaders at that time. Besides, organizational memories are long, as Customs demonstrated in trying to recover its niche in the area of narcotics investigations after having lost it to the DEA. In fact, in the area of intelligence, where every agency participated, many of the efforts of each agency were isolated from the intelligence efforts of other agencies. Each government agency had its own intelligence "division," even as Congress repeatedly called for the centralization of all anti-drug intelligence efforts. What Congress' pleas to centralize intelligence efforts did was to create more intelligence centers that only duplicated the many intelligence activities in which anti-narcotics agencies were already involved. No agency was willing to eliminate its own internal intelligence division, even if it participated in centralized efforts such as EPIC, in favor of a government-wide anti-narcotics intelligence matrix. Every case in the area of anti-narcotics intelligence appears to confirm the point that agencies value autonomy very highly. This point is reinforced by the 2004 *9/11 Commission Report* on the fragmentation of the intelligence community on the issue of terror. To this type of duplication but simultaneous isolation the Commission attributed a great deal of the lack of success in preventing the September 11 attack on New York and Washington. In general, government agencies dislike centralization, as clearly seen when SOUTHCOM's CINC, George Joulwan, attempted to create a centralized roster for all aircraft activity in South America that was aimed at coordinating all the air-related activities of all U.S. anti-drug agencies. He, like Thurman's intelligence centralization efforts earlier, was unsuccessful. Agencies preferred to have complete control of their own aircraft activities. This case too lends additional support to the idea that agencies value autonomy very highly and prefer to be kings of their own dominion.

A Bureaucratic Growth Theory: Bureaucratic Politics *and* Organizational Culture

To reinforce one of the most important lessons regarding the general finding that all agencies value resources but that they do not pursue them randomly and imperiously, it is useful to consider organizational culture and bureaucratic politics together. Evidence points to the fact that while resources are highly valued by nearly everyone, government agencies like to pursue and receive resources for specific activities that the agency values. These activities are in turn largely determined by the culture of the organization. For example, DEA did not pursue resources to engage in the areas of eradication, interdiction, or even education and prevention. Instead, DEA pursued resources in the area of investigations—or even more specifically instigation and prosecution of drug cases. Because the focus of the agency is largely individuals and organizations as law breakers, DEA sought resources to grow in that area. Eradication, interdiction and education strategies were simply not the focus of DEA. Rather, more traditional law enforcement activities were at the core of the way the agency perceived its function and its members had all the basic attitudes and assumptions that accompany such activities well ingrained. The military is a similar case. It clearly rejected a somewhat promising money-line because it did not consider drug law enforcement anywhere near its preferred and valued activities—and the solution to the drug war was anything but close to the means that the military prefers to use. Even potentially imperialistic agencies, like DOMS, which fervently sought the international drug mission, justified the added mission and resources arguing that "they were already doing that anyway." The growth ambitions of DOMS followed closely the lines of the way the agency viewed itself and its social function.

It appears then that contemplating bureaucratic politics and organizational culture together can help discern that agencies pick their expansionary paths carefully along valued activities that are predetermined by the organization's preferred problems and solutions. Organizational culture operates as the channel or path along which agencies seek to grow. Within the lines demarcated by their organizational culture, government agencies may pursue greater resources more or less aggressively—as evidenced by the varying degrees of lobbying for more resources on Capitol Hill and by agencies' various and varied attempts to capitalize on the increasing federal anti-narcotics budget. In this sense, one could say that bureaucratic politics and organizational culture do not contradict but complement each other. This discovery is fundamental because most students of bureaucracy tend to pit bureaucratic politics against organizational culture in trying to understand how government agencies operate. The reality is that the two lenses, when juxtaposed, may explain in a much more nuanced way the manner in which government agencies prefer to grow. This line of argument stemming from our discovery that organizational culture and bureaucratic politics constitute a single double lens must be explored further in future research. A future volume analyzing the Homeland Security reorganization act of 2002 will look at this point with greater depth.

The Value of Autonomy (Turf)

An important lesson here is that agencies value autonomy quite highly. Although often government agencies have to put up with overlapping lines of jurisdiction, they dislike having them altogether. They seem to prefer to know exactly where some lines of authority begin and where other end. In fact, agencies value their autonomy with greater dedication than they value their resources. This implies that government agencies may be willing to give up resources or not acquire them if their organizational autonomy is threatened by the acquisitions. All of these observations are evident in the anti-narcotics policy field. The State Department also appeared to value autonomy—its exclusive jurisdiction over all U.S. activities abroad, including the international drug war—well beyond any resources it might obtain from participating in the drug war. State did not appear interested in profiting from the drug war. Instead, its actions in the drug war policy sphere appeared designed to prevent further erosion of its supremacy over *foreign* policy. The case of the military also confirms this conclusion. Among the military, there was also a manifest fear that entry into the drug war would subject the military to greater scrutiny from Capitol Hill and that, if the drug war failed, the military would likely be held responsible for that failure. The Pentagon would rather have none of the mission, even if it came accompanied with greater resources. The loss of autonomy is as close as an agency comes to a life-and-death experience. DEA, for example, had to fight three different attempts by the FBI to absorb it—the ultimate loss of autonomy, the death of an organization. This constant threat not only kept DEA substantially preoccupied with its survival, but DEA sought, in different ways, to match the nature and character of the FBI in the belief that equality would ensure its autonomy permanently.

The picture, nevertheless, is not as clear as it seems. Agencies with broader jurisdictions, such as U.S. Customs and the FBI, are less susceptible to capture than agencies with very narrow jurisdictions, such as DEA. Although DEA avoided being absorbed by the FBI, the FBI tried it three times, and only by appealing to the importance that politicians placed on the issue of illegal drugs was DEA able to escape capture. But safe from the FBI for the time being, in the area of investigations, DEA lost its battle with Customs and was forced to share jurisdiction over drug investigations operations—a painful loss of autonomy for the organization. In effect, potential losses of autonomy provoke virulent reactions. The previously analyzed actions by SOUTHCOM also demonstrate this. Thus, all evidence points to the enormous value that government agencies place on their autonomy, even over resources.

Bureaucratic Growth: To Go Where No One Has Gone Before

The cases examined here also suggest that the more crowded a particular policy space is, the more difficult it is for a new agency to make inroads within that area. This finding is important because it indicates that *what the agencies* are involved in a particular issue is not the only thing that matters. Clearly, *how many agencies* are involved also matters. For example, DEA faced fierce resistance to its only attempt to go into the interdiction area largely because that area was already crowded. SOUTHCOM's efforts similarly to centralize intelligence failed. Incidentally, opposition to the military's entry into the drug war did not come only from within the military; LEAs were particularly concerned that the military would crowd them out with its resources—in effect, many agencies feared that they would lose their cause to an "800-pound gorilla." LEAs were originally very cautious about the military's entry into the war on drugs. Quite a few even argued against it. But LEA opposition to the military's participation could not overcome Congress and the President's—the political masters—determination to make the military a participant in the drug war. Clearly, the opposition of an agency to a specific plan finds an important, though not necessarily absolute, limit where congressional and presidential power asserts itself.

In the case of the State Department, a bureaucratic politics analysis proved quite useful. For example, State did not view the international drug war as a major component of its diplomatic efforts to advance U.S. interests abroad. When the drug war became an international endeavor, State was forced to give it greater importance. But it did so defensively, to safeguard its primacy in foreign policy. DOS moved quickly and aggressively to show other agencies that the *foreign* drug war was entirely within its domain and fought more fiercely to defend what they already had, very likely more than what they would have fought to acquire what they did not yet possess.

Curiously, all governmental agencies showed a penchant for taking credit. It is already well known that showing "results" is of paramount importance in the American political game. An analysis of the anti-narcotics policy space confirms this premise. But because measuring results in the drug war is so difficult, agencies employed various methods for collecting hard "stats," which they could use both to argue for greater resources on Capitol Hill and save the agency considerable badgering for not "making a difference in the drug war." Such competition is understandable, of course, given the incentives and disincentives in agency-political master relations in the U.S. government system.

Lessons Learned: Organizational Culture

Organizational Culture and Organizational Preferences

From the lens of organizational culture, our analysis shows that all government agencies, regardless of their nature, develop preferred problems and solutions around the social function that they were created to perform. And when they seek to grow, they grow along the lines of those preferred problems and solutions. In the case of DEA, it appears that its agents had an unyielding faith in the fact that people break the law. When they sought to grow, they did so along the lines of their preferred problems and solutions.

The case of the military is stronger than that of the DEA and thereby an easier case to show the power of an organization's culture. The military's refusal to take on the drug war stemmed from the fact that it did not view law enforcement tasks anywhere near the social function the military was created to perform. Eventually, the military downgraded and outright neglected the drug mission soon after the Bush Administration left office in 1993. The Pentagon's drug war budget considerably decreased after 1992. Its assets dedicated to the drug war also diminished.

Among diplomats the drug war was considered an obstacle to the smooth execution of their tasks: building, maintaining, and repairing international relationships. Again, when State finally decided to make the drug war part of its day-to-day activities, it appeared motivated by the need to prevent other agencies from encroaching on State's jurisdiction over *foreign* affairs.

These cases show that it may be better to look at government agencies through the lenses of organizational culture and bureaucratic politics together in order to get a more accurate picture of the organizational behavior of government agencies.

Subcultures and Organizational Culture

Another important lesson learned in this book is that organizational subcultures are ways of accommodating disparate elements within an agency. Utilizing purposeful and careful subcultural divisions inside an organization to accommodate incompatible sets of tasks is a good strategy to maintain internal harmony. In addition, subcultural divisions do not always have to mean that one subculture has to suffer so that the other prospers. Sometimes subcultural accommodation helps an organization live harmoniously without major rifts. U.S. Customs is a good example of this.

An analysis of U.S. Customs in the drug war showed that sometimes, when organizations are relatively large and cover multiple tasks, the internal cleavages within the organization will follow "cultural" fault lines. U.S. Customs has two principal subcultures, the "inspection" culture and the "interdiction" culture. Contrary to expectations though, both subcultures thrived within the organization with equal force. Neither culture prevailed over the other, nor was there neglect of either of these cultures. The explanation that emerges for this internal harmony is that the two subcultures were simply kept separate. The personnel within each subculture—inspectors on the one hand and interdiction officers on the other—rarely occupied the same buildings or geographical spaces; their missions and activities almost never overlapped. Instead, each culture had its own venue, its own people (from differing backgrounds), and its own geographical location. Interdiction took place in the air and in the sea, nearly completely independent of the "inspection" culture, which conducted its operations along the border and harbors. This bipolarity within U.S. Customs leads to the conclusion that increasing or abundant resources do help organizations accommodate more than one culture.

An examination of U.S. Customs also suggests another refinement for organizational culture analyses: the issue of professionalism. It is worth noting that "professions" may matter more than at first thought for the purposes of "cultural" harmony within an organization's subcultures. Within U.S. Customs, the personnel that tended to go to each of the subcultures generally had a different background. Air interdiction was staffed with former pilots, who were then trained to be agents. The inspection subculture of U.S. Customs appears to be staffed with former military and law enforcement agents who may or may not have been trained to be pilots, but were trained to be Customs agents. The two subcultures of U.S. Customs hardly competed with each other but this situation of conflict was made easier by the fact that resources were abundant and neither culture had to cannibalize the resources of the other.

Subcultures are also useful in other ways. Sometimes creating a subculture for a particular mission that came into being later may help an agency maintain focus on its original mission and tasks and prevent a secondary mission from diminishing its resources and focus. Sometimes, however, a subculture is created to purposefully isolate an unwanted mission or task and then starve it and kill it. The military and the State Department exemplify this. Each created separate units to "handle" the drug war mission, but these units hardly prospered lavishly within the departments. Quite the contrary, they were generally isolated and starved for more resources. This is quite consistent with organizational culture. INM at State was an unwanted bureau because the drug mission was not well liked. INM did not constitute a bureau that any diplomat aspiring to climb the foreign representation ladder would seek out. Many of its activities were subject to the higher priorities of the most important geographical and functional bureaus within State. The small bureau that handled the drug war mission inside the Pentagon was similarly isolated and starved. No self-respecting military man would aspire to head it or to seek promotions or benefits by working the drug war in that office.

Organizational Culture and Individual Personalities

Although personalities, even at the top levels of an organization, normally operate within the boundaries of organizational culture, occasionally they actually reshape it. Alfred Kahn at the Civil Aeronautics Board and J. Edgar Hoover at the Federal Bureau of Investigation are just two such cases. Some organizational choices are undoubtedly the product of the resolve of individuals, as in the case of George Joulwan, or the political and interpersonal skills of the top level officials, as in the case of Carol Hallett. Personal concerns with specific issues also appear to matter. In the war on drugs, the Coast Guard turned out to be a case where bureau chief personality prevailed over organizational cultural elements. Admiral P.A. Yost paid close attention to the drug war during his tenure and made it part of the day-to-day activities of the Coast Guard. He was thoroughly dedicated to "make a difference in the drug war." But his successor, Admiral J. William Kime, was less concerned with the drug war and much more concerned with the environment. His greater concern with the environment led to a downgrading in the Coast Guard's drug war efforts in favor of environmental efforts. Thus, even through the Coast Guard considers both types of enforcement within its jurisdiction, the shift in priorities shows that sometimes the personal preferences of an agency's leaders do make a difference on the priorities of the organization. Nevertheless, none of these individuals changed the Coast Guard's organizational culture in any fundamental way. Interestingly enough, not even at U.S. Embassies did the personality of an Ambassador, a figure that can be quite dominant in his or her environment, make a fundamental long-term difference in the culture of diplomats and their attitude toward the drug war, as the actions of Ambassador Robert Gelbard illustrate.

New Problems, Old Solutions

It is also clear that the pre-established preferred problems and solutions of an agency—which emerge down the line from the social function an organization was created to perform—generally continue in the way the agency interprets and handles a new mission. The case of the military further confirms this hypothesis.

SOUTHCOM employed important low-intensity conflict (LIC) doctrines developed for other purposes to fight its war on drugs. Although over time the military learned to make some adjustments to its LIC concepts that reflected more accurately the business-like style of drug trafficking organizations, it is important to note that SOUTHCOM resorted first and foremost to its LIC manuals in order to fulfill its mission in the drug war. The employment of Cold War-style war games for developing a military strategy for the drug war is also noteworthy. The resort to these games shows that the military's anti-drug efforts were circumscribed by the way the military does things.

Finally, the case of the military illustrates that a governmental organization's bureaucrats may only perceive those consequences that they are trained to identify. This confirms the insightful observations of Robert K. Merton, when he argued that people inside organizations adhere to rules originally conceived as instrumental in such a way that they become an end onto themselves. In effect, the members of an organization acquire "a pronounced character of the mind," and interpret life situations in conformance (or non-conformance) with the organization's rules. A cop, for example, is not trained to identify the important negative consequences of certain law enforcement actions on the diplomatic relations of the United States with a host country. The soldiers, who took over numerous buildings of the Panamanian government in 1989, were not trained to treat the many documents they guarded as prosecutorial evidence for a future trial, as already analyzed. Similarly, the case of the State Department also confirms this important premise of organizational culture. To many diplomats the "drug war" at home did not even appear as an important component of the overall U.S. anti-narcotics strategy. It was simply outside the radar of State.

In general, there is no way in which agencies engaged in the function they were created for will be able to reconceive and redefine themselves to accommodate the necessities of a new policy problem because their organizational culture is likely to demand that they define the problem utilizing their basic assumptions and attitudes and that they use their day-to-day tools to solve the problem. In effect, a new policy problem comes to an agency in danger of being adapted and reshaped to be solved through old solutions.

Bureaucratic Politics *and* Organizational Culture

Seeing Through a Double Lens

Enough evidence has emerged to show that bureaucratic politics and organizational do not compete with one another in explaining organizational behavior but that they are actually complementary. Upbeat reporting—the tendency to report rosy scenarios and downplay negative information—for example appears consistent with both models. Whether bureaucratic politics or organizational culture best explains an action depends on the motivation behind the intention of the actor—something difficult but not impossible to find out. If an organization is motivated to engage in upbeat reporting because of its own need to obtain a good report card from its political masters, to make an argument for increased resources or greater autonomy, to raise the reputation of the agency or to avoid harsh oversight from the organization's overseers, then bureaucratic politics is helpful. The case of the State Department shows that upbeat reporting (e.g., about the behavior and accomplishments of foreign governments) is done when the organization perceives threats to the performance of its primary tasks (e.g., to build, maintain and repair relations). This motivation points to organizational culture at work rather than bureaucratic politics.

In the case of subcultures, it is clear that both bureaucratic politics and organizational culture can work together to better explain organizational behavior. The already analyzed case of U.S. Customs, for example, suggests that agencies often cope with divergent internal cultures by separating and compartmentalizing them and thus attain what is a quintessentially political goal.

There is also something that could be termed "cultural" opportunism. The case of the military illustrates what is meant by this. As already stated, the military was forced to enter the drug war by its political masters. Facing a budget crunch, however, there is evidence that some military organizations employed the anti-drug budget to keep some programs alive, to train their personnel, and to cover reductions in flying hours' and steaming days' budgets. This implies that agencies undergoing budgetary cuts will sometimes embrace a new mission but will interpret it and use the additional resources in such a way that they reinforce what the organization is already doing.

The case of DEA also revealed that sometimes agencies operating in the same policy space need to make considerable adjustments to each other's culture in order to function well together. The contrast between DEA and DOS was a useful exercise inasmuch as the approach of each agency to the drug war highlighted the culture of the other organization. This process of accommodation and adjustment, however, can take a very long time.

Another curious lesson taken from a simultaneous analysis of the organizational culture and the politics of bureaucracy of drug war agencies relates to the fact that not all agencies view each other as competitors, even if they operate in the very same policy area or are even assigned to the same tasks. Although sometimes agencies cooperate for political reasons, it is clear that a degree of cultural compatibility can help quite a lot. The Coast Guard and the Navy found it very easy to cooperate. Cooperation between these two agencies was facilitated by their "cultural compatibility." Similarly, U.S. Customs and SOUTHCOM did not see each other as rivals or competitors. Instead, they cooperated fully in the air interdiction area, analogous to the Navy and the Coast Guard's motivations. These pairings of agencies allow us to see that within certain degrees of cultural compatibility, the structure of incentives, an element more closely aligned with bureaucratic politics, is quite reinforcing of these partnerships.

A fundamental point that arises from our study of bureaucratic politics is the problem of bureaucratic growth. If a theory of bureaucratic growth is to consider limits to growth, the simultaneous study of bureaucratic politics and organizational culture reveals that bureaucratic growth has limits set by the culture of the organization. The Coast Guard, for example, grew almost exclusively in the drug maritime interdiction area. It essentially withdrew from all air interdiction efforts, even though that was an area where there were assets acquired. The Coast Guard was already culturally predisposed to define the problem as one of maritime interdiction and to push for a maritime solution for itself. This might have facilitated its giving up air interdiction in favor of U.S. Customs. Similarly, DEA sought greater resources but the arguments for growth reveal a desire to increase funds for DEA's preferred activity, drug trafficking investigations. Rarely did DEA argue for more money for education and prevention, eradication or interdiction. U.S. Customs sought to grow principally in two areas, investigations and air interdiction. It did not seek to participate in eradication efforts nor was it interested in conducting drug busts in the streets of Chicago or New York. It sought to grow in specific, preferred environments. These cases demonstrate that agencies do not seek to grow indiscriminately. Instead, agencies choose carefully the areas where they are to grow and these areas are often guided by the culture of an organization.

Conclusion

Governments are complex networks of organizations, with their own distinct dynamics. Indeed, even though I chose bureaucratic politics and organizational culture as analytical paradigms, precisely because they are different, make different assumptions, and follow different inference patterns, by now, it is clear that both are quite useful to explain the behavior of government agencies. As this work developed, it became clear that neither bureaucratic politics nor organizational culture is useful on its own. It is *together* that they attain their utmost explanatory power. In explaining bureaucratic growth, a constant problem for scholars of government, the models do an excellent job together. Agencies do pursue greater resources, but their pursuit is shaped and colored by the pre-established cultural preferences of the organization. In other words, culture appears to place natural limits on bureaucratic growth. Thus the apparent incommensurability of the models—that bureaucratic politics analyzes the interaction of an organization with other actors in its environment and that organizational culture examines the agency from within—turned out to be an advantage, rather than a disadvantage. The interaction of a government agency with other actors in its environment appears determined by the way the organization sees itself and the way it conceives its mission in society. One cannot, for example, argue that bureaucracies are imperialistic, without discussing in what direction or how much or how fast that imperialism is growing. If we claim that bureaus pursue greater autonomy, we also have to argue that they do not depend altogether for it on their political bosses or the other actors in their environment but that they carve niches for themselves and avoid overlaps in a policy space in order to maximize their autonomy. This choice is largely shaped by the preferred problems and solutions of the agency.

Similarly, this study discovered that even though organizations want greater resources and autonomy, they are far from pursuing these everywhere all the time. Instead, government agencies use windows of opportunity to push their preferred problems and solutions to the forefront. These windows of opportunity may arise from new legislation, the disappearance of an agency, larger budgets, changes in the national mood, a new administration, and so forth. They are, in effect, an opportunity for an agency to advance its agenda and dampen other problems or proposals. In the drug war, it was relatively evident that agencies did take advantage of the opportunities provided by increasing budgets as well as the prominence of the drug war among elected officials.

But windows of opportunities have to be entered in time because they are generally scarce and short in duration. Along these lines, personalities begin to matter. Who heads an agency and what skills the officials possess are important in leading an agency in the direction that it desires to go. As it became evident, sometimes a window of opportunity was wasted because an agency's managers did not possess the skills or the channels of action to take advantage of it. Other times, however, astute leaders were able to take enormous advantage of these windows of opportunity to enhance both the resource endowment and autonomy of their agencies.

Finally, this work is a step in understanding how bureaucratic politics and organizational culture actually work together to explain agency behavior. More and deeper research looking at more cases beyond the drug war are needed in order to discern even more nuanced ways in which bureaucratic politics and organizational culture can help us understand agency behavior and, ultimately, why governments do what they do and how bureaucracies contribute to the success or failure of a policy.

Notes

1. By FY2000, the anti-narcotics budget was hovering around $20 billion dollars.

2. Interestingly, John Kingdon develops a similar conclusion in *Agendas, Alternatives, and Public Policies* (Glenview, IL: Scott, Foresman and Company, 1984); 212-215.

Bibliography

Books

Aberbach, Joel D., Robert D. Putnam, and Bert A. Rockman. 1981. *Bureaucrats and Politicians in Western Democracies*. Cambridge, Massachusetts: Harvard University Press.

Aberbach, Joel D. 1990. *Keeping a Watchful Eye: The Politics of Congressional Oversight.* Washington, District of Columbia: The Brookings Institution.

Allison, Graham T. 1971. *Essence of Decision: Explaining the Cuban Missile Crisis.* Boston: Little, Brown and Company.

———, and Peter Szanton. 1976. *Remaking Foreign Policy.* New York, New York: Basic Books.

———, and Philip Zelikow. 1999. *Essence of Decision: Explaining the Cuban Missile Crisis.* 2nd ed. Boston: Little, Brown and Company.

———, and Morton Halperin. "Bureaucratic Politics: A Paradigm and Some Policy Implications." In *Theory and Policy in International Relations*, 40-79. Edited by Raymond Tanter and Richard H. Ullman. Princeton: Princeton University Press, 1972.

Axelrod, Robert, ed. 1976. *The Structure of Decision: The Cognitive Maps of Political Elites.* Princeton, New Jersey: Princeton University Press.

Bagley, Bruce M., and William O. Walker, III., eds. 1994. *Drug Trafficking in the Americas.* Boulder, Colorado: Lynne Rienner Publishers.

Bardach, Eugene. 1998. *Getting Agencies to Work Together: The Practice and Theory of Managerial Craftsmanship.* Washington, District of Columbia: Brookings Institution Press.

Baum, Dan. 1996. *Smoke and Mirrors: The War on Drugs and the Politics of Failure.* Boston, Massachusetts: Little, Brown and Company.

Bendor, Jonathan B. 1985. *Parallel Systems: Redundancy in Government.* Los Angeles, California: University of California Press.

Bertram, Eva, et al. 1996. *Drug War Politics: The Price of Denial.* 1996. Berkeley, California: University of California Press.

Blais, André and Dion, Stéphane, eds. 1991. *The Budget-Maximizing Bureaucrat: Appraisals and Evidence.* Pittsburgh, Pennsylvania: University of Pittsburgh Press.

Builder, Carl H. 1993. *Measuring the Leverage: Assessing Military Contributions to Drug Interdiction.* Santa Monica, California.: RAND.

Builder, Carl H. 1989. *The Masks of War: American Military Styles in Strategy and Analysis.* Baltimore, Maryland: The Johns Hopkins University Press.

Bullock, Ian, Oliver Stallybrass, and Stephen Trombley, eds. 1988. *The Harper Dictionary of Modern Thought*, rev. ed. New York, New York: Harper and Row.

Campbell, John Franklin. 1971. *The Foreign Policy Fudge Factory.* New York, New York: Basic Books.

Chepesiuk, Ron. 1999. *Hard Target: The United States War Against International Drug Trafficking, 1982-1997.* Jefferson, North Carolina: McFarland & Company, Inc., Publishers.

Collier, David. 1991. "The Comparative Method: Two Decades of Change." In *Comparative Political Dynamics.* Rustow and Erickson, eds. New York, New York: Harper Collins.

Crane, Diane. 1994. *The Sociology of Culture: Emerging Theoretical Perspectives.* Cambridge, Massachusetts: Blackwell Publishers.

Dexter, Lewis Anthony. 1970. *Elite and Specialized Interviewing.* Evanston, Illinois: Northwestern University Press.

Diamond, Michael A. 1993. *The Unconscious Life of Organizations: Interpreting Organizational Identity.* Westport, Connecticut: Quorum Books.

Doig, James W. 1965. *The Assistant Secretaries: Problems and Processes of Appointments.* Washington, District of Columbia: The Brookings Institution.

Downie, Richard Duncan. 1998. *Learning from Conflict: The U.S. Military in Vietnam, El Salvador, and the Drug War.* Westport, Connecticut: Praeger.

Downs, Anthony. 1967. *Inside Bureaucracy.* Boston, Massachussetts: Little, Brown and Company.

Eckstein, Harry. 1975. "Case Study and Theory in Political Science." In *Handbook of Political Science*. Fred Greenstein and Nelson Polsby, eds. Reading, Pennsylvania: Addison-Wesley.

Elwood, William N. 1994. *Rhetoric in the War on Drugs: The Triumphs and Tragedies of Public Relations.* Westport, Connecticut: Praeger.

Frankfort-Nachmias, Chava and David Nachmias. 1992. *Research Methods in the Social Sciences*, 4th ed. New York, New York: St. Martin's Press.

Friman, H. Richard.1996. *NarcoDiplomacy: Exporting the U.S. War on Drugs*. Ithaca, New York: Cornell University Press.

Fuss, Charles M., Jr. 1996. *Sea of Grass: The Maritime Drug War 1970-1990.* Annapolis, Maryland: Naval Institute Press.

Geertz, Clifford. 1973. *The Interpretation of Cultures.* New York, New York: Basic Books.

George, Alexander and Timothy McKeown. 1985. "Case Studies and Theories of Organizational Decisionmaking." In *Advances in Information Processing in Organizations*, Vol. 2. Robert Coulam and Richard Smith, eds. Greenwich, Connecticut: JAI Press, Inc.

Gormley, William T., Jr. 1989. *Taming the Bureaucracy: Muscles, Prayers, and Other Strategies*. Princeton, New Jersey: Princeton University Press.

Halperin, Morton H. 1974. *Bureaucratic Politics and Foreign Policy*. Washington, District of Columbia: The Brookings Institution.

Hart, Patrick t'. 1994. *Groupthink in Government: A Study of Small Groups and Policy Failure*. Baltimore, Maryland: The Johns Hopkins University Press.

Hilsman, Roger. 1967. *To Move A Nation*. Garden City, New Jersey: Doubleday Company.

Holden-Rhodes, J. F. 1997. *Sharing the Secrets: Open Source Intelligence and the War on Drugs.* Westport, Connecticut: Praeger.

Huntington, Samuel. 1961. *The Common Defense: Strategic Programs in National Politics.* New York, New York: Columbia University Press.

Katzenstein, Peter J., ed. 1996. *The Culture of National Security: Norms and Identity in World Politics.* New York, New York: Columbia University Press.

Kaufman, Herbert. 1981. *The Administrative Behavior of Bureau Chiefs*. Washington, District of Columbia: The Brookings Institution.

Kerwin, Cornelius M. 1994. *Rulemaking: How Government Agencies Write Law and Make Policy*. Washington, District of Columbia: CQ Press.

Kingdon, John W. 1984. *Agendas, Alternatives, and Public Policies*. Glenview, Illinois: Scott, Foresman, and Company.

Knoke, David. 1990. *Political Network: The Structural Perspective*. New York, New York: Cambridge University Press.

———, and Franz Urban Pappi, Jeffrey Broadbent, Yutaka Tsujinaka. 1996. *Comparing Policy Networks: Labor Politics in the U.S., Germany, and Japan.* New York, New York: Cambridge University Press.

———, and James H. Kuklinski. 1982. *Network Analysis.* Beverly Hills, California: Sage Publications.

Kozak, David C. and Keagle, James M., eds., 1988. *Bureaucratic Politics and National Security: Theory and Practice.* Boulder, Colorado: Lynne Rienner Publishers.

Laitin, David D. 1986. *Hegemony and Culture: Politics and Religious Change Among the Yaruba.* Chicago, Illinois: Chicago University Press.

Lakatos, Imre. 1970. "Falsification and the Methodology of Scientific Research Programmes." In *Criticism and the Growth of Knowledge*. Imre Lakatos and Alan Musgrave, eds. Cambridge: Cambridge University Press.

Legro, Jeffrey. 1996. "*In The Culture of National Security*". New York, New York: Cambridge University Press.

Lasswell, Harold D. 1938. *Who Gets What, When, and How*. New York, New York: McGraw-Hill.

Lewis, Eugene. 1980. *Public Enterpreneurship: Toward a Theory of Bureaucratic Political Power: The Organizational Lives of Hyman Rickover, J. Edgar Hoover, and Robert Moses*. Bloomington, Indiana: Indiana University Press.

Lipsky, Michael. 1980. *Street-Level Bureaucracy: Dilemmas of the Individual in Public Services.* New York, New York: Russell Sage Foundation.

Malamud-Goti, Jaime. 1992. *Smoke and Mirrors: The Paradox of the Drug Wars.* Boulder, Colorado. Westview Press.

March, James G. and Olsen, Johan P. 1965. *Handbook of Organizations*. Chicago, Illinois: Rand McNally.

———, and Herbert A. Simon. 1958. *Organizations.* New York, New York: Wiley.

Martin, Joanne. 1992. *Cultures in Organizations: Three Perspectives.* New York, New York: Oxford University Press.

Meier, Kenneth. 1993. *Politics and the Bureaucracy: Policymaking in the Fourth Branch of Government.* Belmont, California: Wadsworth Publishing Company.

Menzel, Sewall H. 1997. *Cocaine Quagmire: Implementing the U.S. Anti-Drug Policy in the North Andes-Columbia.* New York: University Press of America, Inc.

Menzel, Sewall H. 1996. *Fire in the Andes: U.S. Foreign Policy and Cocaine Politics in Bolivia and Peru.* New York, New York. University Press of America, Inc.

Merton, Robert K. 1968. *Social Theory and Social Structure.* New York, New York: The Free Press.

Murphy, Jerome T. 1980. *Getting the Facts: A Fieldwork Guide for Evaluators and Policy Analysts.* Santa Monica, California: Goodyear Publishing Company, Inc.

Neustadt, Richard. 1960. *Presidential Power: The Politics of Leadership.* New York, New York: Wiley.

Newsom, David D., ed. 1990. *Diplomacy Under a Foreign Flag: When Nations Break Relations.* Washington, District of Columbia: Institute for the Study of Diplomacy.

Nicolson, Harold. 1988. *Diplomacy.* Washington, District of Columbia: Georgetown University.

Niskanen, William A. 1998. *Policy Analysis and Public Choice: Selected Papers by William A. Niskanen.* Northhampton, Massaschusetts: Edward Elgar.

———. 1971. *Bureaucracy and Representative Government.* Chicago, Illinois: Aldine-Atherton.

Perl, Raphael F. 1994. *Drugs and Foreign Policy: A Critical Review.* Boulder, Colorado: Westview Press.

Peters, Guy B. 1988. *Comparing Public Bureaucracies: Problems of Theory and Method.* Tuscaloosa, Alabama. The University of Alabama Press.

———. 1978. *The Politics of Bureaucracy: A Comparative Perspective.* New York, New York: Longman Publishers.

Rachal, Patricia. 1982. *Federal Narcotics Enforcement: Reorganization and Reform.* Boston, Massachusetts: Auburn House Publishing Company.

Reisner, Marc. 1986. *The American West and Its Disappearing Water*. New York, New York: Viking.

Reuter, Peter, Gordon Crawford, and Jonathan Cave. 1988. *Sealing the Borders: The Effects of Increased Military Participation in Drug Interdiction.* Santa Monica, California: RAND Corp.

Ripley, Brian. 1995. "Cognition, Culture, and Bureaucratic Politics." In L. Neack, J. A. K. Hey and P. J. Haney, eds. *Foreign Policy Analysis*. Englewood Cliffs, New Jersey: Prentice-Hall.

Ritti, R., and G. R. Funkhouser. 1993. *The Ropes to Skip and the Ropes to Know: Studies in Organizational Behavior*. Columbus, Ohio: Grid.

Rogowski, Ronald. 1974. *Rational Legitimacy: A Theory of Political Support*. Princeton, New Jersey: Princeton University Press.

Rosati, Jerel A. 1993. *The Politics of United States Foreign Policy.* New York, New York: Harcourt Brace College Publishers.

Rourke, Francis E. 1984. *Bureaucracy, Politics, and Public Policy.* 3rd ed. Boston, Massachusetts: Little, Brown and Company.

Rubin, Barry. 1985. *Secrets of State: The State Department and the Struggle Over U.S. Foreign Policy*. New York, New York: Oxford University Press.

Scharpf, Fritz W., ed. 1993. *Games in Hierarchies and Networks: Analytical and Empirical Approaches to the Study of Governance Institutions.* Boulder, Colorado: Westview Press.

Schilling, Warner R., Paul Y. Hammond and Glenn H. Snyder. "The Politics of National Defense: Fiscal Year 1950" in *Strategy, Politics, and Defense Budgets*. New York/London: Columbia University Press, 1962.

Selznick, Philip. 1957. *Leadership in Administration*. Evanston, Illinois: Row, Peterson, & Co.

Sharp, Elaine B. 1994. *The Dilemma of Drug Policy in the United States*. USA: HarperCollins College Publishers.

Stanley, David T., Dean E. Mann, and James W. Doig. 1967. *Men Who Govern: A Biographical Profile of Federal Political Executives*. Washington, District of Columbia: The Brookings Institution.

Stearns, Monteagle. 1996. *Talking to Strangers: Improving American Diplomacy at Home and Abroad*. Princeton, New Jersey: Princeton University Press.

Taw, Jennifer Morrison, Peter Persselin, and Maren Leed. 1998. *Meeting Peace Operations' Requirements While Maintaining MTW Readiness.* Santa Monica California: RAND.

Verba, Sidney, and Gabriel Almond. 1963. *The Civic Culture: Political Attitudes and Democracy in Five Countries.* Princeton, New Jersey: Princeton University Press.

Walker, William O., III, ed. 1991. *Drug Control Policy: Essays in Historical and Comparative Perspective.* University Park, Pennsylvania, The Pennsylvania State University Press.

Wilson, James Q. 1989. *Bureaucracy: What Government Agencies Do and Why They Do It.* New York, New York: Basic Books.

———. 1978. *The Investigators: Managing FBI and Narcotics Agents.* New York, New York: Basic Books.

Articles

Art, Robert J. "Bureaucratic Politics and American Foreign Policy: A Critique." *Policy Sciences* 4:4 (December 1973); 467-490.

Barker, George. "Clientelism in Economic Reporting." *Foreign Service Journal* (June 1989); pp. 42-48.

Bendor, Jonathan and Thomas H. Hammond. "Rethinking Allison's Models." *American Political Science Review* 86: 2 (June 1992); 301-322.

Brightman, Robert. "Forget Culture: Replacement, Transcendence, Relexification." *Cultural Anthropology* 10:4 (1995); 509-546.

Cheney, Richard B. "War Against Drugs." *Defense* 89 (November/December 1989); 4.

Clark, Peter B., and James Q. Wilson. "Incentive Systems: A Theory of Organizations." *Administrative Science Quarterly* 6:2 (September 1961).

Desch, Michael. "Culture Clash: Assessing the Importance of Ideas in Security Studies." *International Security* 23:1 (Summer 1998); 141-170.

Destler, I. M. "Making Foreign Policy: Comment." *American Political Science Review* 66 (1972); 786-790.

Duncan, W. Jack. "Organizational Culture: 'Getting a Fix' on an Elusive Concept. *The Academy of Management EXECUTIVE* 3:3 (1989); 229-236.

Elgström, Ole. "National Culture and International Relations." *Cooperation and Conflict* 29:3 (September 1994); 289-301.

Elkins, David J. and Richard E. B. Simeon. "A Cause in Search of its Effect, Or What Does Political Culture Explain? *Comparative Politics* 11:2 (January 1979); 127-145.

Ellison, Brian A. "Autonomy in Action: Bureaucratic Competition Among Functional Rivals in Denver Water Politics." *Policy Studies Review* 14:1/2 (Spring/Summer 1995); 25-48.

Gelb, Leslie H. "Muskie and Brzezinski: The Struggle Over Foreign Policy." *New York Times Magazine* (20 July 1980); 26-40.

Goodin, Robert E. "The Logic of Bureaucratic Backscratching." *Public Choice* 24 (1975); 53-68.

Gormley, James J. "Reflections of a State Department Drug Warrior." *Foreign Service Journal* (June 1992); 31-34.

Headrick, Thomas E. "Expert Policy Analysis and Bureaucratic Politics: Searching for the Causes of the 1987 Stock Market Crash." *Law and Policy* 14:4 (October 1992); 313-335.

Hermann, Richard. "The Empirical Challenge of the Cognitive Revolution: A Strategy for Drawing Inferences About Perceptions." *International Studies Quarterly* 32 (1988); 175-203.

Hilsman, Roger. "The Foreign Policy Consensus: An Interim Report." *Journal of Conflict Resolution* (December 1959); 361-382.

Johnston, Alastair Ian. "Thinking About Strategic Culture." *International Security* 19:4 (Spring 1995); 32-64.

Kaarbo, Juliet. "Power Politics in Foreign Policy: The Influence of Bureaucratic Minorities." *European Journal of International Relations* 4:1 (1998); 67-97.

Krasner, Stephen D. "Are Bureaucracies Important? (Or Allison Wonderland)." *Foreign Policy* (Summer 1972); 159-179.

Kunioka, Todd and Lawrence S. Rothenberg. "The Politics of Bureaucratic Competition: The Case of Natural Resource Policy." *Journal of Policy Analysis and Management* 12:4 (1993); 700-725.

Laitin, David D. "The Civic Culture at 30." *American Political Science Review* 89:1 (March 1995).

Larson, Deborah Welch. "Research Note: Problems of Content Analysis in Foreign Policy Research: Notes from the Study of the Origins of Cold War Belief Systems. *International Studies Quarterly* 32 (1988); 241-255.

Macey, Jonathan R. "Organizational Design and Political Control of Administrative Agencies." *The Journal of Law, Economics, and Organization* 8:1 (1992); 93-125.

Merton, Robert K. "Bureaucratic Structure and Personality." *Social Forces* 17 (1940); 560-568.

Mosher, Frederick. "Professions in Public Service." *Public Administration Review* (March/April 1978); 144-150.

Munck, Gerardo L. "Canons of Research Design in Qualitative Analysis." *Studies in Comparative International Development* 33:3 (Fall 1998).

Newsom, David D. "Are Diplomats Patriotic?" *Foreign Service Journal* (March 1989); 30-35.

Page, Edward C., and Linda Wouters. "Bureaucratic Politics and Political Leadership in Brussels." *Public Administration* 72 (Autumn 1994); 445-459.

Pateman, Carol. "Political Culture, Political Structure, and Political Change." *British Journal of Political Science* 1:3 (July 1971).

Rhodes, Edward. "Do Bureaucratic Politics Matter? Some Disconfirming Findings from the Case of the U.S. Navy." *World Politics* 47:1 (October 1994); 1-41.

Rodman, Peter W. "The NSC System: Why It's Here To Stay." *Foreign Service Journal* (February 1992); 24-26.

Rosati, Jerel. "Developing a Systemic Decision-Making Framework: Bureaucratic Politics in Perspective." *World Politics* 33 (1981).

Rosenberg, Tina. "Unholy Alliance: Latin American Militaries and the War on Drugs." *Foreign Service Journal* (November 1991); 24-27.

Schein, Edgar. "Organizational Culture." *American Psychologist* 45:2 (1990); 109-119.

Simon, Herbert A. "Decision-Making and Administrative Organization." *Public Administration Review* 4 (1944); 16-25.

Smith, S. "Policy Preferences and Bureaucratic Position: The Case of the American Hostage Rescue Mission." *International Affairs* 61 (1985); 9-25.

Valenta, J. "The Bureaucratic Politics Paradigm and the Soviet Invasion of Czechoslovakia." *Political Science Quarterly* 94 (1979); 55-76.

Welch, David A. "The Organizational Process and Bureaucratic Politics Paradigms: Retrospect and Prospect." *International Security* 17:2 (Fall 1992); 112-146.

Wildavsky, Aaron. "Choosing Preferences by Constructing Institutions." *American Political Science Review* 81:1 (March 1987).

Williams, Gary. "State Department Narc." *Foreign Service Journal* (August 1990); 22-26.

No Author. "The Posse Comitatus Act: A Principle in Need of Renewal." *Washington Univeristy Law Quarterly* 75:2 (Summer 1997).

Monographs

Equipped for the Future: Managing U.S. Foreign Affairs in the 21st Century. The Henry L. Stimson Center. October 1998.

Congressional Documents

U.S., Congress. Committee on Armed Services. *Narcotics Interdiction and the Use of the Military: Issues for Congress*. Report of the Defense Policy Panel and Investigations Subcommittee. Proceedings of a Seminar Held by the Congressional Research Service. 100th Congress. 24 August 1988.

———. Committee on Armed Services. *Military Role in Drug Interdiction, Part 2*. Hearing before the Investigations Subcomittee. 101st Congress. 18 April 1989.

———. Committee on Governmental Affairs. *Federal Drug Interdiction: The Role of the Department of Defense*. Hearing before the Permanent Subcommittee on Investigations. 101st Congress. 9 June 1989.

———. Committee on Foreign Affairs. *Review of the International Aspects of the President's Drug Control Strategy.* Hearing before the Committee on Foreign Affairs. 101st Congress. 12 September, 1989.

———. Committee on Armed Services. *Military Role in Drug Interdiction, Part 3*. Hearing before the Investigations Subcommittee. 101st Congress. 21 September 1989.

———. Committee on Foreign Affairs. *Review of the International Aspects of the President's 1990 Drug Control Strategy*. Hearing before the Committee on Foreign Affairs. 101st Congress. 27 February 1990.

———. Committee on Government Operations. *Report 101-991*. 101st Congress. 30 November 1990.

———. Committee on Foreign Affairs. *Andean Strategy*. Hearing before the Subcommittee on Western Hemisphere Affairs. 102th Congress. 26 February 1991.

———. Committee on Foreign Affairs. *The Future of the Andean War on Drugs after the Escape of Pablo Escobar*. Joint Hearing before the Subcommittee on Western Hemisphere Affairs and Task Force on International Narcotics Control of the Committee on Foreign Affairs. 102nd Congress. July 29, 1992.

———. Committee of the Judiciary. *FBI and DEA: Merger or Enhanced Cooperation?* Joint Hearing before the Subcommittee on Civil and Constitutional Rights and the Subcommittee on Crime and Criminal Justice . 29 September 1993.

———. Committee on Government Operations. *International Narcotics*. Hearing before the Legislation and National Security Subcommittee of the Committee on Government Operations. 103rd Congress. 7 October 1994.

———. Committee on Foreign Affairs. *International Narcotics Control and United States Foreign Policy: A Compilation of Laws, Treaties, Executive Documents, and Related Materials*. 103rd Congress. December 1994.

———. Committee on the Judiciary. *Enforcement of Federal Drug Laws: Strategies and Policies of the FBI and DEA*. Hearing before the Subcommittee on Crime. 104th Congress. 30 March 1995.

———. Committee on Transportation. *Coast Guard Interdiction Mission*. Hearing before the Subcommittee on Coast Guard and Maritime Transportation of the Committee on Transportation and Infrastructure. 104th Congress. 1 August 1995.

U.S., Senate. Committee on the Judiciary. *Drug Policy in the Andean Nations*. Hearings before the Senate Committee on the Judiciary. 101st Congress. 6 November 1989, and 28 January and 22 March 1990.

———. Committee on Foreign Relations. *Andean Drug Initiative: Hearing Before the Subcommittee on Terrorism, Narcotics, and International Operations*. 102nd Congress. 20 February 1992.

———. Committee on International Relations and Caucus on International Narcotics Control. *International Narcotics Control and United States Foreign Policy: A Compilation of Laws, Treaties, Executive Documents, and Related Materials*. 105th Congress. September 1997.

GAO Reports

"Issues Surrounding Increased Use of the Military in Drug Interdiction." 1988. Washington, District of Columbia: General Accounting Office.

"Over-The-Horizon Radar: Better Justification Needed for DOD System's Expansion." 1991. Washington, District of Columbia: General Accounting Office.

"The Drug War: U.S. Programs in Peru Face Serious Obstacles." 1991. Washington, District of Columbia: General Accounting Office.

"Drug Control: Inadequate Guidance Results in Duplicate Intelligence Production Efforts." 1992. Washington, District of Columbia: General Accounting Office.

"Drug Control: Coordination of Intelligence Activities." 1993. Washington, District of Columbia: General Accounting Office.

Other Government Documents

Memorandum from the Office of the Assistant Secretary for Force Management of the Department of Defense. By Dale H. Clark, Director for Requirements, Plans, and Programs. June 1989.

Information Memorandum for the Secretary of the Treasury. By Salvatore R. Martoche, Assistant Secretary for Enforcement of the U.S. Treasury Department to Secretary Brady. No date (c. April 1989).

Baker, James, III. *Democracy, Diplomacy, and the War Against Drugs*. United States Department of State, Bureau of Public Affairs. Washington, District of Columbia. 22 November 1989.

United States Budget. 1991, 1992, 1993, 1994. Washington, District of Columbia: Government Printing Office.

U.S. Customs Update 1992. 1992. Washington, District of Columbia: Department of the Treasury, U.S. Customs Service.

International Narcotics Strategy Report. 1992. Washington, District of Columbia: Department of State.

The Development of the Base Force: 1989-1992. 1993. By Lorna S. Jaffe. Joint History Office of the Office of the Chairman of the Joint Chiefs of Staff.

National Drug Control Strategy Report. 1994. Office of National Drug Control Policy. Washington, District of Columbia: The White House.

Unpublished Works

Ferrara, Joseph A. 1995. *Defense, Disasters, and Drugs: Understanding Policy Implementation*. Ph.D. Dissertation: Georgetown University.

Harrington, John Douglas. 1996. *Neglected U.S. Military Missions: Contending Theories of Bureaucratic Politics and Organizational Culture and the Case of Air Lift Mobility*. Ph.D. Dissertation: Georgetown University.

Other Documents

The Washington Post. 13 May 1989.

Air Force Times. 2 October 1989.

USA Today. "Military Options in the War on Drugs. 7 July 1990.

The Houston Chronicle. 28 June 1992.

The Commercial Appeal. 28 June 1992.

The Washington Post. 31 October 1993.

The Washington Post. 13 March 2000.

Index

About the Author

Dr. Tony Payan is an Assistant Professor of Political Science and International Relations at the University of Texas at El Paso. He obtained his Ph.D. in International Relations from Georgetown University. His research and writing focus on foreign policy of the United States, Mexican Foreign Policy, the United States-Mexico border, and United States-Mexico relations. He is the author of several articles and papers on these subjects. He is the author of *The Three U.S.-Mexico Border Wars: Drugs, Immigration and Homeland Security* and co-editor of *Gobernabilidad o Ingobernabilidad en la Región Paso del Norte* (with Dr. Socorro Tabuenca). He also serves in the editorial board of *Nóesis*, a Mexican Journal of Social Sciences, and as co-editor in chief of the *Journal of Law and Border Studies*. He is currently working on a third book on the foreign policy of the Vicente Fox Administration 2000-2006.